no place like home

no place like home
Notes from a Western Life

Linda M. Hasselstrom

UNIVERSITY OF NEVADA PRESS

Reno & Las Vegas

University of Nevada Press, Reno, Nevada 89557 USA

Copyright © 2009 Linda M. Hasselstrom

Manufactured in the United States of America

LIBRARY OF CONGRESS CATALOGING-IN-PUBLICATION DATA

Hasselstrom, Linda M.

No place like home : notes from a Western life / Linda M. Hasselstrom.

p. cm.

Includes bibliographical references.

ISBN 978-0-87417-796-1 (hardcover : alk. paper)

1. Hasselstrom, Linda M. 2. Women ranchers—South Dakota—Biography.

3. Ranch life—South Dakota. 4. South Dakota—Social life and customs.

5. South Dakota—Biography. 6. Cheyenne (Wyo.)—Biography. 7. Community

life—West (U.S.)—Case studies. 8. Social change—West (U.S.)—Case studies.

9. Human ecology—West (U.S.)—Case studies. 10. West (U.S.)—Rural

conditions—Case studies. I. Title.

F656.4.H37A3 2009

978—dc22   2009015669

The paper used in this book is a recycled stock made from 30 percent post-
consumer waste materials, certified by FSC, and meets the requirements
of American National Standard for Information Sciences—Permanence
of Paper for Printed Library Materials, ANSI/NISO Z39.48-1992 (R2002).
Binding materials were selected for strength and durability.

University of Nevada Press Paperback Edition, 2010

19   18   17   16   15   14   13   12   11   10

5   4   3   2   1

ISBN-13: 978-0-87417-831-9 (pbk.: alk. paper)

For Jerry

MY SUNRISE,
MY SUNSET

Contents

Acknowledgments   ix

Prologue: A '54 Chevy Named Beulah   1
Selling the Ranch   9
Dear John: How to Move to the Country   31
The School Bus Driver Waved   41
Laughter in the Alley   46
Tomato Cages Are Metaphors   53
A Rocket Launcher in the Closet   62
The Beauty of Responsibility   67
Watching for Grizzlies Anyway   69
He Pinched the Burning End   77
Shoveling Snow in the Dark   83
Stalking Coffee in Sitka   89
Recycling Freedom   99
Tattoos and a Thong   103
Learning the Names of Cows   107
How to Live at the Dump   114
It Doesn't Just Happen   125
Making Pottery out of Sewage   132
Pray for Me I Drive Highway 79   138
The Stolen Canoe Mystery   145
Playing Pool with the Cat Men   151
Sounding the Writing Mudhole   160
Investigating the Heron Murders   176
Who's Driving the Subdivision?   184
Overlooking Antelope Ridge   192
Epilogue: Waiting for the Storm   203

Additional Resources   207

Acknowledgments

A brief version of "Selling the Ranch" appeared in some western newspapers as "A Dispatch from the New West Battleground," syndicated by Writers on the Range for *High Country News*.

"Dear John: How to Move to the Country" appeared in slightly different form as "Dear John: Moving to the Country," in the "Death of the New West?" issue of *divide*, August 2003, pp. 14–17, published by the Program for Writing and Rhetoric, University of Colorado at Boulder, Colorado.

"The School Bus Driver Waved" was published in some western newspapers as "Aggressive Waving," syndicated by Writers on the Range for *High Country News*.

An early version of "The Beauty of Responsibility" was published as "Responsibility" in "What the World Needs Now: Twelve Honest Answers," *Orion*, Spring 2002, vol. 21, no. 2, pp. 32–33.

"Watching for Grizzlies Anyway" was published in slightly different form as "The Wild Boy and the Community Stew" in *Owen Wister Review*, 2007, ed. Ken Steinken, pp. 74–79.

Jane Kirkpatrick's words in "Recycling Freedom" are quoted with permission from her novel *Hold Tight the Thread* (Waterbrook Press, Colorado Springs, CO, 2004).

An early version of "Tattoos and a Thong" appeared as "Thermopolis, Wyoming," *Northern Lights*, vol. 16, no. 3, p. 9.

"Learning the Names of Cows" and "Investigating the Heron Murders" were published in early versions by *Great River Review*, Spring/Summer 1998, no. 28, pp. 65–76. Different versions of "Learning the Names of Cows" and "The Case of the Purloined Canoe," retitled "The Stolen Canoe Mystery," were published as "No Place Like Home" in Richard L. Knight et al., eds., *Ranching West of the 100th Meridian: Culture, Ecology, and Economics* (Island Press, Washington DC, 2002).

"Pray for Me I Drive Highway 79" was first published in *Paddlefish*, Mt. Marty College, Yankton, SD, 2008.

"Sounding the Writing Mudhole" has been much revised since it appeared as "Reimagining Windbreak House" in *Michigan Quarterly Review*, Winter 2001, vol. 40, no. 1, pp. 74–90.

An early version of "Who's Driving the Subdivision?" was published as "When Flooding Drops a House in a Hayfield" in *High Country News*, September 2007.

no place like home

Prologue: A '54 Chevy Named Beulah

No matter how far you have gone on a wrong road, turn back.
—*Turkish proverb*

I've lived in western communities most of my life. During my practice marriage, I dutifully accompanied my first husband to central Missouri, eventually escaping from that swampy region pursued by hairy spiders larger than my hand. In the three decades since, I've stayed in the high western plains, writing about the quirks of humans, animals, and plants of this arid region.

My mother was also escaping an unsuccessful marriage when she jumped on a midnight train in Edinburg, Texas, worried because, at age four, I spoke Spanish better than I spoke English. Whenever I woke from a nap, I heard thrumming of the train wheels and her voice lecturing me about the dangers of a drinking habit like my daddy's. She found refuge briefly with relatives in Wyoming, then dropped me off with her mother on a ranch in southwestern South Dakota while she looked for a house and job in the nearest sizable town. In Craven Canyon, my grandmother Cora Belle taught me how to use the outhouse and wood-burning stove; I helped feed her chickens and carry water into the house to heat in the kettle when we washed dishes. Each evening I cleaned and lit the kerosene lamps so we could read. Mother found work as an executive secretary and settled me into a little house on Fifth Street in Rapid City just in time for the legendary Blizzard of 1949. When I was nine years old, mother married John Hasselstrom, and we moved to his ranch near Hermosa, where I was able to grow up in the kind of community that causes bouts of nostalgia, especially among people who have never lived in one.

The Hermosa grade school contained the first through fourth grades in one room, the fifth through eighth in another. My fellow students had known each other since birth; even their grandparents had grown up together in the same county, so they formed a tight clique. Henry Bale, the janitor in the basement, became my best friend. He kept the ancient furnace burning, cleaned the bathrooms, and told me stories about Hermosa characters, including the grandparents of the kids who wouldn't talk to me. Sometime during that first year in the country I started carrying tiny notebooks in the hip pocket of my jeans and writing down my thoughts and questions.

Everywhere I've gone since then, for almost sixty years, I've carried some kind of notebook, and I'm still writing down more questions than answers.

My mother drove me six miles to school on a gravel road unless the weather was bad enough for my father to drive, or keep me home to help him feed the cattle from a hayrack pulled by a team of Belgians, Bud and Beauty. We finally got a telephone when I was in high school, connecting with several other families on the local party line, and soon knew each other's voices so well that raising the receiver for a couple of seconds provided enough information to start or confirm a rumor. As we talked, our voices gradually faded. Finally one person bellowed, "I can't hear you with all those rubberneckers on the line!" The clatter of receivers being replaced echoed down the lines, mile after mile. Accepting a date or whispering a confidence was as public as, and faster than, the weekly county newspaper.

Our town and county were mostly Republican, Protestant, and Caucasian, but other differences didn't matter when men, women, and children fought prairie fires or gathered for the annual county fair where everyone bid on the quilts made by the church ladies. By the time I entered high school, I was steeped in country pursuits: demonstrations for the Buttons and Bows 4-H Club, horseback tricks for a precision drill team, showing cattle at the fair, and working on the ranch when I wasn't studying.

NATURALLY, I wanted to go to college as far away from home as possible, but my parents wouldn't let me leave the state, so I attended the University of South Dakota in the eastern corner. Married to a divorced Baptist minister the year after graduation against my parents' wishes, I took two teaching jobs in Columbia, Missouri, and learned something about being a stepmother when my husband's children visited. We eventually moved back to the ranch, where we built an apartment on the side of my parents' house. The move was supposed to save our marriage, and for a while it seemed to work; I helped my father with ranch chores while my husband wrote. Sometimes I scribbled a few lines on a scrap of paper; he supplemented our income by working as a traveling writer for the state arts council. We started a publishing company named Lame Johnny Press after a notorious stagecoach robber and horse thief who was hanged by vigilantes a few miles away.

In 1972, a flood that killed more than two hundred people washed away the company that had just printed the first issue of our quarterly literary magazine, *Sunday Clothes*. By the time I realized my husband was still dallying with any nubile nymphet naive enough to fall for his line, he'd run the magazine deeply in debt. I kept publishing the magazine to pay off creditors, changed the name of the press, and eventually brought out twenty-two books. One day I realized I'd printed the work of more than five hundred artists and writers from South Dakota and the surrounding states, but fewer than a fifty of them were paying the five-dollar yearly subscription rate. I dumped the remaining issues of the magazine in the garden for mulch, and wrote a poem. Twenty years later when a neighbor plowed the same garden spot as part of my move back to the ranch, no trace of the magazines turned up. My garden therefore created a perfect metaphor about the durability of man's creations when they are tucked in the bosom of nature.

Following mother's advice always to have something to fall back on, I'd earned an MA in American literature, which made me too expensive for local teaching jobs, so I kept living in the apartment attached to the ranch house. My nebulous plan for the next fifty years of rural life involved ranch work and best-selling novels. I found encouragement in this folly when I sold a rough movie script about the life of Crazy Horse to actor Tom Laughlin, who was riding high on his Billy Jack movies.

Writing steadily soon taught me that I couldn't successfully make things up. I read environmental magazines to broaden my understanding of land use, discovering that few people who actually worked on the land had, or made, time to write about it. So I turned to nonfiction, explaining ranching to people who seem to think cows are more destructive to land than elk, deer, and bison. The job requires trying to explain why our seemingly endless prairie grasslands are so important to the nation. First, grasslands produce naturally healthy food with relatively little effort when cattle, chickens, and other meat-producing animals are allowed to follow their legacy of grazing on native vegetation. The plains also provide pure air, open space, and loyal citizens. When a California publisher produced my first published book, the usual slender volume of verse, I was forty-one.

Meanwhile I fell in love and married again five years after my divorce, to another father on the rebound, George R. Snell, who loved muzzle-loading rifles and wilderness camping. I worked with my father and second husband on making the best use of the flora and fauna that shared the land with the cattle we raised. As an only child, I expected to inherit my father's ranch, work it with George, and keep writing those best-selling novels in my spare time. I hadn't ever been able to afford an impractical white Stetson, but my cowgirl fantasy was intact.

AS I GREW AND CHANGED, so did the neighborhood. The highway was paved, and eventually turned into a divided four-lane. Our county has no zoning, so homes of every price range from trailers to mansions sprouted along the gravel roads winding up into the tree-covered hills. The children of these new residents might attend our schools, but their parents drove to Rapid City for jobs, church, restaurants, and shopping. Young men who used to work on ranches in the summer got bigger wages building a missile base that was never armed, then moved away. George and I made local friends by trading labor in the old-fashioned way, but we also went to potlucks in town where some of the guests wouldn't eat out of pans that had ever touched meat. Everyone, vegan and cow-raisers, loved the star-gazing parties on our deck in January.

We'd been married less than ten years when George died. After several untreated strokes, my father ordered me to stop writing or leave, and accused me of trying to steal his ranch. I endured his mad behavior for a while, but bought into a retreat in Vallecitos, New Mexico, in case I needed another home. Finally, I rented my house to a writer and took refuge with our friend Jerry in Cheyenne, Wyoming, while I decided what to do next.

IN NOVEMBER 1990, Jerry and I went to Scotland. On Thanksgiving, our fifth day in the country, we woke up in Dornoch, breakfasted on blood pudding and gave thanks, visited a bookstore, a butcher shop, and the Abbey Church at Holyrood House, and drove north along the narrow coast road past quiet fishing villages. Dunrobin Castle was closed to tourists; Jerry tried a couple of doors and found them locked, so we admired the dormant gardens and a Pict symbol stone. We spotted Cairn Liath by its shape; there was no sign. We climbed a fence and explored, thinking of the families gathering here when lookouts spotted raiding Norse sea-wolves. In Bora, we bought handwoven blankets from a shop that was closing because, the grim proprietor said, she couldn't compete with cheap goods made overseas. Ninja turtles were for sale in the same shop where I bought a dozen pair of classic woolen tights. Our Thanksgiving lunch was fresh fish and chips wrapped in newspaper. We parked facing the harbor, and ate while a single fishing boat tried to fight through the gale on one side of us, and a lone golfer blasted golf balls against it on the other.

Our drive along the northern coast of Scotland featured everything the tourist guides probably mention: sunshine, crashing waves, spectacular views of the ocean including a giant wind generator at Berriedale. A series of one-lane hairpin curves set Jerry to mumbling about Wyoming highways until he figured out the way to gain the right-of-way: never look at the oncoming driver. By the time we got to Dunbeath, we had realized the Scots don't erect signs pointing to the sights, so we were looking over both shoulders, seeing brochs, standing stones, and cairns on every rise of ground. Some were actually ancient stones, but most were sheep. At 3:40, nearly sunset, we reached Hill O'Many Stanes, and walked among twenty-two rows of 250 standing stones. In the near darkness, they looked like the ghosts of the Caithness residents who made them centuries ago. That night we stayed at the Portland Arms Hotel in Lybster, and met Duncan. Before sleeping, I recorded that encounter, "Playing Pool with the Cat Men," in my journal, along with speculations about what makes a community, and why a little fishing village in Scotland should remind me so much of the South Dakota ranching community where I grew up. Without knowing it, I had begun writing this book. "How long does it take to write a book?" readers often ask. "All the years that you've lived," said Ed Abbey.

MY FATHER deftly disinherited me before dying in 1992, so that I had to sell his cattle to pay his unpaid bills. Then I sold my herd and borrowed money to buy the ranch. I leased it to a neighbor since I had no cows and my house was still occupied by renters. As soon as mother was settled into a nursing home, she revised the past until she could almost believe I was the daughter she'd always wanted; she died in 2001.

For my fiftieth birthday, Jerry built me a kaleidoscope, filling the object chamber with bright bits of glass. Each time I turned it, the glittering picture shifted; no two views were the same. Later that year, a Minnesota press published my fifth book; I dedicated it to my father.

In my study in our two-story house above one of the busiest streets in Cheyenne, I wrote and rewrote Duncan's story. I also began recording memories of other kinds of communities to which I had belonged: buckskinning groups, and the bluegrass fellowship of Missouri musicians underlying the society of college professors. While I settled into Jerry's circle of engineers, geologists, and highway crews in Cheyenne, and found the best routes to the grocery store and library, I realized I was reliving an experiment: country girl moves to town. (Friends from Boston, New York, Los Angeles, Seattle, San Francisco, and other urban hives laughed when I called Cheyenne a "city.") Some folks wrote to tell me that leaving the country meant I'd left my subject matter, and that I'd never write anything worthwhile again. But I couldn't stop thinking, and thinking requires me to write. It seemed to me that if I could figure out how to create a community in Cheyenne, I might gain some insight into whether the subdivisions and ranchettes invading my rural district would ever coalesce into real communities—and how I might help the process.

DRIVING BACK AND FORTH between my South Dakota and Wyoming homes, I've thought about how we decide where home is. I've always said I'm from Hermosa, South Dakota, but the longer I stay away, the less I know about its daily activities. I pay taxes and contribute to several local volunteer fire departments, but I haven't swung a wet sack at blazing grass for years. Meanwhile, in Cheyenne, I likewise pay taxes, but my attempts to find compatible friends have met with mixed success.

In part, I blame the fact that Cheyenne, like most other cities, is burning down. Good people fight crime, homelessness, rising taxes, noise, and poverty, trying to pretend their hair isn't on fire. Naturally, we each tend first to our own spouses, children, homes, but I believe my home is more secure if my neighbor and I know and trust each other. Some communities are naturally short-lived; the buckskinning camps where George and I lived for a few weeks a year vanished when we pulled up the tipi stakes, though the friendships sometimes lasted for years. And I'm hardly an authority on great communities. The prairie people who raised me were stiff-necked, stubborn, and judgmental; the Lakota in our neighborhood say that the smart pioneers went to Oregon. Despite my modern reading material and liberal leanings, I sound more like my grandmother every day. A cantankerous lot, my relatives and their neighbors disagreed more often and more bluntly than we dare today. Still, they created strong bonds with each other and to their settlement because they all took responsibility for, and depended on, one another.

LIKE MOST PEOPLE, I moved away from my parents as part of growing up in a world convulsed with contradictions. The men my mother wanted me to marry as soon as they became lawyers or doctors went to Vietnam and learned to kill. Students who flunked my classes wrote angry letters to me from jungle foxholes. The Summer of Love coincided with the Tet Offensive. Gathering on the quad to protest the war, we were jeered by the ag students and cowboys, and surrounded and beaten by armed Missouri troopers. We bellowed with Country Joe McDonald and the Fish, "Whoopee! We're all gonna die." Students in the dormitory of the girls' college where I taught in Missouri cheered when Martin Luther King was shot. The details differ, but the same mayhem fills today's news.

Humans are so full of contradictions it's amazing we can talk to one another at all, let alone be politically correct. A writer friend reminds me that even the factor that distinguishes us from animals, our ability to walk upright, is an intricate balancing act by muscles in complete opposition to one another. The medicines used to treat George's Hodgkin's disease kept him alive for ten years before the side effects killed him. Some days when

I'm filled with hope for the human race, I still find myself singing the Tom Lehrer song about the joys of a spring afternoon when we're poisoning pigeons in the park.

"THERE'S NO PLACE LIKE HOME, there's no place like home, there's no place like home," Dorothy chanted in *The Wizard of Oz*. She only had to click the heels of her ruby slippers together three times before she was back among loving friends and family and fond memories. When I learned that L. Frank Baum had written his timeless book in South Dakota, I felt as if I were part of his achievement, even though, as usual, my home state wasn't getting much credit for inspiring him. I've been thwacking my heels together ever since, in cowboy boots, in Birkenstocks, in fleece-lined snow-boots, and in squeaky Crocs, tirelessly trying to find the magic path home even though I know nothing is quite so simple. Contradictions abound.

When I first drove away from the ranch in my secondhand, burnt orange 1954 Chevrolet Bel Air (named after my favorite Mormon great-aunt because both were comfortable, sturdy, trustworthy, and strong), I knew I was leaving my real home. Every day I've lived since has challenged that belief. When Jerry retires after thirty years with the Wyoming Department of Transportation, my SUV will follow his pickup to park beside a tiny travel trailer, part of our plan to try new things. We carry with us experiences and tales from living in other places, along with differing ideas about how we might create a life together on this ranch. We plan to enjoy exploring outward from what has always been the center of my universe. No, we patiently tell neighbors and friends, we aren't going to buy any cows, or bison, or horses.

"Storytelling," said Hannah Arendt, "reveals meaning without committing the error of defining it." A reader may interpret some of these narratives differently than I do. Each story that follows is, however, part of my definition of the home place for which I am still searching.

Selling the Ranch

In April 2000, I attended the auction of a ranch near mine in rural western South Dakota. That single sale changed our lives, put an end to the community where I grew up.

The ranch owner whose death caused the sale—I'll call him Paul—had been one of my father's best, and most close-mouthed, friends. I remembered his parents, square-built, hardworking, red-faced Germans who taught their son to make the ranch more productive. Their philosophy matched my father's: never spend any money.

Paul had gradually expanded the ranch by buying scattered bits of pasture and hay ground on which he raised fine Hereford cattle. Too busy to court a wife, he worked the place with his parents, and then with a succession of hired hands, none of whom stayed long. One man who left Paul to work for my uncle said, "I didn't mind so much when he told me how to fix fence. Any man might have different ideas about that than his neighbor. But when he started telling me how to tie my shoes, I decided to move on."

After his parents died, Paul, whose social life had pretty much consisted of leaning on the pickup in the pasture visiting with his neighbors, managed to marry a woman about his age with grown children. He confided to my dad that she spent most of her time driving to town to shop and get her hair fixed. She also entertained, because I remember going with my mother and a group of women to the historic stone house where they lived, a former station on the stagecoach line between Cheyenne, Wyoming, and the Black Hills gold fields. I loved the house's compact rooms, its three-foot-thick stone walls. The rancher's new wife complained loudly, her vivid red curls bouncing, that she couldn't pound a nail in the stone walls! Couldn't hang a picture! And the rooms were so small! And he wouldn't let her build more rooms because it would cost too much money! She looked slyly at us as she said he had a lot of money, and we all looked away. Money was a subject we never discussed; most of the women in that room, my mother included, didn't even know how much land their husbands owned. I suppose her children visited the ranch, but I don't recall ever meeting them. Paul always drove through his pastures and went to town alone in his pickup.

As Paul aged, several of us tried to buy the pieces of his land adjoining our ranches, but he wouldn't discuss selling separate pastures. Since he hadn't managed to found a family, we knew the ranch would likely be sold at his death. He'd built a good working place on hard work and frugality. His parents had raised him to get the most value from every single penny, and land prices rose steadily in our area as ranchers sold off plots along the highway for homesites.

What was he thinking? Ranchers ought to be among the most realistic of people, since they are likely to encounter birth and death in the corrals as soon as they can walk. But sometimes, like my father, they behave as if they are immortal. I don't know the details of Paul's will. Soon after his death, we began to hear rumors that his widow's children couldn't agree. Someone wanted money, but others wanted to see the ranch continue to operate. The widow couldn't run it alone, and none of her children had ever lived there. The solution: sell to the highest bidder and divide the spoils.

Naturally, since they'd never lived in our community, it probably never occurred to them to consider what the sale of the ranch might do to the neighborhood. Worse, neither did Paul, who had spent his whole life there.

We're all taught, after all, to be independent, to defend our rights, to say that what we do on our own property is nobody's business but ours.

Each time I drive home to the ranch since the sale, I am amazed at the speed with which our community is disintegrating, almost as fast as a bulldozer can roll. Within months, the results of Paul's sale were scattered through the pastures: houses three times the size of the one where Paul's parents lived long and productive lives. I look at these expensive piles and remember Paul, and shake my head. If he'd tossed bombs through our windows, or set fire to the churches and the post office, we'd have thrown him in jail and repaired the damage. We can't fix this, and few of us would even acknowledge that we should.

He didn't understand what he was doing. As our community turns from a home into a string of bland subdivisions, fast-food joints strung along the highway, and exhaust fumes, I will date its death from April 6, 2003. We'd already seen the effects of such sales, so ignorance is no excuse.

Ranchers who don't consider the future, don't plan how their ranches will change ownership in an organized way, are the direct cause of many of the ranchette subdivisions in the West. The remaining ranchers like to blame this destruction on "Californians," or "newcomers" moving into our communities, but it's our neighbors, mostly dead and thus safe from our anger, who started this.

A WORKING, VIABLE COMMUNITY can't be evaluated by looking only at the cost of its houses or the cars in the garage, any more than we can judge how wisely a woman will raise her children by adding up the cost of her clothes. People who equate land with money can only sell it to realize its value. No matter what we say about our values and our morals, the way we are building our society demonstrates that money is what we really care about. Mollie Beattie, a director of the U.S. Fish and Wildlife Service, once said, "What a country chooses to save is what a country chooses to say about itself."

Drive the main highway into your community and remember how it looked ten years ago, fifteen, fifty if you are old enough. What you see is what you and your friends value, an announcement to every passerby of what you hold most dear.

VISITING BEFORE THE AUCTION, neighboring ranchers expressed doubts that this would remain a working ranch, and mumbled that Paul's daddy, old Thee, would be spinning in his grave.

The auctioneers' job that day, of course, was to sell the land for the highest price possible. This auction firm had specialized in selling ranch land for years. They'd had experience with the land rush, selling lots in the Black Hills, but I imagine they weren't sure anyone would be interested in homesites on our arid prairie. While it's prime grassland for raising cattle, it lacks trees, in part because it lacks water; there are no natural creeks or lakes, and drilling wells is tricky. The auctioneers, knowing that people looking for homesites would want trees, produced a color brochure with photographs of trees. We ranchers, used to looking at detail, noticed right away that the photographer had showed the same scraggly pines from several different angles, and pointed out to each other the tract described as "wooded" contained only one tree.

Tracts to be sold adjoined several of the ranches owned by the folks who visited with me in the hallway before the sale. When I suggested that we should cooperate to buy particular pastures to keep them agricultural, keep them from being homesites, nobody was interested. "I wouldn't want to tell anybody what he could do with his land," they said.

AS SALE TIME NEARED, the ranchers moved into chairs in the center of the room, the brims of their broad hats level over their sun-browned faces, their jackets buttoned unless they'd gained too much weight over the winter. Their wives sat beside them, hatless but wearing their coats and holding their purses on their laps. Significant, I thought.

Some of the ranchers glanced over their shoulders at the men in the back of the room as they sat down, but after that they looked straight ahead, though none of them were actually wearing blinders. They listened with their arms folded until the bidding was well started. Then some pulled notebooks and pencils from their shirt pockets, making notes and shaking their heads.

In the back of the room, thinner men stood or leaned against the wall wearing stonewashed denim jeans with the bottoms tucked into boots so everyone could admire the audacious colors and intricate stitching. Their western shirts were snapped at the cuffs; their faces and hands were white, their fingernails even and clean. One wore a bolo tie centered with a piece of turquoise the size of a half dollar. Several wore rings; few ranchers who still have all ten fingers wear rings. One or two wore leather or sheepskin vests. I saw a cap with a Nike logo, but most left their silver hair uncovered, fluffed and shiny and brushed back so it barely touched their collars. Each had a calculator in a vest pocket; several had a tiny phone clipped somewhere. One had a wire around or in his ear and a speaker by his mouth and murmured constantly into it. Several well-polished women stood against the wall for a few minutes before flouncing into chairs. Before that day, I might have said it was impossible to flounce in a leather miniskirt. Every few minutes one of the women would flip open a cell phone and listen, or talk, or both. One or two left the room muttering.

The ranch was advertised for sale either as a single unit of 1,977 acres, or as "nine Tracts, 75 to 680 acres." The auctioneer gave a little spiel about Paul, about how hard he'd worked before leaving the place to his widow and her children.

An electronic screen at the front of the room listed the nine tracts of land. The auctioneer briefly described the sale plan. First the individual plots would be offered for bid, but those offers would not be final, only "hold" prices. Then the ranch would be offered for sale as a whole, and anyone who wanted it would have to put up more money than had been offered for all the separate parcels. If the ranch did not sell as a unit, the separate pieces would be auctioned again, and this time the winning bidder would have to pay whatever was bid. Audience members murmured and looked at each other, looking puzzled.

The auctioneer started the bidding with Tract 1, the home place with the historic stone house. "Headquarters," he called it, a word Paul would never have used. The sales brochure described it as a "classic native-stone ranch home with three bedrooms, bath, kitchen-dining, and basement." In a row ahead of me, the widow looked around the room, her mouth as tight as it was the day she was telling us how small and inconvenient the house was. I could visualize the warmth of the stone walls as the sun set on a winter day, the "stone-and-pipe-fenced yard," never cluttered with machinery or junk, the small two-car garage, and the trim outbuildings including a couple of red-painted sheds, tin-roofed cattle shelters on the north side of the plank corrals.

The auctioneer's voice began to ring and soar as he rattled off numbers. "What am I bid for this fine ranch headquarters? Who wants to start it at five thousand dollars an acre?"

The ringmen took their handheld microphones and circled the room, rolling their eyes, and waving a hand in the air, shouting "Hup!" when they had a bid. The auctioneer looked carefully at each bidder, probably matching him to a mental file. The ranchers and observers in the middle of the room didn't want to turn around, but we rolled our eyes left and right under our hat brims, trying to track who was bidding and how—by touching a hat, with a nod, with a credit card flipped in the air.

As the auctioneer pronounced each high bid, the amount per acre was listed on the screen. The auctioneer never uttered the word "sold," because no money or land would change hands in this round of bidding. The top bid for each tract of land, called a "hold" bid, was simply recorded on the screen at the front of the room, suggesting what the buyers in the room or connected by telephone were willing to pay.

The amounts listed as bid for all the tracts on the board added up to an average of $485 an acre. Already, the sale had made history in our county. One bidder had offered more than $1,000 an acre for two parcels totaling 150 acres, with no well or other improvements. That bid was roughly five times the value of the land on the tax rolls.

FOR THOUSANDS OF YEARS, this land had existed as arid prairie grassland, home to meadowlarks and red-tailed hawks, badgers and bunnies, and a variety of grazing animals — antelope, bison, cows. This morning it would become something else: development land, homesites: an investment.

Moreover, the sales accomplished in this few hours of bidding would permanently change—raise—the value placed on all the land in the county by the assessor. After years of being grassland, valued for what it could produce, for the rich tangle of roots under its surface, the grasses waving in the sun, the meat made of those grasses by deer and cattle and antelope, its worth would now be calculated on the sale price on this particular day. Its best product, the grass, might even be deliberately destroyed by people who wanted greener grass, or trees that couldn't be produced without artificial enhancements. And the so-called value of every acre of ground in the entire county would be questioned.

A few people were going to make a lot of money on this sale. How much, I wondered, would this sale cost all of us when our property taxes were next assessed? The costs of this sale would be mounting for years as people left this room thinking of their land more as a commodity than as a home.

A recess was called, and some folks got up to go to the restroom or pace and visit in the hallway. In the women's bathroom, a woman who had ranched with her son a few miles south of us since I was a little girl asked me if I was planning to buy anything. "Haven't decided yet," I said in true rancher fashion. In fact, like everyone in the room, I had to apply for a bidding number before the sale if I was planning to buy, so I lied.

Watching the woman primp, I remembered when she'd enlivened our community gossip when she married an old bachelor rancher forty years ago. He'd been a fixture at the county fair for years, white-haired and frail, sitting on his horse in the parade. Everyone had been surprised after his death when she'd settled down to running the ranch instead of selling it, though there were always rumors about her hired hands. Now she was getting set to reap the rewards of that investment. Her ranch lies along the highway, but the house is invisible behind huge old cottonwood trees a quarter mile off the road. The entrance is guarded by a bold plank gate, always shut, and a big NO TRESPASSING sign. Gossip says she keeps a rifle by the front door and can hit the gate with her first shot every time. Her son disappeared for thirty years or so, but has recently been spotted at local bars, looking like he's been insulted by everyone he's ever met.

"Well," she said, "I came here to find out what kinda prices we're lookin at, case I want to sell out, but this is too low; I wouldn't take less'n $1500 an acre for my place," she declared, tucking a bright red strand of hair behind one ear.

AS I HEADED BACK TO MY SEAT, the local representative of the Nature Conservancy stopped me and said he'd like to discuss a conservation easement on my ranch. I tried to explain that I was a writer concentrating on a scene as well as a rancher who might be doing business, but he didn't listen. My neighbors think conservation easements mean turning the land over to the government, and that the only thing worse would be giving it to a national environmental organization. This man has been in this community for years, yet he seemed unaware that I might not want to be seen talking to him in front of this group. "Call me next week," I said once, but he moved in front of me, leaning close. This is one reason some environmental groups make little headway in ranch country: they pay no attention to local moods, ideas, customs, or even economics. Focused on winning, on their terms, some seldom ask advice from longtime residents, or listen when it's offered.

Finally I yelled, "Get away from me. I do not want to talk to you."

"I'll call you," he called after me. He didn't.

By that time, a man I'd wanted to talk to had turned away, and auctioneers were turning on their mikes. I lost an opportunity that might have
made a difference in what happened next.

In the next phase of bidding, the land was offered for sale as an entire
ranch. Anyone who bought it as a whole had to bid more than the hold bids
offered for the individual tracts.

Some flaws in this scheme are obvious. Bidders did have to register to
buy, giving some assurance that they had enough money to cover their
bids. I wonder how many ranches sell as a single unit at this kind of sale.
The first bidders do not have to put their money where their mouths are;
they could conceivably run the bids up to a figure no other bidder could
top to buy the entire ranch.

Even if someone bought the whole place, there was no guarantee it
would remain a working ranch, of course. A buyer might still subdivide,
either intentionally or reluctantly if he had bid more than he could afford.

If the ranch did not sell as a single unit in the second round of bidding,
the real sale would begin. In the third and final round of the auction, pieces of land would be sold separately—really sold—to the traditional highest
bidder.

This is a devilishly clever way to sell land if maximum profit is the only
goal, as it usually is. The first round of bidding may draw bids only from
the eager people who don't understand what's going on. Even if they realize that they are not really buying the land—and some of them never do,
no matter how many times it's explained—they may be tempted to bid and
bid and bid. Often, this serves only to announce to the serious bidders how
much money they will risk.

Meanwhile, serious buyers can calculate how much they will have to
spend for what they want. During the recess, bidders who may have mis-
calculated whipped out their cell phones and called—brokers? bankers?
Others left.

Pacing the floor outside the auction room was a man whose fantasy
about a house in the country had already cost him money. The day he'd
come to look at the parcel of land he wanted, his pickup's catalytic converter set a fire. Our attorneys eventually forced him to pay the volunteer
fire department's expenses, and compensate us for our grass and buildings.

In the first round of the sale, he had placed a bid on the tract he'd inspected the day he set the fire, the largest at 680 acres. I'm not sure if his bid had been highest in the hold round, but as he swaggered back into the room, he scowled at me. Perhaps he had temporarily forgotten that if his bid was successful, we would be close neighbors.

Now that the opening skirmish was over, the auctioneer grew solemn. The oldest one took the microphone and talked a little about Paul and ranching and the traditions of agriculture and the community. He explained that the second round of bidding was only for buyers who wanted the whole ranch. He talked about the condition of the grass, and showed us on the maps where the wells and dams and water tanks were. He explained that a local ranchers' group had run a pipeline across several of the pastures, and that purchase of the land entitled the buyer to use the pipeline—but only for watering cattle. If the buyer wanted to build a house, he couldn't use the water for that. Moreover, he'd have to join the water organization, and their rules were complicated; the buyer would have to talk to them about membership.

Then he handed the microphone back to the younger auctioneer, who said, "Aaaaaaaalll right then, let's sell this ranch."

Everyone in the center of the room stopped breathing. But we didn't stop thinking. I looked at the list in my hand. Tract 1 contained the stone house. In the front row, I could see the widow, her hair still the same unlikely red, still unnaturally curly, looking grimly around the room. She nodded as the auctioneer described the house and outbuildings, how well built and well kept they were, how hard the rancher had worked to keep everything in tip-top shape.

Then he began his call, soliciting bids at $600 an acre. His employees circled the room, their collars undone, hair awry, waving their arms and moving close to the buyers standing around the walls of the room, especially the ones who stood with their arms folded and who, according to the whispers around me, had more money than God.

I kept looking at the list. Tracts 2, 3, 4, and 5, the pastures surrounding the old stone ranch house close to the highway, were the visible heart of the ranch, though the best grassland and best hayland lay elsewhere. All my life, driving by these level pastures on the highway, we'd looked at Paul's Hereford bulls. Their white faces shone against their red curly hides, the wide horns swinging rhythmically as they paced toward water.

For a while, my father also raised registered Herefords, so we'd bought some bulls from him. I always enjoyed those bulls, because they were so gentle I could ride several of them, and scratch behind their ears, drape an arm casually across one of the massive horns.

Of course fifty years of feeding Herefords were only a fragment of that land's history. The bison herds thundered along this broad valley that circles the Black Hills, moving in and out of its sheltered valleys with the seasons, searching for the best grazing. They were followed by the hunters, Lakota and other tribes. This flat area on both sides of the highway south of Rapid City is said by archaeologists to contain dozens of sites of hunting camps and villages; only a few were excavated ahead of the highway expansion. Then came the Cheyenne-to-Deadwood stage, following a route that meandered back and forth through the valley, shifting with snowdrifts and spring rains. My father had pointed out where the trail wound through our pasture, and a neighbor has a collection of ox shoes he picked up where the trail crossed his fields. On top of the ridge south of my house are stone cairns that mark a trail to homes of settlers who homesteaded closer to the Badlands. Walking beside their teams, they moved rocks out of the trail as they headed west to join the stage road on their way to town for provisions.

As the bulldozers scrape off the topsoil to build houses, these clues to how people once lived here may be obliterated. If the new owners can find water when they drill, someday they may sit in their living rooms with a great view of the Badlands watching their sprinklers keep invasive grass alive and never know about the families who lived there before them. Perhaps their tenure will be no longer than that of the nomads who preceded them, but surely they will do more damage because they own more destructive tools.

Once the sale is over, the grass will never be pasture again, but homesites. The tipi rings and bison bones and fire pits of the ancients will be covered with concrete and steel and wood. The stage trail will disappear under asphalt.

Tract 6, 520 acres, lay south of a pasture I consider one of my best despite its lack of water. Once, our cattle had been able to drink from a big dam built across one of the deep rocky gullies, but the dam has been dry for a decade or more because of a continuing drought. My father drilled several wells, and once even hit a small flow of water. None of the pumps we tried, including an expensive solar model, were able to pull enough water from the rough clay-filled ground to provide for even a small herd of cows. Finally, we set up a cattle tank on a flat plateau, bought a plastic tank that fit our pickup, and began hauling water to the cattle there. Filling the tank and hauling the water took several hours a day, so we used the pasture just enough to keep the grass healthy and vigorous. Despite the dry years, the pasture gained some moisture because it lay close to the edge of the Black Hills, in the rain shadow, so grass grows hip-deep in some areas.

Just south of that pasture lay the rocky conical hills of Tract 6, with a little topsoil over ancient piles of gravel. Paul, knowing that only the roots of the buffalograss held the soil on those steep slopes, never kept his cattle in the pasture for long. Cattle don't especially like to climb hills, so they'd used the hilltops mostly for catching a breeze on hot summer days.

One of the detriments of the land as pasture was its roughness; the western edge held part of a deep valley where we wouldn't want our cattle to be caught in a snowstorm because it would be difficult to get to them. So we generally kept cattle there during the hottest part of summer. After drinking each day, cattle lie around digesting, chewing their cud. Toward evening, as cooler air flowed down from the hills, they'd begin to chew and nibble away from the tank. They seldom reached the most distant edges of the pasture before they were thirsty and turned back toward the tank. Now I lease the pasture to another neighbor, who has land next to it, so that his cattle can drink at his well-filled tank when they are thirsty.

Since the grass grew thick on the pasture's outskirts, we often left a horse there alone in the fall, so we'd have one on that side of the highway if we needed to move cows, and to give her rest. Near some trees at the extreme west end of the pasture, water seeped steadily into a pool the size of my cupped hands, providing enough for the horse and the other animals that shared the pasture with her.

Nearby, coyotes denned in broken clay bluffs. Once, an otherwise good neighbor drove into our yard with a pair of coyotes dead in the back of the pickup. Their bodies were so big their tails dragged the ground. My father, who never let anyone shoot coyotes on our land, knowing how much good they did us as scavengers of the dead and eaters of gophers, meadow mice, and other crop-damaging rodents, came out of the garage with his face white and grim to talk to the neighbor. And then the man told us he'd shot the coyotes on our land, near the den. I walked away. After my father died, I made a point of informing those neighbors that while they were welcome to walk onto my land to hunt deer or antelope, they could not shoot coyotes.

Tracts 7 and 8, containing seventy-five acres each, lie across the highway from my house. I had suggested to a couple of my nearest neighbors that we pool our resources to buy them, and then work out who would own them. The owner had never grazed them heavily, because the windmill that supplied the only water was temperamental, and the well connected to it shallow.

THINKING OF THE WELL triggered a memory. I may have been twelve when I climbed the windmill with my father. I think Paul was sick, and knew the windmill was on, and had asked my father to turn it off. We drove the old 1951 pickup across the road, which was gravel then, and into the pasture and stood at the base of the windmill looking up. My father pointed out the lever that had to be pulled down and fastened to stop the windmill's furious turning.

He asked me if I was afraid of heights. "Yes," I said, looking at my boots, mumbling, embarrassed. "Well, so am I," he said, "but we have this job to do."

So we both climbed the windmill, me following him, our hands sweating, clinging to the rungs, talking about how scared we were. At the top, we turned off the windmill, and then relaxed a little, enjoying the view. He let me figure the lesson out for myself: that being scared didn't mean not doing something that needed doing.

My rancher neighbors didn't want to buy the pieces of land, though they lived closer to them than I did. "Nobody will buy those to live on," scoffed the older one. "There's no water, no trees, no shelter. When you've lived as long as I have, Linda, you'll learn not to get all upset over these things." He brought his checkbook to the auction, but never touched it.

THE AUCTIONEER, unable to get a bid on the entire ranch at $600 an acre, tried to draw out a bid of $500. Then he turned off his microphone and conferred with one of his partners in whispers.

"Well," he said, "we can't sell it for less than the average of the hold bids; that's $485 an acre. Anyone want to put in a bid at $485 an acre?"

He sang his song again while the ringmen moved through the room pointing at various buyers, trying to make somebody nervous enough to raise a hand. The men identified by the crowd's whispers as the ones with "deep pockets" kept their hands in them.

South Dakota statistics say that about ten acres is required in our arid area to feed a cow unit, consisting of a cow and her calf. Experienced ranchers understand that in a dry year, double that acreage, or more, may be required, plus supplementary feed. Cattle operators prefer that the cattle they run "pay for themselves." That is, sales of the cattle in any given year should be enough to pay the rancher's expenses that year—fixing fences, buying school clothes, buying supplementary feed for the cattle, gas, everything. Rarely does this happen; ranchers borrow money, finagle for the latest federal disaster payments, take chances.

Around 1,975 acres were being sold that day, or grazing for 197 head of cows in a good year—and we hadn't had a good year for more than a decade.

That figure doesn't allow for the acreage a rancher would need to deduct for buildings, for the proposed highway, for rocks and ridges that grew no forage. By frugal living, Paul had made a living by running fewer than 200 head of cattle.

As the auctioneer pleaded with the crowd, I realized that he assumed that no one in the room could afford to buy the ranch in order to make a living from it. The man who knew its every blade of grass, who had tightened his belt and its fences, was dead. Even an owner who wanted to run cattle on the ranch would have to learn fast and spend almost nothing in order to make a living from the ranch. And that wasn't going to happen. The auctioneer was trying, correctly, to sell it to someone who wanted a second home, a deduction, a toy, an investment—something other than a working ranch.

Even if the ranch sold as a working ranch, its position in our community would change. No longer would a family who owned it join a church, contribute to a fire department, show up on the fire line next to us. He wouldn't drive into the yard and lean against his pickup in the sun to visit. If he wasn't ferociously wealthy, he wouldn't have time to visit because he and his wife would need good jobs to pay for their ranchette lifestyle and the gas they'd use driving back and forth to town.

Several of the auctioneers' assistants walked in small circles, talking softly into phones, turning their backs to read off the prices bid in the earlier round, nodding, turning back to look at some of the potential buyers in the room.

The auctioneer tried lecturing: "There's some of you that can afford to buy this whole ranch, and you're gonna be sorry tomorrow that you didn't do it."

"This is the perfect gentleman's ranch," said the auctioneer in a voice that he might have used to invite a lady into his bedroom. "And Paul was a perfect gentleman, a good rancher and cattleman. This ranch has been well taken care of. You could walk right into this, a turnkey operation."

No one bid. Another recess was called. The conversations in the corridors and the women's bathroom were briefer, but more intense. Many women glanced in the mirror, looked sidelong at one another, and then left in a hurry, with no chatter, no trust. The men stood in the halls, hands in their pockets, bouncing up and down. A few spoke into their cell phones. Several wrote in their pocket notebooks.

"We need to know where we are," writes Scott Russell Sanders, "so that we may dwell in our place with a full heart." For each home ground, he insists, "we need new maps, living maps, stories and poems, photographs and paintings, essays and songs." Paul lost his chance to write the story of the land to which he devoted every bit of his energy, every day of his life; no one will ever know the words he didn't record. This soil will be home to a new generation, though I cannot visualize their stories, poems, or songs; still, I am notoriously narrow-minded.

THEN EVERYONE TOOK SEATS and the auctioneer began his explanation: This time when the tracts of land were called off, bids would be accepted only from buyers who had registered with the auctioneer. No buyer could leave the premises after the sale without writing a check for a percentage of the cost of what he bought. Gesturing to several employees with cell phones, he said some additional potential purchasers would be following the action and bidding by telephone. Of course, no one in the audience would know if the auctioneers' employees were actually talking with anyone or not.

During this round of the auction, some bidders raised their hands for the first time; after all, they knew everyone else's limit. Observers whispered, "He's a doctor," or, "He's in real estate." Someone whispered "Yuppie scum."

During the second part of the sale, the auctioneers answered some questions directly, and some inadvertently. Early in the day, one auctioneer had mumbled something about a "proposed highway." Ten minutes later, trying to get a bidder to raise, he said, "Where else are you going to find a site like this on a four-lane divided highway?"

If you are considering buying or selling land, here's an important fact: auctioneers can't be held responsible for their remarks; their job is to make money for the seller. The buyer's job is to beware.

The murmuring conversations that had provided an undertone to the first two-thirds of the sale subsided. Everyone knew that the sale this time would be final.

Many people—let's be direct instead of politically correct, they were all men—who bid in the first round kept their arms folded during the second.

Only the most purposeful bidders moved, and their bids were subtle— the nod of a head, the lift of a finger. Each gesture, after all, represented thousands of dollars. After the auctioneer's cry of "Going once, going twice, going three times," each tract would be labeled "sold" on the screen in the front of the room.

DURING 2005, the new four-lane highway called the Heartland Expressway was completed past much of the land sold that day. Each time I go home to my ranch from my city home, I examine what the buyers of those tracts have done with them.

The stone ranch house on its 153 acres sold for $1,050 per acre, a total of something like $161,000. The house and outbuildings have not changed.

The yard now contains pink and yellow playground equipment, especially vivid against the pale green buffalograss. Made of plastic, I think, the slide looks bloated, as if it is filled with air.

Tracts 2 and 3 are each around seventy-six acres, and each is accessible both from a county road and from the highway, so they seemed likely to sell as homesites. The sales brochure describes them as if they might be part of a ranch: as "excellent native pasture." One has a stock dam, but both are treeless, and neither has a well or other "improvements." They sold for $725 and $900 an acre, respectively.

Within a year or two, Tract 3 contained a house and garage, and a few cows grazing around the buildings. Considering the long drought, I hope someone is giving those cows considerable supplementary feed.

Tracts 4 and 5, at 160 acres each, soon sprouted large houses. The grass damaged by the building operation is not recovering in the fierce drought. On Tract 5, two huge ochre boulders, probably found while the basement was being dug, provide an entrance, but there is no functional gate. A decorative sign over the driveway calls the place a ranch. The house's big glass windows face mostly north, into the prevailing wind.

Tract 6, a total of 520 acres in the shape of a backwards p, lay south of my favorite pasture, its rolling hills covered with tall native grasses. At auction, it brought $775 an acre, or close to a hundred thousand dollars. Six months later, it was a subdivision, Heartland Estates. A large ad in the local real estate sheet advertised "Horse Ranchettes! Fresh Country Air! Privacy! 28 prime Parcels Ranging from 6 acres to 26 acres."

The ad continued, "Beautiful acreages of various sizes with views of Harney Peak, Mt. Coolidge, and the Badlands. Water included in most lots. Riding trails; Park area; Doublewide or stick built homes! Covenants are Horse Friendly!" Wondering about that ad saying water accompanied "most" lots, I learned a single well would serve much of the development. And the price? "$29,000 for 10-acre parcels without water."

Let's see now—that means in April the buyer paid, or promised to pay, $7,750 for ten acres of paradise with nothing on it but the breeze and some grass. Four months later, he was selling that same ten acres for an additional $21,250. His expenses included surveying the lots and bulldozing the narrow trail that led from the county road to the narrow parcels so prospective buyers could visit. Developers drilled a well that served some of the properties, though I saw no evidence a pipeline had been laid, indicating the buyers might have to pay to get water from the well to their acreage. They did. Three years later, one "estate" owner said he had to install two pumps to move water from the well to the house.

Most of the buyers placed their houses on top of the rocky little hills. Even from a distance I can see gouges in the skimpy vegetation, gullies forming where someone has driven, washouts forming along vehicle tracks. We've had little rain, yet the lower slopes of many of the hills are beginning to erode and slump. Ignoring the scarcity of water and the nonexistent or thin soil, some of the subdivisions' residents have optimistically planted trees. If they can afford pumps powerful enough to suck water uphill to their unnatural garden plots, the soaking will only make the hills slump faster.

A geology graduate student at the School of Mines and Technology who was conducting a soil survey of the area said several subdivision residents asked him to tell them where their land began and ended.

These folks moved to the country, surely, because they wanted what the country life offers; so we have much in common. I've always found solace in the silence, punctuated by the howl of coyotes and the sleepy calling of birds. The darkness allowed me to see the stars shining brightly enough I could walk around my house without a flashlight. The Heartland ranchette residents have erected security lights that shine all night long. Without the lights, or with direction lights pointed at garages and pathways, no one on the highway would know they were over there.

Now when I step out on my deck a mile away, I have to shade my eyes in order to see the ground in front of me, or the stars. Consequences.

A SINGLE BIDDER bought Tracts 7 and 8, directly across the highway from my house and retreat. For 150 acres, he agreed to pay $157,500, or $1,050 per acre, planning to raise horses.

The day of the sale, the 157 acres I own across the highway from his purchase was assessed at $218.68 per acre. Now the "value" of my land will be assessed as if I, too, wanted to build a horse barn. Because of his purchase, the county will now want to zone my land for development instead of as agricultural property.

According to my deeds, I also own drainage rights on that expensive land, which a lawyer tells me means he can't pollute the drainage. That is, if I detect a speck of horse manure in the water that flows onto my land from his, he has violated the drainage agreement.

How do I enforce this, I ask my attorney, who explains that we can only find out by taking legal action *after* damage has occurred.

These were the plots my neighbor said were worthless, that no one would buy. He practically patted me on the head for even considering such a silly idea as buying them to keep them out of the hands of a developer.

Within a couple of weeks, the buyer had called me and offered to buy my ranch.

No thanks, I said.

Well, he'd found himself a little short on his auction purchase. How about if I bought his million-dollar house on a lot in the Black Hills?

Nope.

Nevertheless, he quickly built a huge horse arena, and a large barn with living quarters above it.

The horses may be deaf, because they are apparently trained to the beat of music that can rattle my windows a half mile away. The first time I called to complain that the noise was disturbing the paying customers of my writing retreat, the phone rang unanswered at 9:00 P.M., at 10:00, at 11:00, at midnight. So I called again at 6:00 A.M. Sorry, said the groggy young man who answered; he couldn't hear the phone ringing because the music was too loud. Exactly, I said.

Then a sign went up advertising the facility for sale, the price dropping as the months passed. Before long he'd carved several house lots out of the edge of his property, presumably subdividing to pay off his loan, and now the lights of several more houses glare all night long. Gigantic logs frame one driveway, and from them hangs the legend "Everything is Everything."

THE LAST PARCEL TO BE AUCTIONED, Tract 9, was the largest, 680 acres of, as the brochure said, "rolling hardgrass pasture with high pla-teau view of Mt. Rushmore and the Black Hills." The description was writ-ten to lure homesite buyers, since deer and cattle don't care much about the view. Besides several spring-fed ponds where I'd seen huge turtles, the property had a flowing well, a well with a windmill, a stock dam, and a "stock dam on community pipeline." The auctioneer stopped the sale to explain that the organization that administered the pipeline did not have to admit a new owner to their ranks.

The brochure also noted "legal access by section line," which should have been a warning to the wary. The other tracts had been open to inspection for months, but the auction brochure specified that this tract, which lay between my ranch and the one my uncle had owned, could be viewed only at designated times so that we could watch for fire and damage. "Close all gates," added the auctioneers, "respect the neighbors' livestock and property, and do not enter if wet." Alert prospective buyers should have understood from this verbiage that while my neighbor and I couldn't stop a new owner from reaching his property, we might not be particularly cooperative. And if he'd heard about the fire set by the beer salesman, he understood our concerns.

Paul had to drive or truck his cattle miles to reach this pasture, so he used it less than he would have if it had been closer to his other holdings. He often took his cattle home in the fall before they had done more than nibble at the best grass, and he kept the fences tight. We worried that a new neighbor might not understand how much of the quality of the land and its wildlife depended upon this gentle use and care, especially if the land was sold for a homesite.

The hold bid still showing on the board at the front of the room was $325 an acre. I remember my father telling me how his father had bought nearby land for ten or twenty dollars an acre after settlers abandoned it in the drought years of the Dirty Thirties. Out of the corner of my eye, I could almost see my father and his friend Paul sitting somewhere in the room, hats on their knees, shaking their heads in disbelief at the prices being paid.

The bidding on that last parcel of land started there, at $325 an acre. The beer salesman raised his hand right away, then turned to stare hard at me and folded his arms, resting them on the beginnings of a potbelly as if his job was finished. Perhaps his bid was the hold bid, and he thought no one would raise it.

Before beer boy could inhale, the auctioneer was calling a bid of $400 an acre. He sat up, spun around to stare at me, and then seemed to focus his eyes just beyond my shoulder. That confirmed my suspicion that my neighbor, who bought my uncle's ranch and leases mine, was bidding.

This piece of land lies between his ranch and mine. Even one house would create too many complications to calculate. In the week before the sale, I'd asked him if we could work together, perhaps splitting the cost of the land, dividing ownership. He'd been noncommittal.

The beer man raised his hand once or twice more, but someone in the back of the room was bidding. Between those bids and my neighbor's, the beer man just couldn't keep up.

Then the auctioneer cried, "Sold!" and entered $500 an acre on the board in front of us, and the sale was over. The beer man leaped up, shoving chairs and trampling toes, eyes fixed so sharply on me I thought he was going to attack. Instead, breathing as if he'd run a mile, he lunged out of the room.

Voices rose as I turned around. My neighbor's face was the color of the grass I've found growing under old boards around a deserted homestead. His wife was gazing at him, patting his back. He cleared his throat several times and said, "I guess I better go see my banker."

That land cost him $340,000, not counting interest on the loan he would need.

Neighbors crowded around him, talking and shaking his hand. I kept looking at him and them, trying to figure out if their congratulations meant they were really happy for him, or they were glad they'd kept their hands in their pockets.

"No way cows are going to pay for that," someone said.

AND THAT'S THE PROBLEM. Cows won't pay for the land. My father didn't teach me anything about financing a ranch, but the principle is clear: profits have to justify expenses. You can't pay more for a machine than it will ever produce. Grassland has historically produced grass, which feeds cows as a cash crop, along with scenic bonuses like antelope, bison, deer, coyotes, and predatory birds. So a rancher shouldn't pay more for the land than he will get when he sells the cows, though those returns may be spread over many years. The cycle was reliable when the price of grassland was tied to the ranching economy. Now other factors, like tourism and the real estate business, have begun to dismantle that working partnership.

Even if the drought ended today and the grass grew knee-deep in that pasture and cattle prices doubled, 680 acres will feed no more than 68 head of cows. In a way, my neighbor is betting the rest of his ranch against this acreage. My uncle Harold sold him that ranch on generous terms so the land would stay together, to be the home of a family that would go on raising cattle for generations. That's how he explained it to me and others who might have expected to profit from his death, who might have expected to inherit some of his land or his money. I felt so proud of him that day, so pleased for him as he looked into the future knowing a good rancher would be running the place he loved and cherished, and not caring that the family would not be of his bloodline.

And now, because Paul couldn't figure out how to plan ahead, or was afraid of wacky environmental ideas like conservation easements, and because the beer man wanted a house in the country, my neighbor may lose that family ranch. I nod at him and turn away, wondering what my uncle would say. He did the right thing, knowing what he knew when he died. He thought, as I did, that his ranch and that of his brother would come back together as a working unit, the way it was before their wives squabbled. He didn't care if the name on the deeds wasn't Hasselstrom; he wanted that particular grazing business to support a ranching family. He expected that our neighbor and I would help each other, and work to make our community better. This sale has shown us how fragile such a plan can be. My neighbor must run the ranch that is now his in the way he believes to be the best.

One bidder who owns another ranch in our neighborhood, besides at least one helicopter and one island, had dropped out of the bidding, shaking his head. Now I heard him say, "I believe I'll go back to California. This is getting too rich for my blood."

As far as I know, that 680 acres is the only part of the ranch Paul built that will remain, for now, in grass. And there's no guarantee how long my neighbor can keep it that way. Most of the other buyers planned to build homes, or subdivide immediately. If anything goes wrong in their lives that affects their finances, the quickest way to make money will be to sell part of the land they have bought so dear.

After the sale, the widow wandered around the room, almost in tears, saying "I didn't think they'd sell it in little pieces; I thought somebody would buy the whole thing." No one listened. If she believed a rancher would buy the land, she was the only one in the room who thought so.

If she really didn't want it sold in pieces, she should have considered the alternatives. Her children, who wanted their share of the money from the ranch, didn't come to the sale. They'll get their checks by mail and will never understand what happened here today. Maybe as they drive by the subdivisions they'll gesture out the window and say, "My stepdad used to have a ranch—I think the house was over there behind that row of little blue trailers." The widow is headed for a retirement village in town with, she tells us, a hairdresser on the staff.

For this modest 1,977-acre ranch in country that is not mountainous or glamorous, seven high bidders paid a total of $1.4 million, an average of about $731 an acre, or triple what the county assessor said the land was worth. Every piece of land in the county will now be reevaluated, by its owners as well as by county tax experts. The ripples of increased valuation will spread.

More subdivisions means the land neighboring my ranch will be taxed as development property rather than agricultural property, taxed on what it might "produce" if sold to the highest bidder. Such land will no longer be valued for its ability to produce feed for beef cattle and thus food for humans. Higher taxes for ranch land creates more pressure to subdivide. The people in those houses will eat beef raised somewhere else.

WALKING OUT OF THE BUILDING after the sale, the ranchers settled their hats on their heads and yanked the brims down level.

They said, "It coulda been worse."

They said, "That's just the way it goes."

They said, "It's not as bad as if it was a trailer park."

Nobody said, "We just destroyed our community."

Dear John: How to Move to the Country

We met after I focused my camera on your charred pickup, and you yelled and ran toward me.

I mentioned in my normal speaking voice that you were trespassing on my land.

You glared, moving closer to demonstrate that you are taller and outweigh me, and yelled some more.

I stood my ground.

There we were: the rancher and the guy who wants to move to the country, a classic New West confrontation.

You stepped closer, took a deep breath, and waved your hands in my face, talking loudly.

I'm liberated enough to interpret such behavior as an effort at intimidation, so I turned my head to direct your gaze to my vehicle. Right away you noticed the woman observing alertly from the passenger seat, and her German shepherd with his head out the window staring at you, lip curled and hackles raised.

You took the hint and stepped back without learning about the pistol under the driver's seat. Our modern shootout involved phones, lawyers, and answering machines. I wish we could have continued to negotiate face to face until we both calmed down. This letter will have to suffice.

I'd like to publish the photograph I took, post it larger than reality on a billboard beside the four-lane highway. Behind you stretches a line of vehicles. A pickup tows a flatbed trailer hauling the burned-out shell of the new pickup you drove to look at the land for sale. Behind that is another pickup and trailer towing the front-end loader you used to clean up the debris from the fire you caused. Behind that is the SUV you drove onto my land the second time you trespassed.

I wasn't fast enough to click the shutter on your two sidekicks, the driver and passenger of the second pickup, as they traded a flat brown bottle back and forth, sipping while they listened to us talk.

The photo might be educational, especially to potential residents of our neighborhood. Folks shopping for ranchettes should know vehicles can start prairie fires. Perhaps I could add a headline explaining that firefighting costs are billed to the vehicle's owner. We ranchers and our neighbors have fought a lot of fires caused by drivers tossing cigarettes out car windows; older residents even remember one fire started when a horseshoe struck a spark from a rock. We believe in people taking responsibility for their actions, so when we know who started a fire, we send them a bill. These assessments help us pay the expenses of our volunteer fire departments, but we don't catch most of the inadvertent arsonists.

The problem started with catalytic converters. Strict air pollution laws in some states—not this one—forced automakers to add converters to most trucks. But drive one of those trucks a half hour out from town, as you did, and then drive it into the tall grass of a good rancher's pasture and you may start a prairie fire, as you did. Fire-conscious ranchers and people concerned about wilderness lands bought trucks without the converters as long as they could. But we were not a big enough demographic, as the marketing folks say. To maximize profits by reducing the expense, automakers simply made converters standard equipment. Ranchers are normally law-abiding, but when we buy a new pickup, we disable the converter, breaking the law in order to save our livelihood.

So converters helped inspire those NO HUNTING OR TRESPASSING signs along the highway: people who drive all over the pasture looking for game can set too many grass fires, even if they aren't in the city habit of tossing cigarettes out car windows. Yet we often welcome hunters, if they ask permission and agree to hunt on foot. When they have game to retrieve, we'll let them drive to it if they have no catalytic converter. Some of them don't know what a catalytic converter is, so sometimes we load up fire-fighting equipment and go along to pick up their deer, or take them in our own pickups.

You crossed my land legally the first time, to look at land for sale in what used to be a rancher's pasture adjoining mine. Because of the high fire danger, neighboring ranchers had already spent considerable time haggling with the auctioneer until he posted signs explaining that no prospective buyer could be admitted without a guide. Days of land tours were specified so the neighbors and firefighters could watch for smoke. We were worried not only about fire, but about other damages and losses we discover when strangers get lost, as they regularly do on the prairie whether they are trespassing or not.

Looking for a place to build a new home, you drove to the site on an established pasture trail, parked your pickup by the gate, and drove around on a four-wheeler. We appreciate your consideration.

The fire apparently started as soon as you left your pickup. You blamed faulty wiring, but it's more likely you had driven through tall grass and some lodged against the catalytic converter or tailpipe. The overheated metal probably ignited the grass. On that windy day, we were all lucky the fire didn't burn thousands of acres. An alert neighbor called the volunteer fire department and neighbors came from all directions.

Do you know these rural volunteer fire departments are funded by donations from residents, and are staffed by every able-bodied person who sees the smoke? You look healthy, so if you move here, we'll expect you to fight fires as well as donate cash. We've helped each other for a couple of generations, because we grew up knowing that we were responsible for cleaning up our own messes, or being smart enough to prevent them.

We hope you raise your children the same way, but lately we've found it necessary to pass on these lessons a little more forcefully. We've made our tradition into a new rule: If you start a fire, you pay the bill for fighting it.

Your little fire, I'm told, cost $1,283.60, in addition to the bills my neighbor and I submitted for damages to grass and the cattle shed the fire destroyed. You're lucky the surrounding landowners were so alert and the firefighters weren't busy elsewhere; you got off cheaply.

You sneered when I mentioned my burned shed; it looked pretty rickety to you. The stories behind that farmyard and its buildings are part of my history, part of our community story. I can still hear John Lindsay's soft, precise voice telling how it saved his cows in the Blizzard of 1949.

He'd shut them in the shed and then couldn't get to the corrals while the storm blew. For three days the hungry cows moved around inside the shed, tramping down the snow that blew in through the cracks in the walls. John was afraid to open the doors, afraid the cows had smothered, but when he did they peered down at him, their eyelids rimmed with ice, their backs against the rafters. As the snow slid out the open door, they coasted and tumbled with it.

Maybe local history isn't important to you, working in town. We hope you join a church or some of the local civic organizations, but you may believe you don't have time. Like many people who commute from a country home, you'll leave home in the dark and get back when it's darker, a schedule that doesn't leave much time for neighborliness, let alone enjoying the scenery or knowing much about the place where you live.

Perhaps you think neighborliness doesn't matter. You might want to look up the Blizzard of '49 before moving to the country; you can even find information about it on the Web. Maybe climate change has ended the plains tradition of the deadly blizzard; I think not.

The day we met, you yelled at me that I had no right to accuse you of trespassing again. Besides retrieving your wrecked truck, you bellowed, you'd considerately brought a front-end loader to clean up debris from the fire.

If you'd asked first, I'd have politely reminded you that bringing in four *more* vehicles might start *another* fire. I'd have asked you to bring fire-fighting equipment, and notify the fire department to stand by. If you'd asked.

You apparently thought me rude for mentioning your trespass. Yet if the house next to yours was for sale and I dropped a cigarette and started a fire as I walked through your living room on my way to look at it, and then showed up in your living room the next day with a mop and a shovel, you'd probably call the police. My pastures are my living room, my savings account, and the foundation of my business. Entering without permission is trespassing.

Our visit didn't last long; you kept yelling while I was trying to explain. The entire conversation was too brief, too loaded with macho moves—made by both of us—to settle anything. Since then, I have been nagged by a question you did not answer: Do you understand the consequences of your desire to build a house next to my pastures?

Since we never had that conversation, I'd like to explain what buying a little piece of land in the country requires.

The tract you wanted was landlocked, a term potential country dwellers should know, though it infuriates auctioneers and real estate sales persons. "Landlocked" acreages do not abut a public road and are surrounded by land owned by others. No easy and obvious access exists. The law requires intervening landowners to allow the owner access, but building a road can get complicated.

When I mentioned these difficulties, you seemed unconcerned, but I wonder if you'd thought ahead. Building a road to a homesite in the middle of a pasture takes more than a bulldozer. To build a house on a landlocked lot, you must first negotiate with adjoining landowners on a way to reach your homesite. The law forces us to allow you access, but doesn't specify that we give you a route that is short, straight, or smooth.

Those pastures have existed since homesteading days, with grazing carefully planned around water sources, existing or created by the rancher. So if you buy this acreage, your road must also allow cattle access to that water. Depending on how angry the adjoining landowners are about that fire, negotiating the details of that road might take a while, and cost you some legal fees.

In the old days, once you'd agreed with your neighbors on passage across their land, you'd have started house-building, wearing a two-track trail in the prairie sod as you went back and forth with a team and wagon. Eventually, other folks might have used the road. Without maintenance, such trails can develop into quagmires or blown-out, dusty chasms. In wet seasons, people sometimes drive around the low spots until they've created a broad muddy mess and destroyed a lot of grass. These days most of us aren't willing or able to allow our main road to be so informal; we want an ambulance or fire truck to get in quickly and safely.

A new road now requires an engineering study to determine the best route. The design includes placement of culverts to control water flow and prevent erosion, both to your road and the grass in surrounding pastures. If the road would prevent animals on one side from getting to a water source on the other, you are responsible for solving that problem. You will have to compensate for the loss of water, perhaps by paying for a new well, or building an underpass to allow cattle access to water.

Once the study is completed, your hired contractor must build a road-bed with a solid foundation to withstand hard rains and the daily travel by the heavy equipment that will be used to build your house. Judging from five decades of experience in maintaining my ranch road, you'll have to replace the deep layer of gravel on top every couple of years. Gravel is still fairly cheap, but those mileage charges from the gravel pit really add up.

Since you work in town, remember that a few inches of snow dropped in a stiff wind can completely block these country roads. The last time I called the county snow plow, twenty years ago, the charge was fifty dollars an hour, but he wouldn't plow my drive; regulations prohibit plowing for fewer than three families on one route. Maintenance of our county roads depends, of course, primarily on agricultural taxes; as subdivisions multiply, the county has chosen to clear urban routes first. They don't usually get to our end of the county for a week after a major storm; by then the snow has melted. We don't mind because a snowplow job may cost us a layer of that expensive gravel.

As soon as earthmovers begin scraping out a road or a homesite, removing the native grass that's been growing on your building site for aeons, thousands of thistles and noxious weeds like leafy spurge and spotted knapweed will sprout. Call the extension agent to find out about state and county regulations governing weeds that may be harmful to humans and grazing animals, because you will be liable for their damage both on, and off, your land. Moreover, many of us do not use poisonous chemicals, so you must consult adjoining landowners about eradication methods and be sure neither the chemicals nor the runoff will come in contact with our animals or our ground.

You are also responsible for the actions of workers you hire to build the road. When cattle leave a pasture, their owner is liable for any damages they cause, no matter who opens a gate that allows them to escape. However, if someone working for you leaves a gate open, the rancher will blame you. If your workers smoke and discard cigarette butts that start fires, if they toss out soda cans that slash the hooves of cattle or horses—all those potential damages would be morally your responsibility. Your neighbors will cooperate to be sure these problems became your legal and financial responsibility as well.

Your work and your social life may continue to center around the distant town, but refusal to accept responsibility can cause serious consequences in a community like ours. The rules are changing as new people move in, but those who don't contribute to the country community may lose some of its benefits. Maybe no one will notice if your pickup slides into a drift on a cold day.

Here's an example of how that selective attention can work. One recent day in our neighborhood, I noticed two separate gatherings to brand calves, a job usually shared among helpful neighbors. One man branded twenty-five calves with about twenty-five helpers. The other branded a hundred calves with his wife, a couple of nephews, and an elderly hired hand.

The first man is always quick to respond to his neighbors' needs; the second is always too busy. He's too busy to fix fence, too, so his cows are often on the highway and in neighbors' pastures. For several years, we put them back in his pasture when he wasn't around, but he never seemed to notice or fix that fence. He's not keeping up his end of the neighborly bargain. Now when his cattle get out, we call the sheriff.

You don't plan to run cattle, you say, so who cares what we think? Remember the fire department and the EMTs, all volunteer. They come when they can, but no one checks on why they didn't show up.

Here's another country custom: when you are standing on your own land, repairing the half of the fence to the right is your job. This policy has ruled here as long as white men have been fencing this prairie, and applies to everyone. It's your responsibility to fence livestock *out* rather than a rancher's job to fence them *in*. Paul, who owned the acreage you wanted, was old and had been unable to fix fence very efficiently for several years; moreover, he'd driven off most of the men he'd hired, so all his fences need major work now.

So, let's see, if you'd bought that 680-acre plot, you would own the job of installing and maintaining four of the eight miles of fence surrounding it, about 21,120 feet. Your access road would require another couple of miles of fence, with gates so we could move our cattle and vehicles across. Neighboring ranchers run both cattle and buffalo, so the fence has to be high and tight enough to contain them. A fence of six-foot wooden posts and four strands of tightly strung barbed wire will usually contain cows; buffalo require an eight-foot fence with posts to match. Steel posts are handy because you can drive them into the ground, but a good fence requires one wooden post for every three or four of steel. The wooden posts must be treated to resist moisture and rot, and planted a couple of feet deep and no more than five feet apart. At the corners, set wood posts a little deeper and build cross-bracing; you can look at the way we build ours. If you have gotten to know us, we'll probably be glad to help with the work, though I suppose you'll just hire a fencing company. In 2005, costs in our area were running $1.22 per foot for the fence, and $13.60 per hour for the labor; figure $25,000 in materials alone. Hard to say how fast a crew might work, but the labor costs would probably be double that. All this expense is part of the ultimate cost of your new home.

First, though, drill a well. Someone told me about a guy who bought a country acreage and hired contractors to build the house. When they said it was time to hook up to the well, the owner said, "Well?" He'd lived in town all his life, thought the plumber could just tap into some pipeline somewhere. Of course, some people relish these city slicker stories so much we really can't be sure they are true.

I hear drillers in our area are charging around $20,000 for a 400-foot hole. Of course, there's no guarantee of water, or a sustainable flow. Our water supply here seems to be dwindling as development moves out from town. Rapid City has drilled several wells four thousand feet deep to provide water for its growing population; such wells may suck water not only from deep down, but from shallower wells. A 400-foot well two miles from your fire is already dry; the owners haul water even for bathing. There's no guarantee that any of us will continue to have enough water.

Twenty years ago, local ranchers formed a cooperative to buy the deep wells on what was once a missile site, but buying into the group is expensive. Their bylaws follow a "first in time" protocol: water goes first to the people who pledged their money to establish the pipeline years ago. In addition, the law provides that domestic use prevails over all other uses; homes and cattle get water before trees or lawns. My family considered buying in once, but couldn't justify the expense.

All these are matters that involve interaction with neighbors, so squabbles can develop if you do not keep in touch.

Have I mentioned the dog packs roaming through our herds, chasing cows and wildlife to exhaustion and killing calves? Their owners live on country acreages but work in town all day, so if Rover is sitting on the porch when they come home, they assume he's stayed home. Some local folks just shoot every strange dog they see. Our dogs stay home; their job is to guard the place. If they don't do it, they are worthless, and we expect our ranching neighbors to shoot them.

I'm sure you've noticed that the houses we natives live in are hunkered behind hills and along draws. You may think we're just too dumb to appreciate the view, but houses on hilltops are high maintenance. Wind, hail, and sleet pummel shingles, siding, and windows, and bore through cracks, driving heating costs up. Since I built my house in 1981, I've replaced the roof and siding twice, my windows and insulation once, in spite of the substantial windbreak on the north and west sides.

Considering the risk of fire and the distance your house would be from the highway, you should choose noncombustible or fire-resistant building materials, ruling out log or wood siding and cedar shakes in favor of metal or stucco, brick or stone. Wood stoves or those picturesque fireplaces are the largest single cause of fires in some areas. None of us have burned garbage outside since a new homeowner lit the trash in her burning barrel and went to work. That fire blew several miles; by the time she got off work, she owed the county more for the fire-fighting bill than her house cost.

During snow season, roughly October through May, drifts pile up on the south side of anything. From my dining room window, I can see a hilltop house with the garage door on the south side. Every morning in winter, I can watch the owner get his aerobic exercise shoveling the drift away to get his car out to drive to work.

HUMANS TINKER with their world as surely as coyotes eat mice; it's all natural behavior, but we sometimes forget that our human puttering has a greater effect on the whole landscape. Ranchers can be the best of neighbors; we can still say with a straight face that a man would give you "the shirt off his back" and be telling the truth. But we're sometimes impatient with folks who want to move into an area and ignore the complicated web of custom worked out by several generations of neighbors who have been responsible for helping to keep the whole region in good health economically as well as ecologically. As you look for land in the country, I hope you will visit the local people and ask questions. Learn about responsible and civil behavior as well as the price of real estate. We don't all like each other, but we built our community by accommodating differences, and we think that arrangement should continue to work.

—Sincerely, Linda M. Hasselstrom, rancher

The School Bus Driver Waved

One warm spring day, driving north to my ranch on a Wyoming back road with all the car windows open, I was thinking about unpaid bills when I noticed someone mowing the borrow ditch. When hay is sparse because of drought, many ranchers and farmers take their mowers into the roadside ditch ("borrowed" from the highway right-of-way) to harvest the hay there. After all, it belonged to the landowner before the government decided to *borrow* it for the common good of transportation.

I slowed down and noted that the mower was a white-haired woman wrestling an old tractor along. She grinned and waved while I was still looking her over, so I scrambled to wave back, surprised.

Driving on, I wondered what caused her to greet me. She saw a woman with efficiently short gray hair, elbow out the car window enjoying the sunshine. Perhaps she appreciated the fact that with my window down, I was paying more attention than many drivers do to the country where she lives and works.

She could not have known how fully I recall and miss her life, that I know what it's like to drive a tractor in the itchy heat hour after hour. She may have been grateful I showed concern for her safety by slowing down to pass her.

For a few moments we were linked in our enjoyment of the day. Though I have driven that highway once or twice a week each summer for more than fifteen years, I had never seen her before. Yet both of us "took the time" and "made the effort" to wave and cheer each other in our separate journeys.

If I'd been on a cell phone, I'd have missed that spark of connection.

WHEN I WAS A CHILD living on my family's ranch in western South Dakota, my father waved to the driver of every car we met on the way to town, and that driver waved back. My father might say, "Oh, Gus got a new car," or "Cliff ought to get that headlight fixed." Of course he knew everyone in the neighborhood, but he waved whether he knew them or not.

Since I started commuting to the ranch several times a month, the people who know me still wave if they spot me on the road, in spite of my Wyoming license plates. I like to think that they are acknowledging that I am still part of this community.

Promoters caused our paved two-lane to bloat into a divided four-lane, though Department of Transportation surveys indicated the larger highway was not really needed for the amount of traffic that exists now, or is expected into the next century. This mutation is, I believe, symbolic of the divisions destroying the rural West. Like other tools, notably pistols and cars, a highway can be useful or destructive, depending on how it's operated.

On a four-lane highway, the average driver wouldn't notice her own mother dying of heat stroke in the opposite lane; its size invites and abets anonymity, speed, competitiveness, ignorance of the surroundings—the opposite of what most people say they want in the country. Most four-lanes collect convenience stores and developments the way a prairie dog draws fleas, destroying the countryside we profess to love. If you love the country, I heard someone say recently, live in town.

The South Dakota Department of Transportation condemned part of my pasture land to build the additional lanes for the four-lane. A green street sign now calls my driveway Windbreak Road. Waiting to pull out on a spring day, overwhelmed with the sense of loss, I devise a test of community connection.

Waving in the country has been the subject of too many humorous essays, often written by city folks, so I want my signal to be simple and clear. With my right hand at the top of the steering wheel, palm out, I raise my index and middle fingers. I make this gesture when I can see the oncoming driver's face, allowing time for a response.

My first waving experiment lasts twenty-eight miles, from my turnoff to

Hot Springs, South Dakota, and includes eighty-four vehicles. Greetings are returned by six.

For the next few miles, I review my data. My headlights are on, a universal signal for "Passing is dangerous." Many of us in this neighborhood adopted this custom after losing relatives and friends to accidents on two-lane highways; therefore, the cars showing headlights may have been local. The school bus driver waved, but the highway patrol trooper didn't. I waved three times at three cars too close together, and got no response. The first driver was nervously watching the two behind him. Both of them were riding each other's bumpers, zigzagging, peering ahead, trying to pass in the no-passing zone.

Intrigued by the results, I repeat the experiment from Edgemont, South Dakota, to Lusk, Wyoming, on two-lane SD 18 and WY 18-85, famous for lurking troopers, leaping deer, and speed traps.

The first vehicle I meet is a battered pickup with local plates. The driver's arm is extended along the back of the seat. Surprised, he waves, grins, waves some more. No one waves first. When I wave at two semis hauling hay bales, the first driver looks astonished; the second is talking on his cell phone. A dozen dead deer decompose in the ditch; speeders have made this road a death trap for wildlife. Covering sixty-six miles in sixty-two minutes, I wave seventy-four times and receive only four salutations.

Experiment summary: 158 waves, 10 returned. What might we learn from this waving experiment?

At the very least, my research may indicate plains folk are dangerously out of practice in the traditional friendly western wave. If they just moved here, maybe they don't understand the custom. And perhaps longtime residents aren't feeling friendly in these challenging days.

A friend with whom I discuss my trial suggests that my waving is an aggressive act, and compares it to the traditional New York third-finger wave. She suggests that my waving symbolizes my refusal to adapt to "modern" ways, and calls me "a holdout, a living old westerner practicing neighborliness." (I suspect she really wants to say "old fossil.")

If this is aggression, why not? Let's all start waving at each other on two-lane highways. If your wave expresses your hostility to bigger highways and look-alike communities, that's fine. If it's pure friendliness, that's OK too.

Maybe the jerk tailgating that oncoming car will be so startled he'll drop his cell phone and drive with both hands.

Perhaps we'll start choosing to drive where people wave, relishing the relaxation of lower speed limits on two-lanes the way we adjust our lifestyles in wilderness, the way we are rediscovering cooking under the banner of "slow food." When increased traffic on narrow roads encourages highway planners to push for wider routes, maybe we'll take the next step: discussing with neighbors whether we need a bigger highway before we leap on the bandwagon of support.

Waving certainly won't solve the problems of growth and development in western communities, but we have to start somewhere. Waving a hand is better than brandishing a firearm, and maybe our ulcers won't flare up.

BACK IN CHEYENNE, I ponder my waving experiment as I drive down city streets. Despite my professed dislike of it, city life offers multiple opportunities for casual little exchanges. In the country, I might spend days without seeing another person.

Waiting for my chance to turn left on a busy street, I make eye contact with the oncoming Harley rider and nod as I brake. He nods back, thanking me. We have looked in one another's eyes and communicated. If I'd turned in front of him, he would have had to brake hard or hit me; bikers have been killed both ways by drivers who ignore them. He can tell by my actions that I know about consequences. He may guess, and correctly, that a motorcyclist I love was badly hurt by a motorist who wasn't paying attention.

Entering the post office, I notice the ten-year-old boy holding the door is black and sullen, perhaps just rebuked by his mother, who waits at the curb glaring at him. He expects me to pass through without acknowledgment. When I say, "Thank you, kind sir," he jerks as if I'd hit him, and then grins hugely. His mother and I smile at one another, maybe a little grimly because we both know about alternatives to this harmony.

A FEW YEARS AGO, I was performing at the National Cowboy Poetry Gathering in Elko, Nevada. Each time I stood up to read one of my poems, I saw the same tiny Chinese woman in the audience. Her face was always crinkled in a smile beneath the silver-black crown of her long hair. One day I was able to sit beside her in the audience; when I introduced my-self, she bowed her head. She'd come to the gathering from San Francisco solely to hear me read my work. Her life, she said, was richer because of my poems about butchering and calving, scrubbing parsnips and planting peas, coring apples and drying onions, grass and rodeos and blizzards and my grandmother's hands. Her parents had immigrated to San Francisco directly from China, and her mother's feet had been bound; she'd lived all her life in that teeming city. Beyond that, she couldn't explain the connec-tion and neither can I. We sat next to one another for an hour, apparently content, but did not exchange addresses. If we'd gone to lunch, the thread linking us might have snapped, but if she moved in next door, we'd soon find more common ground. We cannot know in what place or person we may find home.

Brief and often silent communication—glances, nods, acknowledg-ments, phrases, waves—count as part of our ticket to community, to my way of thinking. The important part is that we pay attention to one another in a respectful way, remain aware of possibilities. These mutual recognitions are even more enjoyable when they occur between two people who don't look alike. When the dreadlocked teenager opens a door for the elderly white woman using a walker and she says, "Why, thank you, young man," they unite only momentarily, but such brief fellowship can change lives.

Laughter in the Alley

Soon after Jerry and I bought this house on Warren Avenue in Cheyenne, I began working on the gardens that would eventually dominate my time outdoors here. Our house stands on the corner of a busy street, across from business offices for the school system and a high school for problem students; so a lot of people walk by at all times of the day.

At first, when someone spoke to me, I'd be thinking about the writing waiting in my upstairs study, and be so startled I'd nearly turn a back flip. Eventually, I put my prairie-honed peripheral vision to work and noticed who was approaching, judging whether or not they'd want to talk. Often, the visit ended with my gift of plants or seeds.

Some previous tenant had covered the parkways—that area between sidewalk and the street—with black plastic and gravel. This method seldom kills weeds, and the scraggly growths that pushed through the barriers were ugly and tough. Several trees grew in the parkways, though the black plastic, by funneling rain and snowfall into the street, probably hastened their demise. Most of them died before we'd been in the house five years.

Jerry shoveled up the gravel and hauled it to the alley. Then we ripped up the plastic, and I began trying to bring back to life the gray, tortured soil. While Jerry worked to repair the house—new wiring, plumbing—I remodeled the soil, collecting bags of grass and digging it in along with our household compost.

Several years of work brought the yards inside the fence into bloom, and I gradually filled the parkways with native species that wouldn't need water after they established themselves, and planted hollyhock seeds in the alley.

One day I came home and noticed an elderly woman picking hollyhocks with two little girls. I walked into the alley and recognized the owner of the house next door; she'd raised her children there before turning it into a rental. "I'm showing them how to make hollyhock dolls," she said, giggling. "I hope you don't mind." Mind? I thought I was the last person who remembered her grandmother helping her make hollyhock dolls. Conserving water is probably woven into my DNA, so I never watered the alley flowers; they thrived on their own, the dominant species changing with the amount of moisture we received each year.

Each noon, I harness up the dogs and we walk a couple of blocks in the neighborhood. We go out the back gate, set in a few feet from the plank fence so a small anteroom was formed off the alley. A waist-high block of concrete used to be a trash burner, back when cities could trust civilians to burn their garbage.

As we walk, I automatically collect into plastic bags broken glass and bottles as well as the dogs' leavings, and set up trash cans the wind or stray dogs have knocked over. These walks bring back memories of walking back from kindergarten in Rapid City, cutting through alleyways and vacant lots. I spend time in alleys when I travel with a dog, too. Idling at canine pace, I see mostly the discarded debris of lives in the lanes homeowners consider semiprivate. I seldom meet residents, but visit with maids and maintenance men, telephone repair persons and plumbers. Through knotholes and gaps in privacy fences, I enjoy green and flowery backyards, usually empty or containing only a frustrated dog. Time and expense are lavished on these spaces, but usually they provide no food. And no matter what time of day or week I pass, I seldom see people in their backyards, so these garden rooms seem to provide no repose either.

A few months after I started strolling and tidying in the alley, I noticed several neighbors planting flowers outside their back fences. Some created tiny landscaped areas with attractive rocks and varieties of plants. The garbagemen were careful not to drive over or step on the plants. Soon the children two houses away began setting up little towns in a wide spot beside another neighbor's garage, playing there when the sun was highest because the shade was deep and the alley insulated from traffic noise. Friends who visited from out of town, wondering how I could stand living in the city, walked the dogs with me and said, "It's like a private courtyard."

One spring evening, Jerry and I were grilling steaks for friends in our backyard when we heard young voices in the alley. We peeked through the cracks in the fence and realized a high school couple had tucked themselves into our alcove at the back gate. Sitting on the old concrete garbage burner, they were cooing and kissing, so immersed in romance they had no idea four people were watching from only inches away. As we tiptoed back to our chairs, Jerry said, "Whispering their little secrets." We all smiled, reminiscing.

Thinking how I had settled into this new home, I reread Paul Gruchow's *Grass Roots: The Universe of Home,* and was struck by his definition of inhabiting a place, meaning a person has "learned how to wear a place like a familiar garment, like the garments of sanctity that nuns once wore."

Suddenly our alley had become a habit, had developed a personality, though it wasn't all posies and peace. A block away, the plank fence around one house was used as a billboard to carry a message painted in large red letters: "MARY Don't throw trash in this yard. Use the garbage can you stole from us."

PEOPLE BEGAN TO TELL US they'd altered their evening walk to pass by our flowers. Dog-walkers looked at the flowers, asked me their names, kept their dogs from squatting. More children played in the back alley.

One night a woman parked beside me, leaped out of her car, and said, "Do you mind if we let this butterfly go in your garden?" She opened the car door for a little blonde girl, who nudged the yellow and black butterfly from her finger to an evening primrose.

"When we got in the car, it was fluttering against the window," said the woman, "and I didn't want to just leave it in the parking lot, so I remembered your flowers and drove over here. Blocks and blocks," she said, and blushed.

We'd never paid much attention to the alternative high school across the street until we noticed the DRUG FREE ZONE signs and realized that the ban included cigarettes. Two or three times a day, a cluster of students hustle across the street to smoke, and toss cigarette butts into the flower beds. As the native plants grew taller and dried in the summer heat, I realized my miniature prairie was as vulnerable to a fire caused by a smoldering cigarette as the life-sized one.

One morning when the dogs barked I saw several boys and one angry-looking girl smoking on the corner. I stepped outside. Instantly, the girl spotted me and mumbled something I knew translated to "Authority Figure Approaching." I'd never thought of how I looked from their point of view; they all hunched their shoulders against me.

"No," I said, thinking fast, "I'm not here to chew you out. I just wanted to—er—introduce you to the dogs so they won't bark when you come over here to smoke." I knelt by the dogs, patting their heads.

"My friend has a dog like that," one boy said, bending down to stick his fingers through the fence. "What are they—Westies?" I babbled on about the dogs, asked how school was, and then told them about the flowers and the fire danger. The boys chatted more easily than the girl, who kept puffing her cigarette and squinting through the smoke at me. Surely she didn't see me as competition, so why was she so distrustful?

Eventually, I stepped out to visit with the smokers so often that when they got a new recruit who groaned when I emerged, the others said, "No, she's OK." I gritted my teeth and resisted lectures on smoking, though I couldn't help suggesting that the two pregnant girls do a little reading on what they might be doing to their babies. They just rolled their eyes and puffed.

BRAD ORTIZ, a carpenter, lived two houses away from us with his wife, Jolene, who became a legend in our neighborhood. After a grocery-shopping spree, she was leaving the store, arms loaded and trailed by her three children. A teenage boy grabbed her purse and ran. Dropping the groceries, she told the children to stay by the car and proved she'd been a high school track star. She caught him in seconds, knocked him down, yanked an arm up behind his back, and suggested that a bystander call the cops.

The kid screamed and cried, and bystanders argued she should let him go. "You got your purse back," they said. "And he's been punished enough." She held on until the police arrived; then she pressed charges.

Brad and Jolene's camper was too big to park behind their house, so they kept it across the street. Sometime during that winter, I began to feel as if someone was watching me. Outside, I would feel sure someone was staring, but no one was in sight, no shadow by any of the windows. When I mentioned the feeling to Jane, who lived in the apartment next door, she nodded; several of us had noticed the sensation, but none of us could find a logical explanation.

Then one day Jolene was in her living room talking on the phone with Brad when she saw a disheveled man walking on the sidewalk across the street, not unusual since this is a main thoroughfare between downtown and the homeless shelters and parks on the outskirts. She noticed the man slouch along the sidewalk and vanish behind the camper. But he didn't re-appear on the other side. She shrieked at Brad over the telephone and ran outside, then had second thoughts. By the time Brad got home ten min-utes later, the camper was empty.

Well, almost. The refrigerator, cupboards, and liquor cabinet had been cleaned out; spare tools were gone, and the bedding was filthy, but the toilet and sink were full. Every stranger who walked through the neighbor-hood after that was watched by more than one pair of eyes to make sure he kept going.

ONE JUNE DAY, I heard laughter in the alley, stepped out the gate, and was nearly run over by a bicycle. Several boys and one younger one were racing back and forth. I laughed and waved, then took a minute to enjoy the row of irises against the back fence, in glorious bloom in all shades of lavender and purple, white and bronze.

A few days later, as I was driving up the side street toward home, the older boy and two younger ones zipped out of the alley in front of my car. As I slammed on the brakes, I saw they were looking at me and didn't see the car coming from the other direction. I leaned on the horn, and the driver stopped. The boys U-turned and zipped back up the alley.

I parked in my driveway and marched up the alley to Jolene's back door. All three bikes lay in the backyard, and all three boys were just popping the tops off sodas. Jolene was on her porch. When I explained, she lit into them.

"He said it was OK," they said, pointing to the older boy who lived a cou-ple of houses away. She chewed him out and told her boys they wouldn't be playing with him until they learned how to think for themselves. The older boy left in a sulk, glaring at us. Jolene hollered, "I'll be over to talk to your mother later."

The next morning when I stepped into the back alley to see how many irises had bloomed in the night, every single blossom had been lopped off. The two younger boys were riding up and down the alley, both wearing bike helmets. The older boy was sitting on his bike, watching.

"Hi guys," I said, trying not to snarl. "Glad you're wearing helmets. Sorry I had to talk to your mom, but you know, you could have been killed yesterday. Both cars could have run over you."

By then, I'd gotten control of my breathing and could say I felt badly about the irises, but I knew they hadn't done it. I looked at the older boy, too, when I said it. He stared back.

Later in the morning, I took a photograph of the buds on a huge black iris in front of the house. I'd planted it three years before, and it was almost trembling in its nearness to blossoming for the first time. One hour after I took the photograph, I went out to get the mail. The stalk lay on the ground, the bloom shriveled and flattened by someone's shoe.

The next day Jolene stopped by to tell me what had happened after her lecture to the three boys. First, she reminded me, she'd doled out sodas to all three boys. A few minutes later, she'd gone shopping, leaving the back door unlocked as usual, but taking her children along. When she came back, she found six empty soda cans in the kitchen; the soda had been poured over every carpet in the house. Neither of us doubted who the culprit was.

During the next few evenings, the neighbors discussed the boy and his family and what might be done. I was afraid to mention the iris for fear he would hurt my dogs when they were in the yard alone. If I planted cactus in the alley, Jolene's children and the neighborhood pets would suffer.

Each of us, it turned out, had made a practice of greeting the older boy by name, speaking nicely to him, attempting to make him feel as if he was part of the neighborhood. Jolene had talked with his parents. Someone said his mother, who weighed more than three hundred pounds, was a social worker. His sister, about twelve and seriously overweight, walked around and around the block each evening, glowering, looking at her feet. His father was often in jail, but when he was home could be heard shouting at the children. I'd seen him walking a black Lab without a leash. If the dog didn't come when he called it, he yelled until it approached and then beat it with the leash.

Jane said she'd visited the house once after catching the boy chasing her cat, and seen a dead rabbit in a cage on the front porch. The rabbit was only fur and bones, but its empty food and water dishes were still in place.

IN VARIOUS GROUPS, we talked about the high school boy and his family for weeks, wondering how we could include them, or at least the boy, in the community we shared. Jolene snapped that she'd always welcomed him into her home with her much younger children, and was growing tired of his behavior.

We drifted apart without coming to a consensus. Not long afterward, we stopped seeing the boy around. Rumors circulated: he'd joined the army; he was too young for the army but he'd been sent to reform school; he was in a mental institution. The girl continued to walk around the block every evening, and every few weeks she'd be accompanied by a different yappy small dog. Midnight the Lab escaped from his yard once or twice and confronted me in the alley, snarling with his hackles raised as I backed away dragging my dogs.

I divided the iris bulbs and moved my favorites inside the fence, including the deep purple one, but the others bloomed unimpeded in the alley. Jolene and her husband bought a bigger house and moved away. We heard later they were divorced, but that rumor didn't change our admiration for her brand of citizenship.

Tomato Cages Are Metaphors

My next-door neighbor's car windows are open. Snow is falling briskly, blowing in the windows to fringe the seat belts, piling up on the shoulders of the stained front seats. This is not the first time she has left the windows open.

Krissy is a single mother, chronically short of money. She often has car trouble. Her landlord is her grandfather, with whom my relationship has been cordial, though distant.

So why don't I go roll up her windows? Or tell her they're open? I pace from the front room to the kitchen and back, wishing we were the kind of neighbors who look out for each other.

But we're not.

"Consequences," I mutter, going back to work. She's only a neighbor by proximity. I've been reading P. J. O'Rourke's *All the Trouble in the World*, and quote to myself, "They are people too. They are just as dumb, stinky, and ridiculous as we are."

THAT WAS IN FEBRUARY; the snow had been predicted the day before, but Krissy seldom noticed anything that was not happening to her at that moment.

When Krissy moved into the upstairs apartment, my friend Jane lived on the first floor. She'd known Krissy and her large, loud family for years, and could understand some of the reasons she behaved as she did. We both hoped that this time she might make changes in her life. I also felt compassion for her as a single woman raising a child. Her husband had been abusive, said the grapevine, so I respected her for having the courage to leave him. And I was glad the drug dealers who had recently occupied that apartment were gone.

Before moving in, Krissy visited with her grandfather several times. She'd stride up the walk, pink hair flying, waving her arms and yelling instructions. He spent several weeks replacing appliances, painting, laying new carpet.

Then one Saturday, two pickup trucks and several cars roared up and parked in front of our house. Four or five men piled out, laughing and joking, leaving the car doors open and music blasting. Krissy's things barely filled the two pickups, but her moving party, complete with pizza delivery and cases of beer stacked on the lawn, lasted hours. The guys would carry something upstairs, clunking and banging and cursing, then gather on the porch to drink a beer and smoke a joint, jostling each other to the music's beat. They tossed the cigarettes and beer cans on the lawn and yelled profanities.

Jerry and I were working in the yard, weeding and mowing. When we took a break, we sat in the arbor on the north side of the house, out of sight of the movers. We reminded each other that it's hard to get help moving. Weeding in the flower beds along the street, where my flowers were blooming wildly, I collected the week's accumulation of waste paper and dog feces as well as the fresh beer bottles and cigarettes.

A BLACK FRIEND TELLS ME that she flinches when she is walking alone and meets a white man, just as I sometimes shrink away from a black man. That wince arises, I think, from ancient and universal fears of *difference*. Attending graduate school in Missouri, I met Toni in an English class; our backgrounds were different, but our ideas were similar enough so that we became friends. One evening she asked why I was being so nice to her. So I told her: I'd never known anyone black, and I was curious. She'd grown up in an East St. Louis ghetto and known few trustworthy whites. One memorable night, we went with several muscular friends of hers to a series of jazz clubs in East St. Louis. The men were polite and protective. Yet several times, asked to dance by stunningly attractive women, they turned them down curtly, even rudely. When I asked why, Toni gently explained to me that the women weren't. Women, that is. I'd never seen drag queens.

In a jazz club so small that a band member who moved fast flicked sweat on the audience, the music swelled and scampered and spiraled among the dim lights until the world I'd always known vanished. A woman who had been sitting beside me apologized for leaving in the middle of a tune, but she saw the music in color, she said, and she had to go paint what she was seeing. Suddenly, I was startled to see a white hand wrap around a drink on the table in front of me.

My hand. I sensed that night what has now been proven: we're all pretty much identical; it's not DNA but cultural behavior that separates people from one another, turns fear into anger, distrust, upheaval.

THE SNOW is four inches deep inside the car now, and it's nearly noon. Krissy may still be asleep; she and her friends came home at 4:00 A.M., yelling and slamming car doors. I was awake, knowing her daughter had been upstairs alone since she left for work at dark.

As I begin to review Krissy's transgressions against neighborliness, I accuse myself of being defensive. OK; I am small, I contain multitudes of teeny little faults, and a few great big ones.

WHAT DOES IT MEAN to be a neighbor in a city? When you live close enough to hear each other's arguments, courtesy is important. Krissy failed first in the small courtesies. That moving day, she and her friends laughed and played loud music and drank beer and never spoke to the neighbors on either side. All of us, we said to one another later, were prepared to be friendly, but perhaps we looked hostile, or judgmental.

Over the next few days, she and her friends parked along the street in front of our house. Ignoring the sidewalks, they stomped through the blooms, tossing cigarettes, fast-food cartons, and bottles. Every morning, I collected a new batch of trash, including used diapers and human feces. I never gave in to the temptation to put the bags of trash on her porch.

One afternoon when a pickup parked in front of our house, Krissy and her sister fell out of the back, giggling and rolling around in the flowers. Later, I put tomato cages around several large plants. Tricky things, tomato cages: mine are five feet tall, a series of metal circles linked by thick upright wires, shoved six inches into the ground. In place around a green plant, they are practically invisible even in daylight, and hard to knock over. The wire is tough and springy. Get a leg though one of the circles, and it's hard to get it out again. Every few days I notice that they are twisted or canted over, and I carefully replace them.

I consider my efforts educational. The tomato cages are metaphors. Being neighborly requires paying attention. Some people never notice that smelly garbage bags attract flies, birds, cats, dogs, and skunks. Every day or two, a man I've never seen before emerges from Krissy's door carrying the trash; some leave it by the front step as they drive away, while others lob it toward the garbage cans in back. Krissy never goes to the back alley, so she doesn't know that several neighbors who are tired of shoveling up rotting food and diapers have sent photographs to her landlord.

A half-dozen empty cat-food cans litter Krissy's front porch. She feeds the neighborhood cats, and lets some inside. While waiting for food, the felines relieve themselves on neighboring lawns. Late at night, when Krissy is gone, she doesn't hear the elderly ladies on the other side of the street calling their kitties. Several times when Krissy has been gone for a weekend, I have seen a cat pacing the ledges inside the windows, yowling.

What else did Krissy do that made her an unfit neighbor? One of her windows overlooks my kitchen. Several times, feeling watched, I looked up to see Krissy and her sister making faces at me. Writing, I work in my second-floor study, windows open in warm weather. No more. Even with the windows shut, the glass rattles with the music.

Surely what I write about Krissy shows more about me, and my views about neighborly conduct, than any assertion I could make. Perhaps some of my objections are matters of taste or personality. Culture.

ALL SUMMER, Krissy told Jane, she couldn't sleep; Jane complained about her pacing the floors overhead. So Krissy left her front door open, her daughter asleep upstairs, and walked the surrounding streets.

While she was gone, young men and women knocked on the door, or simply wandered inside. They'd been customers of the previous drug-dealing tenants, perhaps, and didn't know they'd moved. Jane talked to Krissy again and again about the danger to her child, but nothing changed.

Each time I spoke to Krissy about her garbage or her noise, she widened her eyes and promised to do better. That's how she operates, Jane said, and

we laughed, a couple of cynical old broads who never benefited from innocence even when we had it.

Once, at 3:00 A.M., I watched a young man climb up the porch support
posts to the roof, then enter the little girl's bedroom window. I called the
landlord. His wife, annoyed, said he was a nephew.

How would I know? I asked. The next time I saw the boy climb in the
window, I called the police.

Several evenings while Jerry and I sat on our porch at dusk, Krissy and
her friends sat on the concrete porch next door, smoking something that
smelled terrible. I mentioned the smell to a knowledgeable friend. "That's
crack," she said grimly. Several of the neighbors who had identified the
smell spoke with Krissy's mother, her counselor, her landlord, the police.
After that, the smell drifted out the upstairs windows.

ONE MORNING Jane knocked on our door and asked us to come outside.
Both her cars, parked on the street, had been badly dented. A strange
car—smashed too badly to drive—was parked behind them. Jane wanted
the driver's name, and she didn't want to move her cars without an insurance adjustor. And she needed to go to work.

Krissy was home, so Jane tried to rouse her by phone and knocking. Then she called the police and explained that besides the damage,
she was worried about the child who might be upstairs. After the police
arrived, Jerry and I stood in the yard talking with Jane and one officer,
while another sat in the cruiser talking with headquarters.

A motor roared, and a gleaming sports car with aerials sprouting from
every orifice whipped into the driveway. A man with gold earrings that contrasted vividly with his ebony ears and nostrils emerged. He had taken two
steps toward the house before he realized that two police officers and several other people were watching him intently. He spun back into the car,
backed out, and laid rubber going up the street.

Eventually, the police got a court order and broke into Krissy's apartment. They found her in bed, but couldn't find her daughter. Jane, who
went upstairs with them, said drug paraphernalia was fully visible in the
apartment, scattered among filthy clothes and garbage. The police yelled,
shook and slapped Krissy, and poured water over her head before she re-

gained consciousness. Finally Krissy mumbled that her daughter was staying with a relative, and gave them the phone number of the driver who had
wrecked the cars.

A few days later, a police car parked in front of the house, and an officer
knocked on Jane's door. He'd come for more information on the damage to
her cars, but while he and Jane talked in her living room, Jane noticed the
upstairs toilet flushing several times. Suddenly water and sewage poured
through Jane's bedroom ceiling onto her bed.

When Jane pounded on Krissy's door, she came out swinging her car
keys and holding her daughter's hand. Jane told her what had happened.

"Oh," said Krissy, snapping her gum. "The kid flushed a toy down the
toilet. Bye, gotta run!"

In words of one syllable, Jane explained the consequences of that flush,
involving plumbing and cleaning. Later, Jane said she'd found baggies full
of white powder in the sewage on her bed. Days later, when Jane asked the
landlord's help, the smell of sewage was still strong in both apartments.

Jane talked with the landlord, reminding him that for thirteen years
she had found responsible renters for the upstairs apartment, mowed the
lawns, and supervised maintenance of this and several other properties he
owned. The landlord admitted that Krissy had never paid rent; he wanted
to make her pay for the damage to his and Jane's property, but his wife and
daughter, Krissy's mother, wouldn't let him. Jane moved out that month.

TRYING TO BE FAIR, I realize that I resent Krissy in part because I miss
Jane, who was a real neighbor in a house that is only a few feet away. Jane
and I were slow to become friends, but we gradually grew to trust one another. Now there is no one next door who will notice if my house is on fire
or if someone kicks the door down.

After Jane left, Krissy acquired a new boyfriend who arrived each Friday
in a double-cab pickup and roared away early Monday morning. The first
weekend, he bought new garbage cans. Each time he drove up, he came
downstairs immediately with three or four bags of trash. Sometimes, as he
drove away—I always knew, because he gunned the motor—another man
arrived. Sometimes Krissy left and was gone overnight. When she came
home, she always got out of the car talking on her cell phone. Within minutes, she'd get company. During the next three or four hours, I'd notice

vehicles parked with motors running as hollow-eyed youngsters ran into her apartment without knocking, then left shoving a package in a pocket or purse.

"Came for meth, man," said one unappetizing specimen, when I opened the inner door to his knock. He yanked on the screen door I kept locked. "Hey man, lemme in," he said, kicking the door.

After I convinced him to shop elsewhere, I visited the local police station and engaged in a mutually satisfying conversation with a plainclothes officer who specialized in drug-related problems.

ONE SPRING NIGHT I'd been working late at my computer. As I switched off the light, my eye caught a movement in Krissy's window, just opposite mine. A naked man was dancing in her hall, pirouetting with a yellow and orange towel that contrasted vividly with his glossy chocolate skin. The lad had some fine moves I noticed as I dropped the blinds.

At sunrise the next morning, I was in my yard with my first cup of coffee and a camera, happily photographing new blossoms as I did every morning. Krissy's door opened, and the man came out.

When he saw me, he ducked, turned his face toward the street, flipped up his collar, and walked crabwise past my chain-link fence, three feet away from me. He rounded the corner and quick-stepped down the side street.

I'm a writer; I notice things. So his furtiveness made me focus on his license plate and the make of his car. Five minutes later, I was drinking a second cup of coffee on the inside porch when he pulled up in front of my house, talking on a cell phone. He got out of the car, stomped through my flowers, and knocked. When I opened the inner door, I stood well back, with the cordless phone in one hand.

"Why are you takin' pictures of me?" he yelled.

"I was taking pictures of my flowers. Get off my porch."

He stepped closer to the screen door and screamed, "Why you takin' pictures of me, lady?"

"I was in my yard minding my own business. Get off my property. That's your second warning." I held up the phone. He yelled a little more, swore, pounded on the screen door, and then left.

Three minutes later, Krissy knocked. I picked up the phone again.

As I opened the door, she yelled, "Why are you watching us and taking pictures?"

"I'm taking pictures of my own flowers in my own front yard."

"You were taking pictures of us."

"You seem to be paranoid, Krissy. I've heard people who use drugs are often paranoid."

"Why do you hate me?" she wailed.

"I don't hate you. In fact, I want to help you. You should consider putting up curtains if you're going to have naked guys dancing around your apartment with the lights on. All the neighbors got a good look." She flounced away without answering.

Each time the man stayed overnight after that, he parked in the lot across the street, and Krissy hung a blanket over the window.

When the Official Boyfriend arrived on weekends, the window remained uncurtained.

AT 4:00 A.M., I am awake. Jane, who talks often with one of her former landlord's sons, reports that Krissy is pregnant and planning to marry the Official Boyfriend. For days, she has been packing, rushing noisily back and forth in his loud truck. Piles of clothing, garbage, and discarded furniture are scattered in the front and back yards and in the alley.

Lying in the dark, I consider the amount of time I have spent thinking about Krissy. Describing her behavior, I wrote to a friend. Am I becoming a bigot, I asked?

Much of what we call "bigotry," he replied, is just "1. Intolerance for other cultures when, 2. Other cultures blatantly ignore local customs." My anger is justified, he assures me, adding, "If I walked into a synagogue eating a ham sandwich, if I walked into a Taiwanese restaurant and loudly started talking about how Mao Tse Tung was the best thing to happen to China in 2500 years, if I walked down Broadway in Seattle wearing a T-shirt that says "KILL ALL FAGGOTS," I would *expect* to get wildly belligerent responses, because I am blatantly ignoring the local customs. Why should I tolerate *other* cultures ignoring mine?"

Cultural differences. My neighbors and I, discussing Krissy in the alley, agreed that we'd tried to separate our dislike of her illegal activities and the dangers they created for her daughter from our instinctive distrust of her self-centered attitude. We almost apologized to each other for watching her while we exchanged stories of her antisocial behavior. When we weren't being politically correct, we called her a druggie slut. We all know people who used drugs, have known them long enough to watch them marry or not, have children or not, hold jobs or not. We've concluded drug users start out selfish and become more so; they can't be good parents, and more responsible citizens must pay for their mistakes.

Perhaps our neighborly scrutiny helped drive Krissy away. We don't have to watch her anymore, but we didn't solve her problem, or help her children. What will happen if her culture runs the country?

One afternoon as I crossed the busy street with the dogs, I heard a motor accelerate and saw a blue truck speeding toward me. I dragged the dogs to safety and turned as it honked. Krissy, so hugely pregnant her girth was obvious through the passenger window, leered and gave me the finger.

A Rocket Launcher in the Closet

Jerry and I speak of Darrell as "a good neighbor" and grin at each other, acknowledging that the description means something different in town than it did in the country. And it should.

Glancing out my study window on the second floor, I see him hustle across the street. His feet move rapidly, but his torso is rigid, arms held at his sides. I can visualize him as a coyote, zipping from one form of concealment to another, surviving because he's wary.

When I was growing up, "good neighbors" were people my parents had met when they were all in diapers. They went to grade school together in Hermosa, high school in Custer, and stayed friends all their lives. When I went to the city high school, we "country kids" had to stick together because city kids considered us to be low on the social ladder. Most of us married locals and came home to the ranch. If we didn't work on Sundays, we attended either the Catholic Church or the United Church of Christ. In the 1950s, though, my father liked to say with an edge to his voice, some of them "discovered they'd been Lutherans all that time," and built a third church.

That must have been one of the first signs that our community was separating into factions that wouldn't always find ways to work together. Some of those divisions affect us today. But in those days, everyone—even the Catholics, whom we treated as if their religion were catching—fought all the prairie fires, and attended all the funerals, where they leaned on their pickups visiting until time to go back to the UCC Church, the only one with a kitchen. There they ate the post-funeral meal cooked by women from every church in town and several from other counties.

Darrell works for his father, an outgoing insurance salesman whose office is across the street from Darrell's apartment. In the garage below his home, Darrell restores old cars in his spare time. If the older man spots either one of us outside on a warm day, he's likely to drop over to tell us something—anything—for an hour or two. Darrell isn't nearly so forthcoming. If he's not polishing fenders, he's working on the house he owns next door to his garage. He has refinished the floors, repainted the walls several times, and replaced the sidewalks. Yet in a town with high rent and a fluid population, the place often stands spotless and empty, as if Darrell can't bear to fill it with someone else's stuff.

For the first decade I lived in this house, all the windows in Darrell's apartment were covered with sheets of white foam board. Eventually, I noticed the board missing from the window above the side street, adorned with curtains and blinds. Darrell can still shut out the world, but sometimes he doesn't.

Though Darrell works on his antique cars, he's never revved motors in that way that makes my jaw ache. At night, I can sometimes hear him playing his guitar, accompanying his tapes of famous rock-and-roll songs. Even when I'm sitting in the backyard only a few feet below his window, though, I have to concentrate hard to hear him. So one of my primary reasons for calling him a "good neighbor" is that he's quiet. He plays rock music when he's working on a car, but the notes never get much beyond the garage doors.

Garbage is an important part of defining a neighbor, and Darrell puts his into tightly covered cans on the day of pickup. With no pets, he avoids several of the dangers to an amiable relationship: dogs that bark constantly or whose owners allow them to relieve themselves in my flower beds where I discover their gifts when I kneel to pull weeds. I've been known to offer these folks a plastic bag if I'm working outside; they don't usually take it, but sometimes they don't walk by our house again, either.

Furthermore, Darrell doesn't throw parties or drop garbage in the street. Day after day, I watch different tenants of the apartment house across the street dash out, leap into a car, power down the windows, then gather the debris from whatever they had for lunch the day before and toss it into the street. When they pull away, I collect drink and sandwich containers, empty beer bottles, bags and bills from clothing stores. One woman did stop littering, though, after I collected her week's leavings into a plastic bag and tied it to her car's side mirror.

In the country, many of my neighbors were also friends; we visited each other's homes, gave each other gifts, shared potluck meals. Darrell has never been in our house, nor we in his. Sometimes he drives away in one of his cars, but he's often back in an hour. I hear he likes hang gliding and snowboarding, both solitary sports. Another friend says his political views are diametrically opposed to mine, but we've never discussed politics, so that's not a problem. In fifteen years of living next door to this man, I have talked with him perhaps five times a year, rarely for more than ten minutes at a time.

Still, when a man who lived a block away killed himself with carbon monoxide in his garage, Darrell told us he'd known the man in high school, and he was always a little strange. But he shook his head and joined us in sorrow for someone who found life too painful to endure.

Darrell once came to an informal gathering in the backyard of the house on the other side of us, whose landlord often used poor judgment in choosing tenants. We were all drinking beer and talking to the soldier who was moving out of the apartment. "I'll miss you, Joe," I told the soldier. "I always thought if I hollered for help, you'd probably have come running."

"Sure," Joe said, and "I'd have come a'runnin.' I got a rocket launcher in the closet." Darrell nodded as if he'd suspected it all along. Later he mentioned that he hadn't had a drink of liquor for years, and though we were all drinking, no one urged him to break that habit. We talked politics, both local and national, for several hours with no raised voices.

Sometime after that, another neighbor told us why Darrell may be so quiet. He was in a bar in another town one night. She says he drank then, but she doesn't think he drank much. When he left, several men followed him and beat him so severely he nearly died. He was hospitalized for months, she says, and when he got out, he moved into the apartment above the garage and blocked all the windows. "The universe is made of stories, not of atoms," said Muriel Rukeyser in *The Speed of Darkness,* and Darrell has found a way to change the story he might have lived, and to make a life in defiance of evil. He reminds me of a coyote slipping warily through the sagebrush; a coyote is simply part of the landscape with neither hostility nor friendliness.

THIS BLOCK OF HOMES is on the edge of downtown, next to a historic district, so there is constant tension between commercial and residential interests. Our house was built in 1911; Darrell's dad gave us a photograph taken from the top of the state capitol dome showing this house, the one Darrell owns behind us, and two other houses besides ours. Beyond them is bare prairie marked by wagon tracks.

Some fine old houses built after this one have been preserved, while others are deteriorating, or have been remodeled into law offices or apartments. The library a block away will soon be replaced by a bigger building in another part of town. The school across the street is devoted to problem teenagers, who sometimes vent their frustrations by visiting on weekends to skid in circles in the parking lots and toss beer bottles out their jalopy windows. Like most homeowners, we teeter-totter from worry to fear about what might happen before we are ready to sell our remodeled home and move elsewhere. For now, this is our neighborhood, and we watch it uneasily, trying to help it remain the kind of place where we know who lives next door, and we can invite them to sit in the arbor with us to watch the sunset.

One night when Jerry was away on a business trip, the sirens that constantly pass the house veered sharply left and stopped almost at once. Several police and fire department vehicles surrounded the library, red and blue lights flashing. Curious, I slipped out the back door and strolled along the wooden fence toward the alley in the dark.

Nervously alert, I recalled that when I walk the dogs down the same alley in daytime, I find evidence that at night it shelters drinkers, pot, crack, and meth smokers, and drug dealers. I've seen some of the big dogs that bark at us from behind fences turned loose to roam in darkness. Regularly, I find human feces where the neighbors' security lights cast shadows. One night we heard shots and shouts, and watched a man run, yelling and waving a pistol, from the apartment house across the street. We saw Darrell standing on the sidewalk beside our house while police surrounded the man in the school parking lot and took him down without shots being fired.

Standing in the alley, then, I kept my hand on the pistol in my pocket and watched the shadows. As my eyes adjusted to the darkness, I made out a silhouette of a man standing between me and the nearest police cruiser: Darrell. I greeted him quietly, and we stood shoulder to shoulder watching as police cautiously opened doors and flashed lights inside the library. When the police left, we nodded at each other and went back to our respective homes.

Jerry and I have taken various shooting and safety courses and hold legal permits to carry concealed weapons. That means I don't wave my pistol around. I've been assaulted, and choose to carry a concealed weapon as one form of protection. After several neighbors reported break-ins, we put a single bar across the lower half of our most vulnerable windows. Like the pistol, these are only tools, one way to prevent violence. Jerry says we're protecting potential burglars: keeping them out so we don't have to shoot them.

Sometimes, the best weapon is alert watchfulness. When I stepped outside to be a visible witness as a man and his wife screamed and hit each other in the street, Darrell was doing the same a half block away; he, too, had a phone in his hand.

During the daytime, we just nod at each other as we pass, but I know that if trouble happens close by, Darrell and I will be watching. I believe if I climbed the stairs to Darrell's apartment and asked for help, he'd do what he could. Maybe this is as neighborly as Darrell can get after being beaten half to death. Close enough.

The Beauty of Responsibility

My father abhorred "breaking" a horse; we "gentled" ours. When the big sorrel filly with the gold mane was born, I registered her as a half-Arab. Nostalgically, I named her after the mare in the work team my father had been driving when I moved to the ranch. For months we petted and haltered her, training that had turned other ranch horses into trustworthy partners in our work. She was so tall and showy I daydreamed about riding her in some performance.

But Beauty seemed demented, biting, kicking, throwing herself against the fence. Only quick reflexes saved us from serious injury several times. When I returned to the ranch after my sophomore college year, my father said he'd given up on her. She fought everything around her, so her head and shoulders were scabbed with self-inflicted wounds.

"I've never even raised my voice to her," my father said, "but you can never trust her." If we walked through the corral, she'd attack, slashing with her hooves.

A neighbor woman wanted to buy her, implying that we'd mistreated the mare and kindness would cure her, but my father refused. That night he said, "We have to decide what to do with that horse."

Sell her at the regular auction, I said.

How would I feel, he asked, if she killed someone? Or was beaten into submission?

He waited for my nod of understanding and consent. He killed her mercifully, with one bullet in her forehead.

UNDERSTANDING how my compassionate father found, or learned, the moral courage to make that choice for Beauty, and for the neighbor woman or some potential buyer we'd never meet, might teach me how ordinary people grow into graver responsibilities; how any traveler, for example, might try to stop a hijacker.

I believe my father accepted obligations one step at a time, just as he trained a horse. Embracing the small duties of daily life helped him discover his strengths and learn to weigh the consequences of his actions. Lesson by lesson, he gained fortitude until he could choose to accept tasks he might have avoided.

Most of the choices we make about our obligations to the world are not as dramatic as killing a dangerous horse or risking our lives against evildoers. I think, though, that smaller actions accumulate in important ways, so I recycle, compost, and pick up other folks' litter as a down payment on the cost of my comforts to the earth.

"Civilization is just a slow process of learning to be kind," said Charles L. Lucas. Perhaps if we each take a little extra responsibility every day, our world will feel safer, more agreeable.

So when I see the graceful dog darting through the noon rush of speeding cars on Warren Avenue, I shut my Westies in the house, open the yard gate, and lure her inside. She has no tags. I call animal control and spend a half hour I didn't think my schedule could afford helping a soft-spoken man coax her gently into his truck.

Back at work, I decide my actions are a fitting antidote to the kind of poison brewed in little brains and spewed from big mouths. My father, I know now, allowed our investment of time and money in the horse to be outweighed by risk to a stranger, by the possibility the horse's life would become worse. Accepting the burden of her life compelled him, finally, to choose her death.

The animal control officer calls to tell me he identified the saluki by a microchip, and returned her without charge to her overjoyed owner. Today, on my account with the world, I will enter the joy of rescuing the dog against the loss of Beauty.

Watching for Grizzlies Anyway

I've always been intrigued by the way connections can be forged even between people who disagree. The buckskinning camps where George and I vacationed drew a cross-section of some of the most cantankerous outlaws not behind bars. In camp, however, people from every conceivable economic and educational level of society were polite to one another, respected the camp rules, and usually avoided discussing politics and religion. This may or may not have been related to the fact that everyone, from toddlers to ancients, were armed with every weapon available to the fur trappers of the 1830s.

About dark one fall day, an old red vw van, its entire skin decorated with peace signs, hand-painted slogans and symbols, and tattered bumper stickers, pulled into camp, driving slowly along the whole line of tipis and cook fires and staring people until it stopped a hundred yards beyond our lodge. Two women wearing faded cotton dresses, a man in jeans and a dirty T-shirt, and a boy about six years old emerged. The man stretched, yawned, lit a cigarette, and sat down on a log. The women set up a wall tent and carried a cooler and a kerosene stove inside; the boy followed with two bent metal yard chairs.

Then the women started hauling armloads of bundles wrapped in plastic and blankets out of the van. Unwrapping clothes, they hung them from the tent and guy ropes, and from the top rack on the van, dragging the blankets inside the tent.

Clothing traders! The word spread in whispers and giggles. Within minutes, every woman in camp was headed for the tent to look at fringed leather shirts decorated with elk teeth, at leather and wool dresses with beaded and quilled shoulders and hems.

One of the women came out of the wall tent eating a sweet roll. "Look all you want," she said as we fingered fur skirts and beaded moccasins. I found a price tag on a leather dress covered from neck to ankles with yellowed elk teeth: twelve hundred dollars.

The woman waved her sweet roll and said, "If you want to try something on, go on inside."

The club's new bride snatched a dress and ducked inside the tent flaps. A minute later the second woman came outside, holding the boy's arm. "Hiding behind the cooler," she said. "Spying." She threw him to the ground and he scuttled away.

At dark, when George and his son Michael came back from the shooting range for supper, the old van was still parked in front of the tent, with music blaring from the radio. Red, doing his job as booshway, strolled up to our fire as I dipped a spoon into the stew pot.

"Hey, Red. Have supper with us?" I said, filling a bowl.

"Just ate a sandwich Sandy sent with me; she'll be up tomorrow." He gestured with his cup of beer. "George, I'm going up and ask 'em to move that van out, kinda explain about how we do things in camp. Since they haven't noticed. Come along?"

Mike followed, and while George and Red talked with the man in the dirty T-shirt, he climbed in the van where the boy was fiddling with the radio. After a moment, the music stopped.

Then Mike came back to our fire. "Weird kid," he mumbled. "I told him that we don't have radios in camp, but he wouldn't say anything, just stared at me."

I heard a shout and looked up to see the stranger waving a fist in Red's face. Both George and Red backed up a couple of steps, their hands automatically dropping to the hilts of their belt knives. Then they ambled back to our lodge.

"I take it he didn't want to move the van," I said.

"No, he sure didn't," Red said, glancing over his shoulder. "Said they had valuable stuff in there, worried somebody might steal it. I told him we'd post a watch." He chuckled. "I didn't tell him we'd be watching for grizzlies anyway." As he spoke, the man drove the old van slowly past us, glaring.

"Maybe he'll feel better when he gets to the other end of camp," Red observed. "Some other traders came in—they're not members of the club either—and they're all camped down at that end, close to the parking lot. He wants to, he can ask them to keep an eye on his stuff."

The night was quiet, and in the morning we noticed that the bright clothes were still hanging outside, limp with dampness from the evening's heavy dew. About noon, the three adults emerged from their tent, blinking. The man drove the van back, and smoked while the women stuffed all the clothing inside. Then the three adults drove away.

Later, I noticed the boy sitting on a log at the edge of the woods, and pointed him out to Mike, who strolled over to talk. With another woman, I walked upstream for a bath in the creek above camp. Coming back, I heard voices inside our lodge. Mike and the boy sat on the buffalo robe covering our sleeping bags. Between them was a gallon can of granola, nuts, and chocolate candies. The boy leaped up when I came in.

"It's OK," Mike said. "That's my stepmother."

I hung my towel on the tipi liner to dry and sat down. The boy looked at me, eyes wide. His hair was only a half-inch long, unevenly chopped, with dark patches scattered over his scalp. A piece of skin hung from a scab on his forehead, and black liquid dangled under his nose. As he stuffed a wad of nuts into his mouth with a grimy hand, I saw through his open shirt how close his skin fit over his ribs.

"I think you boys have had enough nuts, Mike. This is our emergency food supply." The boy ran outside before I finished speaking, tripping over the lodge door. "He was really hungry," Mike whispered. "I didn't see him put any boogers in it."

When I told George, he grimaced and said, "Maybe Mike's learning something about sharing, anyway."

"Just so he's not trading granola for lice."

TRADITIONALLY, on the second night in camp, everyone gathers at the central fire pit to share a community stew. In the early afternoon, the men hauled out the club's iron pot, four feet in diameter, erected a huge tripod to support it, laid the fire, and piled firewood nearby. Then they put up a flat piece of canvas supported by poles at the corners, a roof to keep rain or sun off the women as they cooked. As their final contribution to the evening meal, they brought to the fire a case of Annie Green Springs wine with the labels, and the lids, removed.

Then the men headed to the west end of the plateau for games and shoots while the women assembled at the fire with jugs of cooking oil, bags of vegetables we'd grown at home or purchased, and packages of meat. We spent the afternoon sitting on logs and rocks around the fire pit, chopping vegetables and trading stories about the past year.

Once the oil in the pot was bubbling, we stirred in the meat with canoe paddles. This year, it included my beef, an elk Pam's husband had shot, venison, rabbit, and a couple of bear steaks. Dodging smoke, we added in-gredients all afternoon, passing wine bottles as our faces reddened in the heat.

Near sunset, several women hung smaller pots full of oil around the rim of the big one, and began mixing and cooking fry bread. Pam got too close to the fire while dodging a spatter of oil, and the hem of her long dress blazed. Two of us rolled her in the dirt to put it out, and smeared grease on her singed ankle. Then somebody handed her the wine bottle, and we all went on cooking. When the sky grew dark, and everyone gathered for sup-per, the colorful van was still missing.

Two women, both mothers, walked to the wall tent and stood po-litely outside to call to the boy. "Come on over and have supper with us. Everyone's eating at the council fire tonight." No response. As one woman lifted the door flap to call again, we saw the boy bolt out the back.

We formed a ragged line, families bringing their own cups or bowls and spoons, dipping stew from the huge pot and slathering the fry bread with butter and honey. Then we scattered around the fire, eating and visiting. Every few minutes, someone would scan the trees around us and call, "Come to the fire." Several times we caught a glimpse of the boy scuttling closer, but by the time we'd all finished eating, he still hadn't come in. The two mothers took a candle and a plate of food to the traders' camp and left it on the log outside the tent door.

We spent the rest of the evening in a loose circle at the central fire, making music with mouth harps, guitars, fiddles, and drums, and visiting.

One woman saw the boy crouched behind a tree as she walked to the latrine, and a man on the same errand saw him run toward the parking lot. We worried about grizzlies, attracted by the cooking smells. Several of the men were wearing high-powered modern pistols tucked discreetly under their buckskin shirts, and several others mentioned having rifles just inside their lodge doors.

After dinner, we held the club's annual meeting, admired the quilt the women had made, and applauded the winner of the raffle, who immediately wrapped the quilt around her shoulders. We visited long into the night. Neither the boy nor the van appeared.

As I took my first step outside our lodge the next morning, I glanced at the traders' camp. The plate stood untouched, the candle melted. George said the van was not in the parking lot.

At noon, when the camp's kids streamed into the open field in front of the lodges for races and tomahawk throws, we saw the boy creep through the trees to the edge of the group. He wore a loose shirt tucked into the pants that kept sliding off his thin hips, and he was barefoot.

Mad Dog, who was directing the tomahawk throw, marched up to the boy, threw an arm over his shoulders, and hauled him into the group, explaining how the game worked. When another boy offered him a tomahawk, the boy reached inside his shirt and pulled out a man-size hatchet.

Mad Dog pointed at the target, and said something I couldn't hear. The boy swung the hatchet's blunt edge at the man's knee. "Careful," Mad Dog said. The kid stepped closer and swung again at Mad Dog's knee, and I heard a *pop*. Mad Dog roared and grabbed his knee with one hand and the hatchet with the other, bellowing in pain. The boy ran into the woods.

Later, a woman saw the boy on the creek bank, sobbing. She spoke softly, patted his shoulder, dipped her handkerchief in the water, and tried to wipe his face. He picked up a rock and struck her on the forehead, then ran. She lurched back to camp, the handkerchief against her bleeding forehead, swearing under her breath. Several women cleaned and bandaged her wound, and then we all walked over to watch the kids' games. Around the circle, everyone discussed the boy.

"How about calling social services?" said one.

"I hate to do that to anybody," said another.

"He's sure an antisocial kid," quipped the woman he'd clouted.

An older woman shook her head. "Get the government involved, and none of us would ever get outta here."

"But it's awful; he might be abused."

"Maybe he just didn't want his face washed, woman," said Red. "Some guys like to be left alone!"

"Maybe he hasn't been 'abused' quite enough," grumbled Mad Dog, rubbing his knee. "If I'd ever whacked my dad with a hatchet, I wouldn't have been able to sit down for a week, not even to mention the amount of firewood I'd have had to saw because I'd never see the hatchet again."

"What if they never come back?" asked Sandy, Red's wife.

"Then we'll take him home with us," he said, nodding. "We won't hardly notice one more." Sandy rolled her eyes. "And he'll learn pretty quick not to hit people with hatchets."

Following the afternoon's games and shoots, people scattered all over the meadow, admiring wildflowers and each other's handmade weapons, taking walks. I leaned on the tipi, reading and enjoying the murmur of voices, crows calling in the distance. Mike, as usual, lost one of his moccasins, and George, leaning on the tipi smoking his pipe, started making a replacement. We ate sandwiches for supper, then lit the candle lanterns inside the lodge and visited with friends who dropped by. No one saw the boy, but we were all thinking about him.

REMEMBERING YEARS LATER, I wonder if that was one of the nights that our friend Fred and I enjoyed a lively discussion about whatever was going on in politics. He told me he'd been a cop in New York City in the sixties, adding, "I'll bet you were one of those damn hippies marching for peace." I never denied it, and whenever we met in camp, we passed a jug back and forth and talked. One night he began to describe working security during a peace march. He was part of a special squad trained for the violence everyone expected, helmeted, booted, wearing bulletproof jackets and carrying riot sticks and full armament. In tight formation, the men ("We were all men in those days," Fred said, grinning) were quick-stepping up a hill, nervous among thousands of marchers, very aware of being outnumbered.

Then one of the men dropped a bag full of grenades. He made a grab for it, accidentally jerking it open. Dozens of grenades spun and rolled away among the feet of the police and the crowds. The tense captain ordered the men to keep marching. When they reached a cleared area, they formed a defensive square in front of the building they were detailed to guard.

"And by the time we got there," Fred said, "every single one of those grenades had been passed to the front of that mob of protesters, and handed to one of the cops." He shook his head, still amazed.

"I was already pretty frustrated with my job," he added, "so that wasn't the only thing that did it. I looked out at those people through the bars on my helmet, and I thought maybe I'd been missing something." Not long after that, he says, he drove his cruiser up the steps of headquarters, stomped into his commander's office, and nailed his badge to the desk. Then he moved west.

NEAR MIDNIGHT, I stepped out to watch the fog roll down the mountain and across the ground like a snowstorm. Three figures were walking past the dark lodges. A few minutes later, a lamp flared in the wall tent, and I heard shouts.

While I cooked breakfast at the outside fire pit the next morning, the clothing traders were doing the same. Then the women hung the lovely clothes around the wall tent, while the man lounged on a buffalo robe, sharing his plate of food with the boy. I leaned against the lodge with a book all morning. From my vantage, I could see the merchants as well as the rest of camp.

I knew the outhouses in the lower end of camp were nearly full, but after a while I realized that no one was walking our direction to use the empty one beside the traders' tent. No children wandered up to our end of camp to play. For six hours, not a single adult went near the wall tent. And, I realized as I became more absorbed in watching than in reading, no one even looked that direction.

By noon, the woman who was cooking the traders' lunch was looking over her shoulder and dropping pans. After they ate, the man strode toward the parking lot, turning to glare at everyone as he passed. As he marched past each lodge, people evaporated before him. Several people walking among the lodges turned abruptly, but most people saw him coming in time to move without haste out of his path. Two women emerged from a lodge and then, simultaneously and without speaking, ducked back inside. One man who was leaning against his lodge simply stood up and turned his back.

By the time the man reached the other traders near the parking lot, they'd all folded their blankets over their trade goods, ducked inside their tents, and closed the flaps.

SUDDENLY I REALIZED what I was seeing: shunning. None of us had talked about this the night before. Somehow, we'd reached a group decision. The traders had been cut off from the society of our camp, slammed into utter silence. By neglecting the boy, the traders had violated the customs of our small village. By common consent, by agreement so complete it didn't need debate, they had been segregated as effectively as if they'd been locked in jail.

As the man drove his van furiously through the silent camp, raising dust, I closed my book and went inside. George was sitting on the bedroll, smoking, and watching through the door. "George! It's shunning! They're shunning those people!" He nodded. "Did anybody talk about it last night?" He shook his head silently. We slipped outside to lean against the shady side of the lodge and watch.

The man slammed on the brakes when he reached the wall tent, and the women jerked open the side door and started throwing clothes inside without wrapping them. Looking over his shoulder every few seconds, the man tossed the tent poles on top and tied them sloppily. The women folded the tent, tossed it through the door, and squeezed into the front seat. The man shut the van's side door and slid under the steering wheel.

"I don't see the boy," I muttered to George. "What if they leave him?"

"Better off," he said. "He'd fit right in with Red's kids, or one of the others. They'd whip him into shape in a hurry."

The van turned and chugged back along the line of lodges. A small dirty face hung in the back window, nose flattened against the glass.

He Pinched the Burning End

On the ranch, I did a lot of thinking on horseback. In the city, I think best while working in my yard. During our first summer on Warren Avenue, I developed a nodding acquaintance with an old man who lived in the apartment house across the street. He was at least seventy, maybe eighty; sun-tanned, wind-twisted, snow-scoured. He looked like the old cowboys who used to drift around the country working awhile as hired men for one rancher or another.

He reminded me so much of my dad that each time I saw him, I couldn't help wondering if that was the only reason I'd noticed him. Was I judging by appearances, feeling connected with people who look like home folks? The old man didn't move very fast as he watered and mowed the lawn, hobbling around the building's narrow skirt of lawn, but his spine was always straight. He wore caps and plaid shirts with his jeans and work boots. At the end of each day he sat in a straight chair by his front door and slowly smoked one cigarette. When he was finished, he pinched the burning end, then shredded the stub. He'd nod or raise a hand at me before he went inside.

One day six months after we moved in, he finally crossed the street. We both observed that the weather was fine and agreed that it was likely to rain. Then he said haltingly, "I notice that your—man is—ah—gone some of the time. If you ever need help, you just call me, Red." He handed me his phone number scribbled on a little square of paper. I thanked him and he went back across the street, looking a little creaky, but like he might have known how to make a difference in a fight. Still, the gesture counted.

He was being neighborly. We had recognized one another, as rural neighbors do.

GETTING A LITTLE HOMESICK for my hometown, though, usually reminds me of its contradictions. My folks taught me that laws were created to help protect the innocent, and that responsible people obeyed the law. My father's rule was that any punishment my grade school teachers doled out, he doubled when I got home. No arguments; no debate. The teachers were the law. So when I think about homespun wisdom, I often drift back to some incident from my childhood.

Lately, though, the news in my county paper has caused me to consider the consequences of those hometown values. A polygamous cult called the Fundamentalist Church of Jesus Christ of Latter Day Saints is building a compound in the western end of the county. Officials have issued building permits for structures of three thousand to fourteen thousand square feet containing dozens of bedrooms and bathrooms. "These aren't homes," says a neighbor. "They're motels."

Observers who have seen sections of culvert eight feet in diameter delivered to the compound suspect the concrete tubes will be used for tunnels like those in FLDS compounds in other states, allowing residents, especially women and children, to scurry between buildings without being seen. Families living next to the compound say jackhammers and bulldozers run from 6:00 A.M. until 2:00 A.M., despite promises to the county sheriff's department that work will end at dusk. Spotlights are trained on neighbors who walk near the compound or sit on the deck of the house next door. A fleet of four-wheelers patrols the perimeter fence day and night, inside and outside a dirt berm high enough to keep passersby from looking into the compound. Trucks haul water daily from faucets in the nearby towns of Custer, Edgemont, and Hot Springs.

The director of equalization reports that the compound pays about $30,000 a year in taxes on time. Officials say the FLDS has met every county rule and requirement and is breaking no law. Surely this group is a living symbol of the western independence that allows us to do as we please on our own land.

I WAS IN THE DRIVEWAY one spring morning, loading my car for a trip to the ranch to conduct a writing retreat, when I heard a car stop, a door slam, a woman's voice. "Excuse me."

I turned around. She was in her forties perhaps, smiling. "I just wanted to thank you for the pasque flowers." She pointed to the lavender blooms crowded among the sage and creeping thyme. "I've never seen them growing at this altitude before."

"Really? I didn't know that; I just collected some seed where we were hiking, out west of town."

As we talked, she told me that she worked at a nearby mental health clinic. "I used to walk this way to work all the time, but it got too hard to cross the street, with all the traffic," she said, raising her voice as a car stopped at the cross street with its windows open so we could share the rap music. We paused until the driver, cap turned sideways, pulled out into traffic. She looked at her watch.

"I'll be late. But I want to tell you. Last spring, one February morning when everything was dark and gray and I was depressed, I noticed the pasque flowers pushing up, blooming through the snow. I think they saved my life." She smiled, and I nodded.

"So I started to come this way again. It makes the traffic bearable. It almost makes that music bearable. How do you stand living here?"

I shrugged. "I've worn earplugs at night for fifteen years. During the daytime, I pull weeds and breathe deeply."

Looking at her watch again, she said that several times she'd taken extra time to walk along the street, looking at the flowers blooming, marveling at their variety. Despite the fact that I work near a window, and can't break the habit of looking out when someone goes by, I'd never seen her. "This fall, bring paper bags and take seed," I told her.

"I recognized the pasque and the columbine," she says. "What's this one?" she said, starting toward the crosswalk.

"That's oregano; I dry it to use in my kitchen. I have it everywhere because it grows so easily."

"And this one?" she gestured toward a deep blue flower.

"Larkspur, or delphinium," I said, "and this one is . . ." She didn't cross the street for another ten minutes, and never looked at her watch once.

MOST OF THE ART PRINTS in my house are by Andrew Wyeth or Georgia O'Keeffe, painters whose work always renews my enthusiasm for writing. Both portray spacious land and open sky in a way I recognize. Wyeth's *Christina's World* was probably the first representation of art I appreciated, in the form of a print my mother hung in the living room. I was sure the painter had found the woman sitting in tawny grass on a long clean hill not far from our place. Above her stands a tall house and barn almost identical to one near our east boundary, weathered gray by prairie storms. She has turned halfway back toward the house and leans on her hands, leaning into the hill and the wind. I was sure she had done as I often have, walked out onto the prairie to sit hidden by the grass listening to the wind, the meadowlarks, the whisper of possibility. I knew she faced that house with both yearning for its comfort and fear of imprisonment. Surely Wyeth was a local artist, like our Harvey Dunn. But while Dunn showed farmers fencing and plowing the prairie for crops, Wyeth portrayed the point of view I associated with ranching, depicting the openness of the prairie and the sky above it, a place where people lived and worked without changing the landscape much.

My mother never explained what the painting meant to her, but when she took it down years later, she said it was depressing. By that time she'd discovered my father couldn't or wouldn't leave the ranch for vacations. Later, learning Wyeth painted Maine seascapes and that Christina was crippled stunned me. Visiting Maine, I found an art museum where I could get so close to Wyeth originals that museum guards warned me not to let my nose touch the paint. Driving along the narrow, twisty roads to look at leaves, Jerry and I realized we were near Wyeth's home, and were surprised to see so much new construction. Every half mile we passed piles of broken trees surrounding a tall, glassy-eyed house skirted with garages and decks, boats and landscaping. Between these freaks, older homes hunkered among the trees. Signs at the end of their driveways advertised caretaking, lawn-mowing, house-opening, house-closing, and house-cleaning: all the skills and services the natives provide to the new and usually temporary residents. O'Keeffe died before developers began to decorate the landscape that she knew with turquoise-colored coyotes and false adobe mansions, and no hint of these ostentatious newcomers appears in Wyeth's paintings. Perhaps a real artist refuses to be drawn into activism, into the temporary squabbles over the environment, must focus only on the timeless landscape.

ON A HOT DAY IN JULY when I spent hours in the garden, I noticed a strange pickup parked on the street beside our back fence all day. Each time I passed it, hauling trash to the alley, a large dog barked at me from the camper shell on the back. Glancing through the windows the first time, I could see the whole interior, but no food or water dishes. I worked on that side of the house all afternoon, but no one came near the pickup. At dusk, I telephoned an animal control officer. When he pulled up, and I went out to meet him, both Darrell and Red came out too; we'd all called at the same time, and directed the officer to the apartment the dog's owner was visiting.

Later that fall, Red came across the street one day to ask me if I'd like some iris plants from the beds in front of the apartment building. When I went over with my shovel, I realized Red was probably not strong enough to divide the plants. No dirt was visible, just bulbs, like big brown worms frozen as they writhed across the ground. With no dirt to stick the shovel into, I tried prying them up, but couldn't dislodge a single bulb. Finally I decided a little damage hardly mattered since there were hundreds of bulbs, and began chopping at the mat with the edge of the shovel. When I'd lifted off a top layer of iris bulbs, ants boiled up out of the ground, covering the shovel almost before I could swear. I squirted water on the ants until their enthusiasm waned and the soil was soft enough to dig more easily. Over the next few days, I toted hundreds of bulbs across the street, and left the bed neat and healthier.

Every time I took a break from writing, I'd grab a digger, scoop a shallow hole, flop the bulb on the edge, cover the roots, step on the ground to seat it firmly, and scoop another hole. By the time I'd planted bulbs in every spare bit of ground in my yard and given away all I could, I still had dozens left. I dug in more along the back alley, fantasizing about becoming the Midnight Iris Planter, sneaking along all the alleys in the neighborhood, planting iris bulbs.

ON ANOTHER SPRING DAY when I was packing for a speaking trip, I saw two EMTs load Red into an ambulance. When I came home days later, Jerry wasn't sure if Red had come home, and I couldn't tell by watching his apartment windows. Every day, while I worked in the yard, I kept glancing across the street, expecting to see him moving a hose, or having his cigarette by the back step. I wanted to tell him how much I appreciated his neighborliness.

When a FOR RENT sign went up on the lawn, I realized I didn't even know Red's last name. Each time I put an iris in a vase on the dining room table, though, I nod across the street and thank Red for reminding me that some connections work.

Shoveling Snow in the Dark

One of our friends recently told us about a couple who had moved into a Cheyenne subdivision nearly fifteen miles out of town. After the usual rituals of marking their new territory by painting the house inside and out and placing new carpets, the family invited the neighbors on their road to a get-acquainted party. The narrator of this story cynically remarked that probably everyone came because the people who had owned the house before had nearly destroyed it with neglect, and they were curious about the renovation.

During the party, the new owner told everyone that he had a tractor with a scraper blade mounted on the front, and if anyone needed their road plowed free of snow, they should give him a call.

They all looked at him blankly; so he explained, "Well, I grew up on a farm, and that's the way we were raised; we help our neighbors. And heck, back there my neighbors were a mile or more apart, not nearly as close as we are here."

Everyone nodded and went on with their cocktail talk.

Maybe, I suggested, his new neighbors think living in a subdivision is like living in town and don't realize how difficult rural life can be in an old-fashioned plains blizzard. If they've never lived in the country, they may really believe those four-wheel drives will get them to work. Or perhaps some developer told them, or they assumed, that the county snowplow will arrive early the morning after a blizzard to plow out all the roads so they can get to work.

In recent years, though, the people who provide emergency services for

Cheyenne, the police, firefighters, EMTs, and ambulance personnel, have appeared repeatedly before the city council, begging the town to establish some control over subdivisions. Either the developers, who make all the money, or the new residents, should pay for extending emergency services. Emergency personnel say they can't possibly provide safety for such a scattered population.

DURING A SPRING STORM that left six inches of heavy snow, Jerry learned that one of his coworkers at the state highway department was in bed with a bad back. Getting up an hour earlier gave Jerry time to shovel at our house before he drove a couple of miles to clear his friend's walk. The snow kept falling, and on the third day when Jerry went to shovel as usual, another man waved him off, hollering, "I'll get it today. I wondered who beat me to it the other day!" In the dark, they couldn't even see each other's faces.

When I tell the story to one of my rancher friends, she recalls that on her last trip to the grocery store, she overheard a young woman with a cell phone say, "I didn't see any tracks in the snow around your house, so I wondered if you needed anything. I'm at the grocery store, and I could drop something by on my way home." My friend calls this kind of thinking the "homestead mentality" and says, "Maybe you have to be raised with it to know you are supposed to do it. Not call 911 and ask someone to rescue you or plow you out. Or call the cops to drive you to the hospital. Just looking after each other, and quietly getting through a stint of unfortunate weather by relying on each other."

WESTERN CITIZENS endlessly discuss the future of their communities. Zoning is often called "the Z word," so these settlements often don't tackle any tough decisions about their future. They've got all they can do, they say, tearing their hair, responding to the changes and threats they see on all sides. As a taxpayer in two western regions, the small city of Cheyenne in Wyoming and the rural county of Custer in South Dakota, I've spent years watching as citizens cope with new problems. Benighted city governments hand out fat tax incentives to lure monster chain stores to town, fully aware that they trample American workers and local business into the dust. The same civic leaders ignore long-established businesses built by

pioneers who committed themselves to these places body, soul, and finances before the towns even existed.

Open space that also provided fodder for wild and domestic animals
is disappearing under subdivisions throughout the plains. Moreover, the
financial foundations of towns and counties are changing in troublesome
ways. New businesses often cater to new citizens, promising savings and
filling shopping baskets with plastic junk made in a foreign country. While
these businesses may temporarily fill coffers and pockets, the fiscal heart
of many western states has been agriculture and its associated enter-
prises. The new wisdom declares farming and ranching to be old-fashioned
and outmoded, but we still need to eat. Many of the old geezers who established agriculture in this inhospitable terrain were escaping from the
crowded, disease-ridden cities of their time and country. Fully educated
in the dangers of cramming too many people into small spaces, they laid
plans for keeping more distance between people while establishing strong
social bonds. Meanwhile, and more importantly, they fed each wave of settlers, while keeping their land both fertile and productive for a century or
two. Realtors and other opportunists may count their money while these
old-timers drift away, but losing the ability to feed ourselves may be more
than we can afford. Warnings have been uttered for a long time; the speech
William Jennings Bryan made before the national Democratic convention
while campaigning for president in 1896 has become known as the "Cross
of Gold" speech. "Burn down your cities and leave our farms," said Bryan,
"and the cities will spring up again like magic." But destroy the farms, "and
the grass will be in the streets of every city in the country." The grass may
win in the end.

In ever-widening concentric circles around Great Plains towns, the
owners of new homes on an acre or two try to figure out how to make the
austere surroundings of their expensive houses match some fantasy landscape where rainfall is generous. Dreaming of forests to break the persis-
tent wind, they plant twigs and pour water into the gravelly ground, killing
native blooms and grasses that would flourish on natural rainfall. Early settlers with similar dreams fled the prairies in the drought of the Dirty Thirties; the prairie wind and weather has scrubbed away most traces of their
sod buildings. Inevitably, the next drought has begun, and is predicted to
be much worse. Modern houses with log entrance gates, swimming pools,

four-car garages, granite countertops, and plate-glass windows might take longer to decay, unless future settlers mine the ruins for materials to replace the resources we can't renew.

THE SUBDIVISIONS keep spreading and the developers keep making money, and cursing both has become routine among ranchers and environmentalists: at last, something they have in common. The idea of satellite villages outside a larger town is not inherently bad. Thomas Jefferson visualized a population of yeoman farmers, intelligent, well-read individuals who were highly self-sufficient. These ideal citizens could grow much of their own food, depending on the climate and location. With other self-employment, perhaps a blacksmith forge in the barn, or a quilt rack in the spare room, family members could earn cash toward necessities they couldn't make or grow. Trips to a larger town for necessities unobtainable elsewhere would be rare. Much of our pioneering history followed this pattern.

Smart developers in some areas have created subdivisions embracing a similar vision, enabling residents to save both personal and purchased energy by living close to most of their daily needs. In such a village, each age group might find ways to contribute skills, knowledge, and labor according to their abilities. Work and home would be close together, allowing all kinds of beneficial interactions. The residents of such villages stand in contrast to the average American subdivision dweller, racing down the dark highway yelling into a cell phone on the way home or to work. Moreover, savvy developers who follow creative models that encourage community ultimately make a lot more money than those who whack a piece of land into little bits and sell it for shoddily built houses or apartments.

In the Great Plains, though, thin soil and scarce water mean that producing enough food for a family would require intensive labor and considerable experience or a detailed knowledge of the climate. Still, we have most of the knowledge we'd need to make those barren subdivisions more sufficient unto themselves. Xeriscaping, container gardening, Internet connections, fast computers. Technology exists that could make Jefferson's theory a reality, getting Americans out of their gas-guzzling cars and off their asphalt treadmills. They could eat food they grew themselves, get to know their offspring, trade veggies for chickens grown in the backyard instead of those dogs our culture discourages us from eating.

We could make these changes voluntarily. Or we could dither through a couple more wars, a hurricane or two, maybe an economic crisis. Eventually, staying home in the subdivision and growing your own carrots might be necessity rather than choice. Get to know your neighbors now, before you have to.

AT EVERY OPPORTUNITY, I talk to subdivision residents in South Dakota or Wyoming about their new communities. Do you have your own well, I asked one man as we stood in his yard. "Oh yes," he said nodding briskly. "Mine was one of the first, but every house out here has its own well." We both turned our heads and looked around; I counted two dozen houses within spitting distance. "Worries me a little," he mumbled.

How deep is it? I asked. He thought it was about a hundred feet, and had heard that the newest well was deeper.

So I adopted a new conversational gambit at social gatherings. "Do you have a well?" I'd ask. Some listeners would flee without apology. Others said the subdivision shared a well, then explained kindly and in words of one syllable that all they need to know is that water flows from the faucets and that plumbers are in the yellow pages.

When I mention septic tanks at one of these social gatherings, people tend to sidle away to freshen their drinks. I seldom get to ask the next question: What will be the effect of well after septic tank beside well beside septic tank next to well, septic tank, drain field, mile after mile after mile?

Most Great Plains toilets are filled by the Ogallala Aquifer, piped also into our Laundromats, swimming pools, spray parks and drinking fountains, and irrigated crops. Deep and mysterious, this vast lake underlies parts of eight states from South Dakota to Texas, an area of around 225,000 square miles. Near its northern edge lie the Pine Ridge and Rosebud Indian Reservations, with which I am intimately familiar, among the most remote and least populated land in the nation. Working to keep their ancient culture vibrant, the Lakota are welcoming tribal people home, building new houses on reservation land, working together to rebuild tribal community, the extended family or *tiyospaye*. Yet a combination of natural minerals and human contamination has made many Lakota wells unsafe to drink from. The tribe is trying to import water from the Missouri River, two hundred miles away, for drinking and other uses. The plan is called Mni Wiconi, "water of life" in the Oglala Lakota language.

Picture it: the descendants of Custer's conquerors with nothing to drink but the old Muddy Mo, considered by environmentalists and river lovers to be one of the world's most endangered waterways. Since human waste has polluted the drinking water on the remote reservation where industry has never thrived, how safe are the shallow wells of the average subdivision?

Pondering, I run water from the faucet and drink; I don't trust bottled beverages either.

Yet the man's offer of snowplow service to his neighbors suggests that even in these raw settlements full of people who have never lived in a real community, fellowship may grow. After all, crises are famous for calling forth the best in everyone. Even a newfangled gadget like a cell phone might prove to be an asset to old-fashioned homestead thinking. Maybe thirsty subdivision dwellers will take the initiative in community water-saving. Experts say that 50–80 percent of wasted residential water is only slightly used, from dish washing, showers, bathroom sinks, and laundry facilities. Let's hook all those toilets, washing machines, and showers to a recycling system that sends this gray water to nourish windbreak trees, as well as yards with native flora and edible gardens.

Why couldn't a cluster of houses treat its own sewage for fertilizer? A savvy subdivision where residents understand they share the expense of the services they enjoy would be the perfect place to demonstrate the advantages of divvying up the costs of water conservation.

Once mandated to share their wastewater, these folks might dust off their generosity in times of need and help each other in other ways. Even I have fallen easily into the city idea that grocery stores are accessible day and night. Once acquainted, subdivision residents might cooperate in gardening, purchasing organic food, car pooling: the possibilities are limitless.

Stalking Coffee in Sitka

This remains my most vivid memory of Sitka, Alaska: at 7:00 A.M. in a coffee shop, I overheard two women talking about Caroline's wedding.

OK, I eavesdropped. Conversations, letters read upside down on desks, things we see—it's material to a writer.

Listening, I was suddenly more than a bleary-eyed stranger with jet lag, I was part of the neighborhood. I'd been on Sitka for only twelve hours, and I not only knew Caroline, but she'd invited me to her wedding. Smugly, I sipped my coffee and wrapped myself in nostalgic thoughts.

MY VISIT to the most populous spot on Baranoff Island was at the invitation of the Island Institute, a private nonprofit organization that provides a framework for discussions about various aspects of community life, and how best to inhabit the places where we live. I visited Sitka only for the few days of the conference, temporarily attached to that specific group of visitors. Yet I found myself identifying with the permanent residents because I kept feeling as if I'd come home.

Even years later, reading the scribbled notes in my Sitka journal brings to mind animated memories of the conference, faces of people, their voices. Our words, arising from diverse experiences, wove us into a colony intensely concerned with how people live together. The conference community connected, interacted, and separated in a few days, a brief whirlpool within the older Sitka community.

The idea of community in Sitka is very old indeed. Anthropologists say the site was first occupied by Tlingit Indians shortly after the last ice age.

Maybe they didn't chat over coffee, but I'll bet our group would recognize some of the conversations.

Emerging from the plane, I had noticed immediately that I might blend into the scene; we were all dressed in worn, comfortable, sturdy clothes and shoes. No high heels in sight; no successful little suits.

Shortly after the meetings began, however, I realized that I had packed too lightly for June in Alaska. Martha, an Alutiiq whose father was Russian and Alutiiq and whose mother was Scots-Irish, noticed my pitiful shivering. She had once lived in Sitka, and promised to lead me to the "white elephant," as she called the secondhand store. Over lunch, she talked about a federal study costing millions in which scientists tried to count killer whales—orcas—by sitting on the beach waiting for them to surface. When the experts finally asked the old people of her community, the elders pointed out that since orcas are so powerful they can come up under ice and break it, they don't spend very much time near the beach.

Reminds me of South Dakota, I told her, where we spend money for white researchers to learn what the native Lakota people have known for generations. Experts may read and revere statements allegedly made to white conquerors by Native Americans, but rarely ask the opinions of the living natives. We grinned at each other.

I imagine I also told her my theory that hunting-and-gathering peoples were happy partly because the less you carry, literally and figuratively, the more you can gather. Thus, most of my "dress-up clothes" for conferences are secondhand, so if I decide to buy heavy souvenirs—several friends had hinted for frozen salmon—I could eliminate clothing to make room in my luggage. The theory works even better with mental baggage: I try to leave my preconceived notions at home to allow room for new information.

Martha warned me, from experience, to leave my purse in my room, put my money in my pants pocket, and keep my hand on it. So, in the crowded store, when a strange hand slid into my pocket, I turned and smiled sweetly at the young Native man standing so close I could dig my elbow into his ribs, and kept a firm grip on my money until his hand stopped caressing mine and went elsewhere. He shrugged and smiled back.

Then I bought a sweater, a sweatshirt dress, a flat cap, and a pair of wool socks for a total of four dollars. Wearing some of the community's castoff clothes, I felt very much at home.

Later, walking, I reflected how pleasant it was to be in a place where the automobile is not the primary mode of transport. Some of the island's nine thousand residents live on their boats, and others do not own cars, so walkers fill the streets, nodding at one another. Many of the vehicles I saw were pickups with big dogs in the back. In the prairie states where I spend the most time, many people (mostly men) make their dogs ride in the pick-up bed. When a truck goes down the street with a barking dog in back, Jerry says with heavy irony, "Oh look, another dog having fun."

Visiting with other strollers on the grounds of the Sitka Pioneer Home, I learned some unofficial Alaskan history, and tested a new theory: asking about plants is a good way to start a conversation. Some of the facts those elderly folks told me were wrong, but in the interests of our enjoyable chat, I did not feel compelled to enlighten them. Instead, I begin a fantasy I carry still: that I might somehow grow a Sitka columbine on the northern plains.

AFTER DINNER every Sitka evening, I hurried back to my room so I could sit at my window watching people go in and out of the stores across the street, and listen as they stopped to visit and tell jokes. Everyone spoke to everyone else, though their faces were different colors and their clothing reflected varying levels of income. I didn't go to Caroline's wedding, but I watched the bride and groom's procession through the streets, among flocks of people laughing and hugging and throwing rice. The murmur of voices in the streets that night was a little louder, but comforting, as of friends talking in the next room.

In the open windows opposite mine, two children blew bubbles; on my side of the street, people leaning against walls visiting looked up and laughed as the shimmering globes drifted toward them in the quiet night air. Then a slightly older boy riding his bike down the street stopped and used his finger to "shoot" at the bubbles, and the watchers drifted off. Soon children were yelling and skateboarding, with no fear of cars, a practice we rarely see "down below," where most urban areas are too congested for a social life conducted in the streets. Gradually the lights vanished and the children evanesced. Around midnight, when I was enjoying cool air sweeping in my open windows, the sky was still light enough to see fog surge over the mountains like ocean waves.

Only fourteen miles of paved road existed on Baranoff Island, but at 6:45 the next morning a street sweeper roared outside my window. Thoroughly awake, I marched into the dark and drizzly streets stalking coffee, alarming the ravens who followed overhead, screaming warnings. Several blocks of darkened businesses convinced me "early to rise" is not a northern maxim. Stumbling along, I also figured out that the since light lingers so long in the evening, people stay up later, so it makes sense that they don't get up before the sun returns. When I spotted the warm golden light of Lane 7, a bowling alley, I plunged inside, shaking rain off my shoulders without even wondering why a bowling alley was open before sunrise.

The only other customer was sitting in a booth to my left, and we looked one another over the same way we'd have done in a cowboy café in my neighborhood, coming to the same conclusion at the same time: good working folks. He nodded and gestured in a friendly way, and said, "Hank." I nodded right back, said "Linda," and sat down across from him.

Hank was a Vietnam vet, therefore my age, originally from Alabama, he said. A heavy crane operator in Vietnam, he'd worked for a month "driving pile" for houses in a development on the other side of the island, came to Sitka to deposit a big check, and had been waiting several days for it to clear so he could lay in supplies. He was relaxed about the delay. "We stop for rain," he said, and our bond was deepened. "We do too," I responded, though rain is considerably more rare in South Dakota than in Sitka.

Building on our link, Hank and I talked as we chomped piles of fried eggs, bacon, and heavily buttered toast. We both prefer solitude, but he's more serious about isolation than I am: the only way to get to Sitka from his home is by fishing boat or plane. Hank had used his army savings to move to Alaska, looking for privacy and work. On the opposite side of the island, he'd found a developer making use of abandoned buildings on the site of an old military installation. "The man I work for bought a huge tank," Hank said, grinning, "maybe thirty by sixty feet, put a floor down the middle, and cut windows in it. He's got a garage and a shop in the bottom half, and lives in the top." Recycling, Alaska style; my neighbor Harry back home would love it.

Hank bought an old communications building, about 2800 square feet, remodeled and moved into part of it, and parked his Cat (Caterpillar tractor) and other equipment in the rest. "Couldn't afford that much space anywhere else in the country," he said. "I knew I could log, or work for developers operating heavy equipment. I figured if the hired work got slow, I could mine gold on the beach. With that Cat, I can move a lot of sand. You find four or five ounces of gold in a ton of beach sand." Tinkering, he has constantly improved his home with found materials. "I've even figured out how to catch rainwater and run my plumbing."

Hank's literate speech made clear, deliberately I think, that if I was one of those people who think physical work brands a person as uneducated, I should think again. "I have my own private fiefdom," he said, nodding at his coffee cup. "In 1995, I spent $1,100 to live, and $335 of that was for Cat parts."

I told Hank about my writing, in which I argue that the people who do physical work on the land—loggers, ranchers, farmers, miners—should be writing about nature and the environment, since it's where they live as well as work.

Hank thought I was pretty smart, for a writer. I even told him—and I may have blushed—that I'd always wanted a Cat, but none of the men I've loved have ever taken my request seriously. Either that, or they were afraid of what I might bulldoze.

For a while, Hank said, he went to Florida every year to get warm and catch fish, but he couldn't stand the crowds. "Now that the pipeline's running," he said, "Alaska ought to be happy. All those Texans and Okies grabbed their money and went back to where they came from." He shook his head. "But we've got to watch out for the next wave; they'll stay."

Hastily, I explained to Hank—he hadn't asked, reminding me again of the taciturn manners of my home—why I was in Sitka. I invited him to the public meeting scheduled for later in the week so local citizens could speak about specific environmental issues. "Maybe if it keeps raining so I can't work," he said, but the rain stopped, and he didn't appear.

After an hour and a half, our talk wound down, and we stood up to pay our checks. At that moment, I noticed another reason Hank may not like crowds: at five and a half feet, I towered over him.

By my third day in Sitka, time seemed to have stopped; our talks at the conference seemed to go on forever, and yet were endlessly fascinating. My hands cramped as I took notes. Everyone I met seemed to be thoughtful and intriguing, and I wanted to record every word everyone said. This was not entirely due to the fact that we writers spend most of our time alone, not talking.

The way we live, someone said, almost mandates catastrophe. I think it was writer Don Snow who noted that in the middle of a flood, we're all standing on the river bank recycling the same arguments from the past hundred years. He did say this is the "Century of the Unthinkable." Someone else said "Civil disobedience is like sex; if you can remember how many times you've done it, you haven't done it enough."

A retired physician said, "This is the second morning of my life." Tom said that though all the native vegetation near his home in Utah has been altered, "Air connects us." Another person said, "We're just dirt that gets up and walks."

When it was my turn to speak, Dorik Mechau introduced me by noting something I had not: that in both my publicity photos, I was kneeling. That reminded me of John McPhee's line in *Pieces of the Frame:* "I had never been in the immediate presence of a red-tailed hawk, and at sight of him I was not sure whether to run or to kneel." Did I unconsciously kneel for those photographs because of the way I feel about the land that is my home? I'd never considered the idea before.

The notions that churned in the air of Sitka during my visit have influenced my thinking and writing about the ideal of community ever since. And I will always remember how Carolyn Servid asked us each to hold our breath as she opened a tiny, ornate box to show us her treasure: a wee hummingbird feather.

Each afternoon, thinking hard, I walked the streets in sunshine, watching the water and the trees, counting eagles and being astonished by how sweetly the ravens sometimes spoke. Outside an espresso shop one day, I saw a man pacing back and forth, looking at his watch on every pivot. I bit my tongue to keep from saying, "You're not from around here, are you?"

Perhaps that was the day a cruise ship hove into Sitka Sound; hundreds of tourists debarked and scattered noisily to buy souvenirs, laughing and snapping pictures. I slouched along the streets, as resentful as if they were cluttering up the streets of my hometown.

Later, I climbed into a small boat for a tour of the sound with my friend Tim, a forest service wildlife biologist. He used to work in South Dakota, and we'd become friends through a buckskinning club, among other muzzle-loading rifle fanatics.

"I can't swim, you know," I reminded him.

He nodded, and explained that the forest service in Alaska is full of ref-
ugees from the grassland; they've retreated to Alaska because the plains are
getting too crowded.

"None of us can swim," he said. "But the first thing we do is buy a boat,
because the water is the only place we can get under open sky."

We both looked up at the broad sky and heaved huge sighs. "I love trees,"
he said, "but sometimes I can't breathe unless I get out on the water."

So much water, we agreed, is almost hypnotic to plains people trained
to the arid rules of "waste not, want not." Water is the most important
"common wealth" in the Great Plains, probably in the world; and yet no
politician wants to discuss what's going to happen as supplies dwindle and
corporations muscle into ownership of food supplies. We discussed water
as we motored around the sound, watching tourists in sea kayaks, salmon
rolling and feeding. I mentioned that a number of people had asked me
to bring salmon back to them, and I hadn't yet collected any homecoming
gifts. I explained how easily I could make room in my luggage. Tim firmly
dissuaded me from wrestling one into the boat as a souvenir.

We chugged close to a Beaver float plane revving up for takeoff while
Tim explained that a Beaver is the most reliable float plane ever made. He
knew of one that had crashed into the ocean in a remote spot, been hauled
out, and made airworthy again. "If you ever have to fly in a float plane," he
said, "be sure it's a Beaver. You might actually survive if it goes down."

When we drifted to conversation about our days in the rifle club, he
laughed again about the time he came to the ranch for a party with our
rowdy club and noticed the dried hide of a dead calf hanging in the basement. When the calf was born dead, I'd realized that his mother had a
good supply of milk, found an older calf whose mother wasn't feeding him
enough, and used the dead calf's pelt on the hungry calf to convince the
bereaved cow he was hers. Once she'd accepted the calf, I'd kept the hide,
thinking George might recycle it as mittens or a furry bag.

In the middle of the uproarious party, Tim entertained himself and us
by pretending to slip into his federal role. "A bear cub pelt!" he bellowed,
grabbing me by the arm. "You are under arrest!" After we all finished laughing, I asked him, purely hypothetically of course, what a friend of his
should do if she happened to have picked up something on the prairie the
federal government said she shouldn't have.

"Shut the door, you idiot" he snapped. "I'd never open a closed door in a friend's house. But if I were in a friend's house and saw something illegal, I'd have to report it."

"Fair enough," I retorted. "That's all I ask of my government." Then I excused myself and loudly slammed several doors.

We chugged close to the ocean liner and looked up at the towering wall of the hull to the people looking down. Feeling a little sick, we agreed the ocean liner might be a living metaphor for the way visitors can affect any lovely place: a huge presence, beside which the natives seem tiny and distant. Then a motor started and the anchor chain started to rise. Tim turned white and gunned the engine hard.

Baranoff Island, he explained, is almost completely wilderness; people live only in Sitka and one other small town. I'd been struck by Sitka's similarities to my homeland; now Tim reminded me of some of the differences. In South Dakota, we receive an average of nine to sixteen inches of moisture a year; in Sitka, the average hundred-inch yearly rainfall is usually spoken of as "more than eight *feet*." One of my pastures is especially good for summer range because seven native cottonwoods thirty feet tall offer shade. In the Tongass National Forest surrounding Sitka on three sides, towering western hemlocks and Sitka spruce average 160 an acre. The whole island is crammed with wildlife, practically tripping over the scientists observing it.

Tim also answered a big question; all the tourist information I'd seen refers to "brown bears," but the description sounded like the fearsome grizzly to me. Yes, he admitted; it's the same bear. I wonder if the local refusal to call them grizzlies is derived from the ancient native custom of not speaking the words for the most powerful animals, out of respect. About a thousand bears live on the island, though Tim assured me I shouldn't worry; they only come into town during the salmon run.

I looked over the side of the boat, at the silver backs of salmon my size surging past.

"Like now," I said.

"Yup," he said.

THE NEXT DAY, I walked a trail in the Sitka National Historic Park with another conference participant, Lester, an elderly doctor recently retired from family practice, whose daughter lives in Sitka. More athletic people hiked ahead while Lester and I ambled, more interested in visiting than setting speed records.

Had I heard, he asked, that two small brown bears had recently been seen in this park?

I'd heard.

And was I afraid? he said, his glasses glinting as he looked up at me.

Not especially, I said, though I knew Lester had noticed me glancing nervously into the shadows under the trees.

I looked at Lester's laugh-lined face, thought over what I knew of his full and well-lived life, and risked a joke.

"You know what my muzzle-loading friends would say about it, Lester? If we see a bear, I don't have to outrun the bear; all I have to do is outrun you."

Lester laughed so hard he had to sit down on a nearby bench. I sat beside him, and we looked at each other, grinning. Watching Lester give himself wholeheartedly to laughter, I knew he'd given himself to his life that way, and that if a grouchy bear emerged from the woods, we might both die laughing. Not a bad end for either of us, though Lester had done more good for the world than I have.

I USED TO THINK that one person can't make a difference, can't change enough of the evil or misinformation in the world to bother trying. The Sitka conference convinced me of the opposite, that only individuals can make a difference, no matter what the task. Each of us makes a stand where we can, and when we meet someone else who's doing the same thing, we've got a community. Hank, Lester—I doubt I'll ever see either of them again, but it gives me courage to know they are out there. Blessed may they be.

Back home on the prairie, I remember Sitka and practice patience as I write about ranching, about why housing developments should not be built in grassland. When I'm disheartened, I think about the community created by collaborative thought in Sitka. In my journal I find this statement made by someone at the conference: "The health of a place will reflect the health of the consciousness of the people who live there."

Hank, whose name I've changed to protect his privacy, is an important part of Sitka's health. I'm sure Martha still defines sustainability as how she supports her family and her elders. I can still hear Richard's voice saying, "a black bear can out-mind you," calling back my father's observation, "It pays to be smarter than the cow." Nearly every day, I hear Don Snow say, "Every time you buy something, you're voting for it."

The longer I stayed in Sitka, the more at home I felt. Dan Henry said he writes essays specifically to discourage tourism to his home state, so I promised never to move there. That community of the mind we formed during those few days links us anyway; we don't have to live together.

Someone at the conference challenged us to think of it this way: Rate a place you love on a scale of 1 to 10. Now rate what you're doing to save that place from being paved or polluted, also on a scale of 1 to 10. Now compare those two ratings, and act as your conscience moves you.

Recycling Freedom

Back in the 1960s, when I lived in Columbia, Missouri, I rode a French racing bike back and forth between two lives.

By day I wore tidy professional suits to teach English at the University of Missouri and journalism at Christian College for Women (later Columbia College). All my suits had very short skirts, the easier to pedal with, my dear.

By night, wearing jeans and dark turtleneck shirts, I joined scruffy long-haired folks of all conceivable genders and colors to publish an underground, antiwar newspaper. I learned the hard way never to drink from a glass or bottle left sitting on the table; no telling what drug had been added to enhance the drink. Most of my drug ingestion experiences, in fact, occurred by accident in that guerrilla newspaper office.

"Stories are the sparks that light our ancestors' lives," says western writer Jane Kirkpatrick, "the embers we blow on to illuminate our own." But this story is about neither the teaching nor the underground newspaper. After living most of my life in rural South Dakota, I was learning in Columbia how to live in a city. My little white Peugeot racing bike was my passport to a new life. I zipped around town to all the places I was supposed to be, dodging traffic in a way that amazes me to recall. One of the bike's handiest features was a tire pump fixed between the rider's legs. When a loose dog snapped at my ankles, I snatched the tire pump lose and discouraged the animal with a smart rap on the snout. Once a man grabbed my ankle and jerked, perhaps in an effort to get acquainted. A whack on his wrist and I was gone, waving the pump and cackling in triumph.

When my husband took our car and I knew he'd come back hours later smelling of another woman and mouthing some anemic excuse, I'd straddle my bike and ride out of town, ride under the trees with their heavy leaves until I was exhausted. Rain sprayed from the tires and drew a line up the back of my coat as I pedaled back and forth from my stuffy apartment to my classes. My husband loved my long hair, so I whacked it off and let the rain and wind blow through the short and shiny strands while I thought about divorce.

That, too, is just reminiscence, not the story as I see it now.

WHEN I MOVED from Missouri back to my South Dakota ranch in the late 1970s, I took the bike along, perhaps unwilling to give up those memories of flying through the sunshine and moonlight to the sizzle of its gears. Or perhaps I was just being frugal, like my parents, who never gave up possessions they couldn't possibly use. I got rid of the husband, but the bike hung in the garage for (mumble mumble) years.

When I decided in 1992 to move to Cheyenne, I was broke and disoriented, but it seemed to me that a good environmentalist who had to live in town might fix up an old bike and ride it to save gas.

THE TOOLS ARE INTACT inside the dusty, stiffened leather case. I try to pump up the cracked tires, and then start calling bike shops to see about replacement parts. Each time I explain how old the bike is, the person on the other end of the telephone laughs.

I ride the bike around the block once or twice. My legs shake a little, but I figure that in a week or two I can get back in shape. Considering how much money I might save on gas—a lot more than I saved in the sixties—I sit down in the canvas chair on the porch to rest.

Swinging gently, I watch the traffic pass on Warren Avenue. Big trucks, noisy little cars that sound like lawnmowers fueled by meth, lumbering Hummers. Some drivers yappity yap on cell phones or light cigarettes, driving tons of speeding steel one-handed. Others scream at their children; some are children screaming along with a rap song. The crippled woman who works in the administration building across the street waits and waits and waits for a break in traffic long enough to hobble across the street, knowing no one will stop for her. Two kids on skateboards risk it, yelling as their wheels clatter into the crosswalk and a cursing driver slams on his brakes. Tires squeal for a block as other drivers react. The boys whoop and race away.

An ambulance siren starts four blocks away at the hospital, but most of the drivers don't pull over until it is directly behind them, the horn shivering the foundations of my house.

Let's see now: I am proposing to get on my thirty-five-year-old bike and use my sixty-two-year-old legs to propel myself out into the middle of that.

Hmmm. I drink some more iced tea and dig weeds while I think.

Jerry, who has a mountain bike tucked somewhere in the garage, offers to loan me his helmet. Maybe, since walking the dogs takes an hour a day, I can start slowly by walking the dogs while riding the bike. But the two Westies are short-legged and given to sudden turns after squirrels and cats. I dig more weeds.

The bike stays under the overhang at the side of the house for another year or two before I admit to what I've decided, tie it on top of my car, and haul it back to South Dakota.

ON A SUNNY SUMMER DAY, I drive with my friend Tamara to Rapid City, then east and up a long hill bristling with radar installations into a cluster of modest houses surrounded by patched-together fences, extra cars, stacks of firewood, dogs, and washing machines overgrown with weeds. People look closely at us as we drive past in our unfamiliar car, just the way they do in my country town, but when we wave, everyone smiles and waves back. Many little western towns look like this, if they haven't been invaded by latte-swilling hordes who build houses with high ceilings and four-car garages and plant lawns they hire people to mow. These are the homes of people who are likely to mow those lawns.

At the end of the road is a tall building sided in blue tin. Beside it are rows and rows of bicycles in orderly piles higher than my head.

The sun shines on the concrete in front of the garage, its double doors open, showing neat workbenches where several men are working on bikes. In front, a Lakota man is helping a little boy with black hair and brown eyes climb on a bike. He steadies the boy for a minute, and then watches, hands on hips, as the kid pedals down the driveway. Three or four other children grin and jump up and down.

We unload my bike and turn to find him looking at us.

"Oh," he says, "an old racing bike."

"Is it too old?"

"Nothing's too old." He gently takes the bike from my hands. Wheeling it into the garage, he nods again. The transaction is over. We drive away.

I'D JUST DONATED to the Yellow Bike Program, and thought at the time the project was strictly local. Instead, it may have begun in Portland, Oregon, around 1994, in the best way: with a couple of people who thought it was a great idea. Around the country, Yellow Bike provides bikes, and something more, for mostly poor kids. A child who wants a bike comes to the center, chooses a bike, and helps repair it before taking it home at no charge. Besides learning about generosity, the children pick up useful mechanical and social skills from the volunteers who staff the program.

In our area many of the recipients are Lakota kids whose folks have, for some reason, left their rural reservation homes to live in Rapid City, the nearest town large enough to offer unskilled labor jobs. Someone gave $10,000 anonymously to start the program, and a dozen local businesses became sponsors. The governor sent three people to build the pole building. The organization gets information out to local folks by conducting bike races and rodeos as an excuse to distribute donated prizes, including bikes. By early 2007, more than six thousand bikes had been ridden away from the blue tin building.

Just one more simple little idea that really works. Every time I think of the stories my bike could tell about my adventures in Missouri, I picture a laughing Lakota girl swooping down that long hill, making her own stories, stories that will be part of my community's future.

Tattoos and a Thong

The first time I hear the story, I am neck deep in the Lobster Pot, the hottest pool at the Star Plunge in Thermopolis, Wyoming, soaking winter's aches out of my muscles.

When tension rides our necks, Jerry and I sometimes head for this small town built around hot springs that have been reducing stress for generations. Legend declares that the West's hot springs have always been considered zones of peace, where Native American tribes at war could relax without bloodshed. Lovely metaphor: these pools of pleasure are born of the West's violent volcanic heart, but the peaceful tradition continues.

"I gotta tell you this story," says a teenage male voice, tense and excited. His words echo off the concrete walls. I let my eyes slide past the boy just as he glances around to see if anyone is listening. He is probably high school age, a lifeguard, squatting on the edge of the big pool beside a long-haired older man whose muscles ripple with tattoos.

I squint and look up at the ceiling, thinking how invisible middle-aged women usually are to young males.

He drops his voice. "I was bowhunting last week, about a mile outside of town."

He stops, tries again: "A mile or *less* from town. I just walked up a little draw and sat down in some willows, like a blind you know." He glances around.

"After school. Just thought I'd sit awhile, shoot something if it came by. I'd just got settled when a coyote came along, hunting mice. I thought I'd shoot him if he'd get close. Found two plastic bags in my pocket and rubbed them together, you know, trying to make them squeak like mice. That didn't work; he just kept on sniffing and pawing at rocks. So I just tried a voice call. You know, made a sound like a fawn lost from its mother or maybe hurt. That coyote looked right at me for a minute, then sat down and howled. Just threw his head back, you know, and howled."

The boy looks carefully around the room. I sink a little deeper in the pool, stifling my groans.

The boy goes on. "It wasn't more than a minute before I heard yipping, sounded like it was everywhere. You know, coyote yips, like they do at night when they're hunting."

He glances around, takes a deep breath. "And then eleven coyotes came over that hill from every direction. *Eleven* coyotes! They gathered around the one that howled and sat there, looking through those skinny little willow branches at me."

He stops, looking at the tattooed man as if he expects him to say something, but the man is kicking his feet in the water, not looking at the boy.

"I thought maybe I'd got myself in trouble there," the boy continues. "I only had four arrows. Figured maybe if I shot one or two, the rest would run off. So I shot one arrow to the left, and missed. Shot another one straight ahead at the first coyote that howled, and missed him too. I dropped my aim a little, shot again, and it went over his head again."

The silence lasts so long I open one eye to look. The tattooed man is shaking his head. He says, "It's instinct. The first one thought he had a meal in those bushes."

"Well," says the boy, "I aimed like that." He raises his arm to demonstrate how he placed the bow.

The man waves his hand, cutting off what the boy is trying to say. "You don't have to aim. Just lift and fire if you want to hit them. Get rid of that compound thing with the springs. Get a recurved bow, or a longbow maybe."

The boy stammers in frustration. "I like my compound, but that's not what I meant. I wondered why—"

The man cuts him off. "What good is it? You confessed yourself—I didn't drag that out of you—you missed four times." He snorts.

The boy says. "Three times. But that's not the point. I'm not really sure I meant to hit any of them. I was just scared for a minute. Have you ever heard of that? I mean twelve coyotes gathering around?" He looks right and left. I imitate a crocodile; only my eyes and nostrils show above water.

He whispers, "I was *afraid* of them. Afraid of *coyotes*. Cowardly chicken-eating, sneaky, mouse-chasing coyotes."

The man rolls his eyes. "Anyway," says the kid, "I was kinda glad I missed because then I figured if I'd killed one and the rest came after me I couldn't kill them all, so I might as well relax and see what they'd do. I sat there for an hour while they looked me over, sniffing, looking, and getting closer all the time. Tongues hanging out, but it looked like they were laughing. Their eyes—." He frowns. "They were like this far away." He holds his arms out as wide as he can, and looks back and forth between his hands. "And it was getting dark and hard to see and I was cold and stiff."

"Finally one got around almost behind me, downwind. I was trying to see him without moving too much, and he slipped around to the side. When I turned back to look at the other eleven, they were gone; disappeared so fast I didn't see them go. Just gone." He throws his arms in the air. "Maybe got a whiff of my scent."

The long-haired man holds up a hand. "You gotta get a better bow," he says, standing up. He goes outside and dives into the cold pool. The boy wanders back to his lifeguard perch looking thoughtful.

Red-skinned and trembling, I pull myself out of the Lobster Pot, stagger to the cold shower and pull the rope. I stand beneath the cold shower until I'm blue, trying to figure out how to get the boy to tell me his story, or tell it where he can see me listening.

I breathe deep, making up for holding my breath while the boy spoke. "The simple telling of a story seems to cast a spell in a room," says Susan Chernak McElroy, "instantly creating a gentle air of intimacy and enchantment that warms even the most barren, cold meeting space." Tribal storytellers say there is merit and wisdom for both teller and listeners in repeating any story over and over, for generations, because both groups learn while they pay attention. How many times, I wonder, will this boy repeat his tale? *Mitakuye oyasin*, say the Lakota; we are all related. This boy has been given plenty of concrete advice about hunting and weapons. But he hasn't known, or perhaps has not yet paid attention to, the modest hunters who learned their place in the universe from hunting. Will he tell the story often enough, thoughtfully enough, to understand it? Will he realize the coyotes know him better than the humans who have not really listened to him today?

Thinking Jerry is in the steam room, I push past a torn canvas curtain over the rough rock doorway and stumble into a cave full of thick vapor. Without my glasses, I almost say, "Hi, honey" before squinting for a better look. Nodding back at me is a stranger, a solid stack of hairy, muscled flesh wearing only tattoos and a thong.

I slide past him, noting that many of his tattoos refer to Harleys, freedom, and the American way. I nod. He nods back. Carefully, I lower myself to the slippery wood bench circling the scratchy walls of the room. Water bubbles out of a tall cone built of layers of minerals just beyond my knees, falling into a pool and gurgling away somewhere beneath me. I breathe deep, straightening my back. Soon I realize my breathing sounds a counterpoint to that of the barrel-chested biker beside me.

Then he begins to speak, describing in rhapsodic terms complete with sensory details including smell, taste, sensation, sight, and sound, the breathtaking joy of riding his Harley alone through Wyoming's Red Desert. We share the steam room in perfect harmony as his voice rises with the tendrils of steam. We are silent for a long time. When we gasp simultaneously and stand, he courteously gestures me ahead, and we run awkwardly on the slick concrete and throw ourselves into the cold pool with one immense, resounding splash.

An hour later, sitting in a corner of the outside pool in the sun, I hear the boy begin his story once more.

Learning the Names of Cows

One fall day I stood very close beside my new father in the center of a corral beside the barn and pretended to be brave. Dust swirled around us. A hundred nervous Angus-Hereford calves galloped back and forth, bawling for their mothers, who bellered answers from another corral on the west side of the barn.

The calves, mostly born in March, each outweighed me at least four times, could look me straight in the eyes, and were terrified. This was the first time they'd been away from their mothers and close to humans since they'd been branded in May. As they ran around us, they shied and kicked, rolled their eyes, and bumped each other.

My father turned slowly in the center of the bovine whirlpool, his eyes flicking over the calves as he talked. "That Jersey milk cow's granddaughter sure throws good calves, leggy, but stout," he'd say, and then turn around, looking at calves that all looked alike to me.

"I believe that one with the black circle around her eye is out of that Angus bull I saved, and I like her looks."

I nodded, rolling my eyes left and right without turning my head, trying to spot a calf with a black circle around her eye.

As he pointed out individual characteristics, I realized that he knew which calf belonged to every cow. Only later did I realize that, while most ranchers buy bulls to get new blood into the herd, he was cautiously experimenting with saving some good calves to grow up into bulls. In order for this to work, he had to remember bloodlines so the bulls didn't breed their mothers or sisters. They all looked nearly identical to me: mostly black with white faces, and a few splashes of white on their chests or ankles.

That day, I was still flabbergasted at the speed with which my dream of becoming a country kid had begun to come true. In May of that year, my mother had done what she'd left home to avoid, married a rancher. For most of the next forty years, I would live and work on that land, learning the details of ranching as my father practiced it: taking care of a hundred fifty cows and their calves from birth through death or departure by sale.

I realized that first summer that my father could recount the family tree of every cow he owned, and every calf she'd produced. Why, I asked, did a rancher have to know his cows so intimately?

In order to have thrifty cows that raised strong calves, he explained, we needed to keep in the herd the cows best adapted to the native grasses that grew on our land. We wanted cows that would thrive in our dry summers and cold winters. Our best cows were often bony critters with prominent hipbones. When the neighbors said they "looked like hell," my father laughed and said, "they put the kick in the chicken," meaning they raised a good calf every year.

"How do you tell them apart?" I asked.

"It'll come to you," he replied.

This was the man who, the day I met him, had asked me to choose either a nickel or a dime from his hand, and praised me for picking the dime because it was worth more.

This was the man who, when he learned I didn't know the multiplication tables, devised his own method of teaching me. Each morning he'd open my bedroom door and shout something like, "What's nine times seven?" If I didn't holler the correct answer immediately, he kept yelling a multiplication question as he yanked the covers off my bed.

As I handed him the fencing pliers along some isolated stretch of fence in the pasture, he'd say, "Thanks. What's nine times eight?"

When we went back to the pickup so I could drink from the water jug, he'd pour his coffee and ask, "What's eight times nine?"

At dark, when we rode into the corral after moving cattle from one pasture to another on a hundred-degree day, he might say, "Long day. Are you tired? And what's six times eight?"

Yet his only advice on recognizing cows was, "It'll come to you."

When I protested, he added, "If you're going to raise cattle, you have to learn to pay attention."

LEARNING ABOUT THE LAKOTA who preceded ranchers on these grasslands, I was slow to realize that what my father taught me, like the wisdom in oral cultures, did not come from study as I had learned to do it. School taught me to read, memorize, repeat, but now I understand I learned the facts and beliefs that have been most important to me by apprenticeship, by watching someone who did something well and trying to do the same. Scholars say this method of learning served people in cultures that did not have writing. Tracking with experienced hunters, boys became disciples of pursuit, learning from the prey and the land. Girls followed women in digging healing herbs, harvesting nourishing vegetables, learning a different language from the same domain. Learning by paying attention.

EACH FALL, we gathered the cows and calves from the summer pasture six miles east of the ranch buildings, and trailed them slowly home. The next morning, we eased them into the big corral east of the barn. My father would open the gate to the west pen, and tell me to stand beside it and not let any calves through.

Then he'd go to another gate and move slowly among the cows, carrying his whip. When he had maneuvered a cow close to the gate, he'd point the whip at her, nod at me, and she'd dash past me while he stepped in front of her calf to turn it back. The only time he ever struck a cow with the whip was when she lunged straight toward him, horns lowered. Then his mouth would tighten, and he'd stand firm until she was close, the sharp horns pointed straight at his lean belly. Then he'd snap the whip lightly against her nose, usually only once. She'd pivot and dive through the gate.

After he'd shut all the cows in the corral, we'd walk to the center of the pen with the calves and look them over while he commented on how fat they were from the summer's grass, or that they "looked a little drouthy" after a dry summer produced short grass.

Then we'd begin to sort again: while I worked the gate, he'd point his whip and separate the biggest steers into one pen to be sold. We'd stroll among them, and he'd bark, "What'll they weigh?" The first few years, I'd hesitantly say something like, "Two hundred." He'd frown and say, "Oh, I think they'll do better than that. I'd say three fifty." I was expected to re-member my guess for each calf, as he did, when the weights flashed on the screen at the sale ring the next day.

Next, we'd use the same technique to sort all the remaining heifer calves into a separate corral, where we'd amble among them while he talk-ed about each calf's conformation and ancestry. Finally, he'd put the best dozen in another pen. We'd keep them close to the buildings for the winter, giving them good feed in shelter so they could grow up to be our replace-ments, breeding cows we'd keep in the herd. He looked for cows that were sturdy and calm, so they would raise their calves with a minimum of fuss. They had to be solid, meaty animals, but their size was less important than their thriftiness: their ability to utilize the food we gave them so that their calves grew as strong and lively as possible. His final criterion for each heifer we kept was always "the look in her eye."

Each year, most of the calves we raised were auctioned off at a sale ring. We sold the biggest steers and the second-best heifers the day after we separated them from the cows. We weaned the younger calves as well, animals too young to fit in any of the groups we sold, enduring several days of bawling from the cows and calves shut in separate pens. As soon as the cows quieted down a little, indicating their udders were beginning to ad-just to the loss of the calf, we put the cows into a fresh pasture with good grass so they could gain strength before winter. We kept the calves in the corral, feeding them hay and sometimes grain until they'd gained enough weight to satisfy my father. Then we'd sell them in small bunches, hauled to the sale ring in our old Chevy pickup, matched as closely as possible by size, weight, and even color. Every couple of weeks, he'd pick out a pickup load of calves to sell, choosing calves that were "bloomy:" healthy and at their peak.

My father decided when to sell the calves by considering several fac-tors. The first calves sold were in top condition. They'd spent the summer consuming their mothers' milk and green grass, before they would begin to lose fat as the grasses dried and the weather grew colder. He liked to sepa-rate the calves from the cows in the morning and sell them that afternoon or the next day. By selling them at once, we avoided weaning them, making them stand around in our corrals for weeks, losing weight and bawling for their mothers. Weaning, and the dangers of sickness associated with it, became the buyers' problem.

Once we'd decided on a date to separate and sell the calves, we had to hope that every other rancher in the neighborhood didn't choose the same date, or the price of calves would drop, no matter how good they were. When the calves reached the sale ring, we had to accept whatever price the auctioneer persuaded a buyer to pay that day—or pay a trucker to take the calves home for the long process of weaning, exposing them to the risks of winter and illness.

Most years my father tucked the check in his billfold murmuring, "Topped the market again." During my first year on the ranch, I learned that cash had to last a year, that most of my clothes were secondhand, and that we drove the oldest trucks and tractors in the neighborhood. For years, that's all I knew of ranching economics.

Our family, our small new community, was a single-family, cow-calf ranch, the most labor-intensive way to raise beef. We warmed new calves in the bathtub during March blizzards, saved some of our best male calves to raise as bulls to service the herd, or bought bulls from neighbors rather than at advertised bull sales where prices would be high. We harvested our own hay, and helped the neighbors fight fires. In short, we tried to keep the ranch as free as possible from obligations to the world outside our community. We had to buy certain commodities, like gasoline, that our neighborhood didn't produce, but our major efforts were devoted to being as self-sufficient as possible. We bought locally as many goods and services as possible.

Part of this self-sufficiency, I soon realized, meant that we didn't sell a good cow if she missed calving one year. "That cow's ten years old," my father might say. "Course it's not 'efficient' to keep her. It's not the 'agri-business' way." Then he'd grin, and I knew the cow would remain on our ranch at least another year. As a result, we had cows fifteen years old who'd earned names as we became acquainted with their personalities and idiosyncrasies. After realizing she could outrun most of our horses, we named one cow Whirlaway after a Kentucky Derby winner. Zebra's sides were marked by dark vertical stripes handed down from her Jersey great-grandmother. Can Opener had one short, curved horn; she polished it sharp by rubbing it on fence posts, and poked other cows to make them get out of her way.

Though my father counted every penny we spent—I still can't leave a room without switching off the light—he was more lenient with his cows and the local wildlife. We left broad strips of uncut hay along the edges of fields for the deer. My dad's explanation: "They have to hide those fawns someplace, and if we can't make a living without *that* hay, we better quit."

I was fourteen the first time my father told me to hold my horse in the open gate of our winter pasture and "count 'em in." A hundred bawling cows, horns high, trotted down a rocky gully into the creek bottom and galloped toward the gate where I sat my horse, narrowing the entrance to force the cows into single file. They shoved and crowded, grinding my legs against the saddle and the gate post. I gritted my teeth and kept counting. After a while, I realized that my brain was supplying a comment on each cow. "Ugly's first again, granddaughter of the old Jersey who taught me to milk, mother of Zebra. Second is that cow that butted her baby around the rocks."

"A hundred and four," I said when my father drove up in the pickup, "and I knew every one of them!"

After that, when he sent me to bring in "that cow that got fat while she starved her calf to death," I came back with the right one.

I'd paid attention, learned by experience. Each day's work brought me more intimate knowledge of the cows. When we moved bunches of cattle anywhere, my father led them in the pickup while I followed them on horseback for miles, trailing them slowly so the calves wouldn't turn back, or lose track of their mothers. My father had quickly dispelled my notion that work involving horses was done at a gallop. "Don't *cowboy*," he'd snap. I'd spent hours with him in the barn at night, mostly sitting on a hay bale while we waited for the right moment to pull a calf. I'd stood in a gate, eyeball to eyeball with a cow that bawled and flung snot over her shoulder, trying to scare me out of the way. And every minute of that time, I was paying attention.

Most days in the summer, my mother put steaks on our plates at noon, serving green beans and boiled potatoes on the side, maybe tomatoes from the garden. My father might pretend to forget what we'd named the heifer. "This is that one born crippled two years ago; I kept her, thinking that leg might straighten out, but it never did. She ought to be tender, because she didn't run around much." We always butchered heifers because steers brought more money at the sale ring.

Together, we'd cut into the pink, juicy meat and lift the first bite to our lips. The deep, rich smell and flavor was seasoned by pure grass and water and clean air, nourishing the heifer and us on our own ground. "Grassfed beef," my father would say, and present a brief oration on the folly of wasting corn on these animals that evolved in every bone, sinew, and drop of blood on wild grass. "People must eat that yellow fat just so they can go on diets," he'd say, chewing and smiling at the same time. "Corn's for pigs, or corn bread. Not for cows." I'd savor each mouthful, remembering how I'd carried water to the heifer when she couldn't get up, helped her to stand so she could nurse, watched her gain strength until she could run behind her mother.

I OWNED NOTHING but my horse and saddle, but those cows were mine in the most important sense: we knew each other. We'd spent time to gether, shared experiences, even adventures. Our recognition was mutual, and therefore we treated each other with respect. Each of us had earned a particular place in the community of the ranch, not gained it free by inheritance or purchase: earned it. I had established my place in the community of our ranch by paying attention, and by working to make it better. From work I gained discipline and pride in whatever I did, lessons that carried me into the rest of my life.

How to Live at the Dump

Making pasta sauce in my city kitchen, I'm thinking about the latest environmental news. As usual, a dramatic headline predicted the end of life as we know it, a tired tactic to scare readers into reading adjective-choked paragraphs about the latest crisis. All threats these days are "grave," all public officials "worried." Citizens who live next to giant smoke stacks spewing poisonous vapors don't understand why their hair is falling out because the company pays good and their daddies worked there before they died of the cancer, doncha know. An official assures us everything under the company logo is not only safe but positively healthy, and by the way, the company name now incorporates the word "environment." A scientist from an obscure university provides a paragraph of statistics proving—and that's usually where I stop reading, eyes glazed and jaw rigid.

Because I am a writer, I sometimes try to exercise my mind by summing up one of those scare stories in twenty-five words or less. This exercise generally demonstrates that the story is a web of half-formed ideas, a mish-mash of unsubstantiated remarks.

Reading environmental news is enough—as my dad used to say—"to depress the hide off a skunk." To counter my worry, I like to do something positive about natural resources, since I agree with P. J. O'Rourke that if we want something, we should buy it or work for it. "We shouldn't," he says, "beg it, steal it, sit around wishing for it, or euchre the government into taking it by force." I work at home, spending most of my time in my own house, so my opportunities to fight pollution and waste are handy and personal.

Pouring the last quarter cup of lemon juice into the frying pan with the mushrooms, garlic, and chicken broth, I rinse the bottle and drop it into the recycling bucket with a beer bottle and two tomato cans.

I HAVE LIVED most of my life without garbage pickup. I realize as I write that how unusual it must be; almost everyone pays someone else to haul trash away. In 1952, when my mother became a rancher's wife, no garbage service existed for rural residents. On the ranch we were still responsible for everything we discarded. If we couldn't burn it, we had to bury it in our own pastures, where our cattle ate the grass that made the meat we ate, so we were picky about disposal methods. We even buried burned waste.

Our personal garbage disposal system consisted of two fifty-gallon barrels standing in a triangular open space between the cellar, the garage, and the corral. One was the "burning barrel," and the other was for trash that could not be burned. Before anything reached either barrel, though, it had gone through a series of challenges.

In our family, very little paper got to the barrel. When paper arrived at the house with writing on only one side, Mother reused it; advertising circulars, letters from congressmen: she ripped them into squares and put them into one of several drawers stuffed with pencils, some only an inch long. When my father left a note to tell my mother where he was going in the pasture, or she wrote a grocery list or sent a note to a teacher, they used stubby pencils and paper scraps.

My father even made us take the labels off cans so that if they hadn't burned off, they wouldn't blow away when we dumped the noncombustible garbage in the pasture; she cut those up too. I was embarrassed to hand my teachers a note that had once wrapped a can of beans, but these days, as my mother would not be surprised to learn, I have pencils and containers (usually recycled boxes) of scrap paper beside every chair in the house.

My parents believed in the maxim that one learns by doing, so emptying wastebaskets was one of my chores. When every bit of use had been squeezed out of a piece of paper, it was placed in the burning barrel and confined under a tight lid weighted down with a rock so paper wouldn't blow out. I learned this lesson by forgetting to replace the lid and rock one day. I don't remember what my father said, but, just as he intended, I remember untangling half a barrel of paper scraps from the surrounding trees and bushes, picking bits out of fresh cow pies in the corral, and running wildly through the alfalfa for a larger piece the wind kept dancing away.

What else did we burn? As little as possible. Newspapers, until I began using them as mulch in the garden and around new trees. Tissue paper, including toilet tissue sometimes when the septic tank was getting full. Dental floss, though we kept toothbrushes to scrub the sink. We kept brown paper grocery bags for wrapping packages, and folded Christmas wrap for reuse until it disintegrated from age.

The barrel where we put garbage that couldn't be burned was slow to fill. When mother bought something in a plastic package, she saved it to reuse in the freezer. Six years after she died, I finally hauled the last box of dusty Cool Whip containers out of the cellar.

My father saved tin cans for holding nails, screws, old fuses, and other workshop materials. He had cans of straight but used nails, and cans of rusty bent nails. On rainy days when I was ten years old, he'd sometimes give me a pair of gloves, a hammer, and a can of rusty nails, and set me to work straightening them by hammering at them on the floor of the garage while he whistled "Red Wing" and tidied up. Hitting my fingers with the hammer didn't get me out of the chore. In the garage and in several sheds around the yard and corrals, he kept wooden boxes heaped with old parts for the horse-drawn machinery. He lined up the outdated and broken down mowers, sulky rakes, windmill towers, wagon wheels, and other large metal junk on the top of hillsides.

Sometimes, listening for rattlesnakes, he'd grope through the grass growing up through the ribs of an old wagon and find a part he could use. Later, after I moved back to the ranch, I collected some of the metal parts from the horse-drawn machinery to use as candleholders and bookends. After my father died, I filled a trailer box with big chunks of antique iron; my tenant sold it to a recycling company. I gave away antique tractor machinery to anyone who could take it. I even led writers who came to my retreat to the hillside and encouraged them to take anything they found attractive. My father would be astonished to know that some of his treasures may now be part of someone's *decor*. Mostly, though, his hoard is rusting down into the thin soil.

We pried cardboard out of the Miracle Whip jar lids before stashing them with other glass bottles and jars in the cellar. My mother canned some of our food when we first moved to the ranch, but eventually saving the jars just seemed to be a habit; she rarely used them. One drawer in the kitchen was stuffed with plastic bags she'd carefully washed and dried; another held rusty twist ties, string, paper clips, and a half million outdated coupons she always forgot to take shopping.

All this labor, some of it clearly futile, became part of my education in recycling, before the word became part of everyday practice or environmental law. Hard work for little return became ingrained in me, not because it made money, but because my parents taught me that it was the right thing to do.

Every now and then, my father would announce that the burn barrel was full enough; if we stuffed too much paper in, it wouldn't burn well. Then we began the wait for a day with no wind so we could burn safely. My mother stored paper garbage in the house or garage, and nagged until he pronounced the day calm enough. He'd drop a match into the barrel, put a heavy screen over it, and stand close by with a shovel and a hose until every scrap of paper was burned. If the leftover ashes filled less than half the barrel, we could begin emptying paper waste into it again the next day. If the ashes were near the top, we waited several more days. Mother was not happy with the delay, but it was part of our fire prevention program. Every day my father would stir the ashes with a shovel until he was sure they were completely cold. Mother wanted to run the hose into the barrel, but he pointed out how heavy and messy it would be for him to empty. Meanwhile, we collected anything else we needed to get rid of and piled it beside the barrels: pieces of wood too rotted to use, tree branches. Finally, on another calm day, he'd announce that we were going to our dump.

He'd back the 1951 pickup up to the barrels, and I'd help him walk them up a two-by-six into the back. Then we'd drive to the garbage hole. It was always in the same pasture, in a natural depression on a high, flat plateau a long way from water. Every few years, when one hole was nearly full, he'd hire a neighbor with a backhoe to cover it and dig a new hole beside it, burying the waste deep enough so no storm or predator we could imagine would unearth it. He never imagined someone might build a house in that spot, but I realize now that even a full basement wouldn't be deep enough to unearth any garbage that hasn't rotted or rusted away.

We'd drive the old green truck on a two-tire trail out through the alfalfa field. My father got in and out several times, opening and closing most of the wire gates because they were too tight for my childish muscles. In the dump pasture, he'd slowly back the pickup, watching my hand signals until he reached the edge. Then he'd climb into the back. He might pause to point out to me a meadowlark singing on a fence post before grabbing the top of a barrel and tilting it. The trick was to hold it at the precise angle to empty without dropping it into the pit. Inevitably, the wind would puff just as the ashes boiled out of the barrel, and we'd get a face full. He'd laugh, sputtering, and hand me his handkerchief after he'd wiped grit off his face.

I'd climb down the bank to shovel dirt over the broken bottles and smashed cans so they wouldn't blow out. Cattle weren't likely to go down into the steep-sided hole, but if they did, we didn't want them to get cans or glass stuck on their hooves.

Looking back, I'm not sure why he put some household discards in another spot, but I suspect that he didn't want to haul it far, or fill the garbage hole too fast. So an old water heater, an electric stove, tangles of barbed wire, and insulators from electric poles are piled around a beautiful limestone outcropping north of the old ranch house. I also buried my favorite cats there, wrapping them in rags or old blankets, and tucking them into a natural hole in the limestone, and then using bricks from an old schoolhouse we'd demolished to fill in the holes. Not until I'd interred several pets did I realize that the local scavengers—coyotes, skunks, raccoons, badgers—dug out the bricks and gobbled the dead felines the first night after the funeral.

Unfortunately, while we couldn't see this mess from the old ranch house, my house on a hill provides a fine view. Each time I look that way, I'm haunted not only by the ugliness of rusting appliances, but by the waste, the attitude it seems to imply about the prairie's beauty. And yet my father always lectured me about our obligations: picking up after ourselves, keeping the land clean not only for our sakes but for the wildlife and cattle. So I feel responsible, particularly these days when some people think ranchers are careless with land.

Why would anyone imagine a rancher would think treating the land badly might benefit him? Still, some folks mention ranchers as "land-rapers" along with loggers and miners and people whose work requires them to harvest natural resources. My father would be appalled; he taught me we live on the land's well-being. For his honor, as well as my own, I need to remove our junk from the limestone shelf. I've cancelled the garbage service, since it takes waste to a city landfill in another county, merely moving it into someone else's neighborhood. One of our first projects when we move back to the ranch will be devising a system for dealing responsibly with our new garbage, as well as the leftovers, recycling what we can and burying the rest deep.

USUALLY, WE DUMPED OUR GARBAGE on our own land. Once or twice, maybe after I got old enough to start mentioning annoyingly often that we shouldn't be filling the pasture with junk, we hauled something to a dump in the woods near Custer.

I seem to remember that we turned off the highway at a handmade sign that said DUMP, and followed a dirt trail until we came to a gate. I think there was a house of logs, surrounded by more stuff than I'd ever seen in one place in my life.

A man came out of the house pulling his suspenders up on his shoulders, and opened the gate, peering into the truck as we drove past him. The picture in my head is of a bearded man in dirty coveralls with even white teeth. My father pulled the pickup into a circle of trees, and we got out. While my father introduced himself, and the man began looking over the load, I looked around.

Along the driveway were orderly stacks of building materials for sale, bricks here, concrete blocks over there, and piles of rose and white quartz. Pathways between flower beds were bounded with more bricks.

Back in the trees, I could see a small Caterpillar tractor beside piles of dirt. Nearer, one side of the yard was lined with a neat row of stoves, refrigerators, and other appliances in various stages of dilapidation. A young man with a wrench was dismantling one stove and putting parts carefully into a child's wagon beside him. Several appliances stood under a shed roof, with price tags marked in large red letters. When he saw me looking at them, the young man hollered, "I've rebuilt those, good as new." In another area of the yard, glass jars were stacked on wooden racks, graduating from larger at the bottom to smaller on the top shelves. "Need any canning jars?" he called. I shook my head and wandered on. The logic of the yard layout was clear. Items that wouldn't be damaged by weather were grouped together and easily accessible in the yard: tires, car parts, gardening tools without handles, plastic or metal children's toys, some freshly painted. Under the sloping tin roof of a three-sided building—built from scavenged materials said the boy when I glanced at him—were more fragile items: cardboard boxes of all sizes, and household items like dishes, glassware, and bundles of utensils. In one corner was a long workbench with shelves above it holding paint cans.

By this time the boy was following me. "See," he said, "we find the paint in the trash too—that's rust-inhibiting paint, expensive stuff—that we use on the tools and stuff like the kids' wagons. This here's inside paint, and we sell that—here's a nice pink—or we paint furniture with it. When I fix stuff up, my dad gives me part of the money when we sell it. That's how I buy my clothes for school and stuff."

The dump, he explained, was the family business. They owned the land, and contracted with the city or the county, maybe both, to handle the waste. What they did with it was apparently not the concern of any authority.

The boy gestured toward the north. "We raise pigs and chickens and turkeys, all on what people throw away." His voice was beginning to rise with passion. "Need any eggs? And we sell pork, on the hoof or butchered."

"You wouldn't *believe* what people throw away, young lady," said the older man, who had walked up behind us with my father. "A lotta food people throw away is plenty good for people too, and they just *waste* it." The boy looked away, blushing, and I guessed that the family made use of some of that food.

My father and the man shook hands. Our truck was empty, but it hadn't been near the deep pit at the back of the property; everything we'd discarded was reusable. On the way home, my father spoke with admiration of how the dump was run. I wasn't yet a teenager, but I knew how embarrassing it was to wear secondhand clothes and be afraid some classmate would recognize them. My father talked about a day when we might run short on resources, when people might be mining landfills to find stoves and other useful articles. How sensible to organize the dump as a useful business instead of covering everything with dirt. Later, I found John Kenneth Galbraith's comment that, "Just as there must be balance in what a community produces, so there must also be balance in what the community consumes." Since my father regularly read Galbraith, I may have heard those words first from him.

In the middle of ballyhoo about our throwaway society, I began to see articles about charitable organizations that follow the same principles, and employ people who might otherwise be jobless or homeless. More recently, I've noticed articles in popular magazines about businesses like Boston's Loading Dock, a nonprofit retail warehouse that sells secondhand virtually all the building materials a homeowner needs. While some parts of our economy still reward speedy builders who knock down buildings and dump the debris in a landfill, reuse centers allow them to save money by writing off donations of salvaged materials. Are good ideas always reinvented when they are needed most?

MY MEMORIES of the Custer family dump may have been colored by years of reading about countries where families and sometimes entire villages live on what other people throw away. Some populous cities mandate recycling, so I hope the number of Americans who blithely toss garbage without thought is dwindling, though I think many are still ignorant about the consequences of wasteful habits. By contrast, I probably spend too much time thinking about it. When I am considering the purchase of some little electronic gadget, for example, I stand in the store aisle contemplating the fact that if I buy the thing, I will also own the indestructible packaging. The longer I think about the gazillion years the package will lie in some waste repository, the less likely I am to decide I really need it.

IN THE YEARS SINCE visiting that family enterprise, I've inspected many dumps. The operator looks at the load, perhaps charges a fee, and tells us to follow the trail and the pickups ahead of us. We back the pickup up to a pile of waste and begin unloading, surrounded by mixed piles: food lumped on newspaper beside furniture adjoining tree limbs beside gas cans. In the distance I usually hear a bulldozer, pushing dirt over the mangled mass. The operator rarely looks at the dumping customers.

Once, I looked down from the back of the pickup and saw fifteen packages of beef steak, fresh and pink, still sealed in its plastic wrap. I resisted the steak, but became notorious for collecting useful objects. I've scavenged boxes of dishes, sealed plastic bags containing sheets and pillow-cases, furniture. George once tried to sneak off to the dump without me, grumbling when I caught him that I was likely to bring home more than we discarded. Eventually the landfills I frequented posted signs directing people not to take anything; when people ignored the signs, the workers started inspecting the pickup beds as patrons left. These regulations, created for sensible reasons like reducing the dump's liability, always drove me into a rage. I believe with Gandhi that "To believe in something, and not to live it, is dishonest." If we believe in recycling, we should do it at the landfill.

RECYCLING HAS FINALLY REACHED CHEYENNE, where I live with about 50,000 other people, so I've separate bins for glass, corrugated cardboard, newspaper and catalogs, aluminum and steel cans, and plastic. I recycle some magazines by giving them to friends or the library. Most of my clothing, my cookware, serving and dining dishes, Christmas decorations, vases, wrapping paper, books and bookends, picture frames, a sewing basket, rugs and waterproof boots are secondhand.

Under the sink is my compost, in a big plastic bottle that once held laundry soap. I've used the same container for more than a decade, and it shows no sign of wearing out, blast it. Every day I'm reminded of the millions of such containers going into landfills.

Morning's coffee grounds go into the compost bucket, as do some vegetable leftovers. No meat scraps, because once I empty the bucket into my outdoor composter, the odor would attract neighborhood cats and dogs as well as the raccoons and skunks who thrive here, practically downtown. I learned this by having skunks in the backyard, not a good idea when one keeps excitable dogs. And anyway, I have other uses for the meat scraps.

Unfortunately, I can't put my dogs' waste into the compost bin either, because it attracts flies, so I'm forced to tuck it into a plastic bag that the garbagemen will haul away. Imagine the tons of carefully wrapped dog waste that will lie for aeons in landfills.

In hot weather, we disperse flies from the compost by sprinkling wood ash from our grill or shavings from Jerry's woodworking shop over the pile. The resident mice keep it aerated, and entertain the dogs for hours.

Preparing potatoes and carrots, I stuff the peelings in a bag in the freezer with onion skins, the fat I trimmed off yesterday's steaks, and the beef stroganoff we didn't finish last week. I keep two bags in the freezer, one for chicken and pork and one for red meat: beef, venison, elk. When one bag is full, I dump it into a big pot on a burner set at medium heat, add a couple quarts of water, a bay leaf, pepper, and occasionally a complementary herb like sage or rosemary. I slice into it whole fresh onions, peels and all, smash a couple of bulbs of garlic and throw any wilted celery stalks and carrots I find in the refrigerator, along with any leftover bits of soup or stew, and any overripe or insect-gnawed vegetables from the garden.

During the day, the pot boils gently at the back of the stove; when I pass by, I skim off fat. At night I turn the burner low enough to keep the pot simmering rather than burning. After the stock boils for two or three days to reduce in volume, I strain the solids out of the remaining quart or two of liquid and freeze it, creating my own always-unique stock for soups and stews. Since I freeze stocks from dark meat in square containers and light stocks in round ones, I could grab the right stock blindfolded in the dark. Most of the containers are recycled, too. Usually I add the boiled meat and vegetables to the dogs' homemade food, but I must waste the skimmed-off fat. Once I move back to the ranch, I'll feed it to pigs or chickens, completing the cycle of turning old food into new food.

Those huge plastic containers for laundry soap frustrate me; they accumulate faster than I can devise uses. For a recent camping trip, I filled some with water without rinsing them, and labeled them SOAPY. Others I rinsed thoroughly—with the garden hose, beside a tree that needed water—and labeled RINSING. Then we set them on the tailgate of the pickup, and tied a towel to the handle. When our hands were dirty, we opened the petcock on a soapy one and didn't have to look for a bar of soap.

Once a week, one of us hauls our personal recycling containers to the city's big blue bins, where we are rarely alone. Reminding myself that high rollers usually tell me, "Time is money," I make each trip count, just as I did when I lived in the country: when I take the recycling, I get groceries and walk the dogs.

In much of the West, recycling hasn't become a priority; some of our elected officials still apparently believe that transportation costs make recycling financially prohibitive. In most cases they have not factored other costs: buying landfill sites when land prices are being driven up by ill-advised subdivisions, or the cost of shortages of recyclable materials.

At the recycling bins, I often see people with out-of-state license plates carefully replacing in their cars bags of waste Cheyenne doesn't recycle.

"I'm taking it home," one woman from Washington huffed to me, "where people are smart enough to recycle it!"

Like many Great Plains states, Wyoming spends millions of bucks a year on tourism campaigns that primarily advertise the scenery. Instead of hiding more landfills among the mountain views and hoping the tourists will be too busy at the rodeo to notice, maybe we ought to invest in better recycling programs and advertise them.

It Doesn't Just Happen

One Wyoming night, as I tried to sleep above our busy street, a howling roar penetrated through my earplugs. I sat up and looked out the window. Two men knelt beside a city utility truck in the center of the avenue, holding a huge hose and peering into the manhole to the waste line.

With an evil grin and a clear conscience, I drifted back to sleep. Some of my neighbors were paying for their sins or learning from their mistakes. As a graduate of several advanced septic tank seminars, I felt a teensy bit smug until I realized that because this is a city, they don't have to clean up after themselves, so they will not necessarily become more responsible.

When Jerry and I moved into our old house, we planned to do a lot of the remodeling ourselves. Jerry had done considerable carpentry work, and I was an experienced gopher and general handy-person. We spent several evenings examining the oddities of the house and planning changes.

In a basement bathroom, a toilet stood on a raised platform, deftly tucked in beside a shower and a tiny, triangular, antique sink.

"One of the first things I'm going to do," Jerry said, "is tear that toilet out and plug the line."

When I pointed out how handy it would be while I did laundry and he built furniture in the basement, he shook his head and reminded me of the Great Sewage Flood.

On that occasion, I'd driven down from South Dakota for the weekend, but he didn't answer my knock on the door. I found him slumped in the backyard, watching a sump pump pour sludge into the alley. Something had blocked the main city waste line running down the alley behind his house, so the waste backed up the pipeline, following the path of least resistance into the lowest area available: his basement. Two feet of subdivision slime flowed into his workshop and a room containing the exotic woods he'd been buying for years to make furniture and art projects. The gunk flowed around antique stoves, woodworking tools, stacks of stained glass. Wearing gloves to protect ourselves from contamination, we spent two days pumping the ooze out and hauling most of the furniture, wood, books, magazines, and records to the dump.

This time when he said, "No toilet in the basement," I nodded.

A few nights later, coming home from a movie, we heard an ominous gurgling. In the basement bathroom, raw sewage bubbled over the edges of the toilet like lava. Jerry swore while I raced for buckets, rags, and the telephone.

By the time I'd called a plumber who said he'd come by—first thing in the morning—Jerry was trying to unlock the side door, our closest route to the back alley. None of the keys we'd gotten from the realtor worked on that lock, so Jerry broke it with a hammer and chisel, and started hauling buckets of gunk outside.

In the house next door, a man yanked a window up and bellowed curses about the noise.

I called out an apology and added, in reasonable tones, that the basement toilet was backing up, and that we'd had to break the door down.

He slammed the window and, as long as he was up anyway, went to the bathroom.

I know that because I was standing behind Jerry when I heard the toilet flush next door. As Jerry bent to dip up another bucket of sewage from our toilet, fresh waste shot two feet in the air past his nose. He howled curses as he ran for the stairs, but I managed to convince him the man knew not what he did.

We spent the rest of the night hauling guck outside and moving possessions upstairs. By morning, we knew far too much about the health and habits of our neighbors.

When the plumber came the next day, he found a cleanout valve in the soil line just inside the basement wall and ran a power auger into it. While goo emerged from the line into a bucket, he explained that all the houses on the street were connected to a single waste line laid through the backyards to the side street a block away. That line connected to the main waste pipe under the street. Our house, the only one with a finished basement, was the end of the line. Several neighboring houses had been converted to apartments. Since the landlord paid the plumbing bills, some residents didn't seem to care what they flushed. They didn't pay for the consequences.

As the plumber talked, he reeled out of the waste line a whole collection of unsavory objects, including diapers, several kinds of menstrual supplies, plastic bags, cigarette butts, and grease.

"So you're saying," mused Jerry, "that we're the low point on a sewage party line."

The plumber laughed and jumped back as a gush of foamy liquid shot out of the pipe. "Yep. There's still a blockage somewhere in that line," he said. "And one of your neighbors is doing laundry." He peered at the suds frothing about our knees. "Baby diapers, I'd say. Hmm, sick baby."

The next night, the roar of the pump truck woke me again; this time city workers were clearing the line in the side street.

The following morning, I visited all the neighboring houses with notes explaining what had happened, and asking them not to flush any of the things the plumber had found in the line. Jerry removed the basement toilet and poured concrete down the pipe beneath it.

That weekend a plumbing contractor partially blocked the avenue while he dug up our yard to install our new, private waste line. Because we have both earned advanced degrees in waste control, we hoped to fit the line with valves that would open to let sewage and wash water out, but snap shut if fluid under pressure came from the direction of the city's main waste line. The plumber we hired, though, said the valves tend to plug easily, and then they are difficult to clean, so he recommended against it.

When this costly job was finished, Jerry cut off the old soil pipe and squeezed four feet of concrete into it, blocking the connection to the other houses.

"There," he said when he'd finished. "Now if our neighbors flush something they shouldn't, it won't come up in this basement."

So as I dozed off to the tune of the city pump truck in the middle of the block, I was hoping the man in the house next door who'd yelled at us was about to gain some hands-on experience with sewage floods.

The next day, a city inspector knocked on the door and handed me a card listing items that should not be flushed or poured down toilets, sinks, or bathtubs. He apologized for the noise at midnight, explaining that giant clots of coagulated suet blended with diapers and—he blushed and mumbled so I knew he didn't want to mention feminine products—had backed sewage into several other houses.

Grinning, I told him about our private line, and how I'd lived with a septic tank most of my life, so none of that slime had my name on it. Touching his cap, he remarked that most people don't seem to understand waste, and departed.

THE EXPERIENCE SET ME to reminiscing about my experiences in sewage management. I'd studied other subjects with textbooks and professors in suits, but my father taught me the theory and practice of practical septic tank operation right in our backyard. Dealing with our own personal bilge wasn't pleasant, but it provided vivid examples of how causes create effects. Once I realized that in a city I might play host to the wastes of strangers at any time, I learned never to run out of plastic gloves.

Lesson One in Professor Hasselstrom's Septic Seminar was spending several hours finding the tank by digging holes two feet deep along the back of the house until we hit concrete. Leaning on his shovel in the sun, my father would yank his hat off, mop his forehead with his handkerchief, and mumble that this time he was going to mark the spot. "Last time we dug it up, I put a steel post over the lid, but your mother didn't think that looked good, so I put a rock over it, and then I hit it with the mower and moved it and forgot to put it back." We drew a map, with measurements.

Once we struck concrete, we dug outward searching for the handle, sweating on our shovels for an hour before we'd cleared enough space to stand on top of the concrete tank. He lifted the concrete plug with a grunt. Fascinated, I leaned over beside him for a look.

I'm tempted to take on the challenge of describing that experience in vivid sensory detail, but I'll summarize: the tank contained a heaving stew in iridescent shades of green, yellow, dun, and black. I breathed shallowly for a week.

My father explained that I was seeing and smelling everything flushed down our toilet, drained from our bathtub and sinks, or discharged from the washing machine during the past year.

"I ought to make your mother look at this," he said, but we both knew she'd either scream or faint. "Every person who uses a toilet ought to see where it goes."

He grimaced and knelt by the top opening, leaning over to poke a stick into the outlet, trying to see if it was plugged. After a while, he got a longer stick and leaned the other way, poking at the waste line that dumped into the tank.

Eventually, he sighed, remarked that he wished it wasn't Sunday and maybe he should be going to church more often. Then he sluiced himself off under the hose and went inside to call the septic service number we kept on the blackboard beside the phone.

Two hours later, we heard a big truck shift down on the highway and rumble as it geared down for the turn. We'd been hanging around the garage, waiting, and we ran to the driveway to try to head him off before he drove across my mother's Oriental poppy bed.

The driver had been there before. Straight across the poppies he drove, parking beside the septic tank. We heard him chuckle as he climbed down from the cab, pulled on his hip waders, and yanked a stained cap low on his forehead.

He chortled as he lowered himself into the septic tank and splashed around, up to his armpits in gunk. He hummed while he poked an iron rod into the outlet and inlet pipes.

He whistled while he unwound a big hose and shoved it deep into the morass. He leaned on a fender while the hose sucked muck into the truck. Looking thoughtful, he unreeled a high-pressure hose with a nozzle resembling a giant screw, then whistled some more while he jammed it up the various pipes feeding the septic tank. When the tank was cleaner and nearly dry, he climbed out and shook himself like a retriever, flinging gobs of slime over my father, me, the dog, and the white siding on the house.

Then he wiped his hands on his pants, shoved his cap back, and scratched his head, humming some more while he scribbled an invoice. My father took it with two fingers and swallowed twice before he reached for the checkbook in his back pocket and opened it on the fender of the truck.

The man spoke for the first time.

"Good thing ya caught me when ya did," he remarked, pulling a tooth-pick from his pocket and wedging it into teeth I considered remarkably white under the circumstances. "Next week me an' the wife head for Flori-da for three months. Got a boat moored down there, a hunderd-footer. We take 'er out 'n fish fer marlin, tuna, all them big fish. Have 'em processed and shipped back so we kin eat good all summer. Course we gotta freezer full of prime beef, too."

He was laughing out loud as he stuffed the check in his damp shirt pocket and climbed into his truck. My father got in the passenger side to direct him to the nearest alfalfa field where he drove back and forth, spray-ing waste while my father walked back to the house. I helped him put the lid back on the tank while he explained why it was cheaper and more prac-tical to spray homegrown fertilizer over the fields to improve the hay we fed our cattle rather than to pay to haul it away. "Kinda like that recycling your friends talk about," he concluded. "And it's another reason we want only—er—natural waste to go down the toilet."

Then we hosed each other off and went in for coffee. My mother made us leave our shoes at the door, and wanted us to leave our clothes on the back porch, but my father refused. After a few sips of coffee, he said, "Have you ever noticed that whenever someone wants to tell me how suc-cessful his boy is, the kid always has a PhD in something scientific I can't pronounce and works in an office on the east coast? Nobody ever tells me his son is a plumber." He shook his head.

"But when I hire a guy to pump the septic tank on Sunday, he charges a hundred bucks an hour. I thought I was doing the right thing, sending you to college, but if they give any courses in plumbing, you'd better take them. It'll do you more good in the long run than reading Faulkner."

HE WAS RIGHT; most days I could recite more plumbing information than Faulkner's prose. I could probably replace the wax ring under a toilet blind-folded, and my familiarity with the ball cock and its trappings might shock a timid soul who does little to a toilet but push the handle down.

The first lesson was the strongest: no matter where I am, I never put anything down a toilet or drain I'd rather not face a month later.

"Shit happens" reads the bumper sticker, but the statement is not only vulgar and cynical, it's untrue. No form of waste just happens; someone creates it, and therefore we're all responsible for what happens next.

We now know how closely all humans resemble one another, despite our insistence on differences of race, creed, or political beliefs. Here's another thing we have in common: sewage. We can't blame it on the poor or people who believe in a different God or gun owners or whites or Republicans or Methodists or meat eaters. You can't give it up for Lent. I can't feel superior to you because mine doesn't stink. As is the case with breathing air or drinking water, if we're not making sewage, we're dead. Other countries are experimenting with using sewage as industrial fuel, and to heat or cool buildings as well as to nourish soil. Maybe it's time Americans started doing something more useful than flushing it.

Making Pottery out of Sewage

Waste. We all create it, and experts are always searching for ways to make us forget it. In the 1980s, one of my more vivid lessons in septic folly involved the state of South Dakota and the—er—residue created by citizens of Minneapolis and St. Paul, Minnesota. Officials in those Twin Cities were overwhelmed by waste disposal; they were incinerating raw sewage, but even the ashes of human waste take up a lot of space. Sprinkling them around the cities' many parks was apparently not an option.

Eventually, city authorities contracted to pay millions of dollars to a company called Consolidated Management Corporation to haul away tons of incinerated sewage.

"Away" turned out, as it usually does, to be somebody else's backyard.

CMC convinced South Dakota's leaders to accept trainloads of the stuff, promising to build a mill to turn the waste into paving materials and fertilizer.

Fertilizer and highways made of sewage weren't the only benefits our fair state was going to get. No sirree.

Perhaps CMC officials did some serious marketing research. Did they take a hint from the state's history and recall that wild nationwide gold rush to Deadwood, how a glittering lure and the siren song of the dance hall girls brought thousands of seekers to town? Some people just can't think straight when gold is mentioned.

With straight faces, company leaders promised that there was gold in that fecal matter. Cash in that caca, dollars in that doodoo, fivers in that feces.

Environmentalists rolled on the floor laughing when the company solemnly promised to mine the sewage ash to recover gold. Surely, we gasped, holding our sides and trying to stifle our giggles, nobody was going to take this seriously. Not even our legislature, notorious even today for blunders that make thinking citizens blush and throw mud on their South Dakota license plates.

State officials believed every word.

We activists thought we were fighting and winning some mighty environmental battles in those days. Hindsight shows how naive we were; we had no idea what greed, stupidity, and lies could accomplish in a state where people are so honest and gullible that million-dollar deals are still made on a handshake.

CMC promised to mine sixty million bucks worth of gold from the sewage ash. After a century of watching the Hearsts dig glitter out of the biggest open-pit gold mine in the world, Dakotans had grown fond of the stuff. So, even though they wouldn't actually get the gold, the state signed up.

Next to money, the next strongest magic word is "jobs," and CMC promised the project would bring three hundred jobs to the southwestern corner of the state. Because this region survives on agriculture and mining, citizens live perpetually in hard times. For months, the company ran ads for the project in state and national newspapers. Workers, the pitch promised, would be given technical training with complex modern equipment, so that they might advance to better jobs in this or another technical field. And probably take those skills to another state, no one said.

Never did the ads published or broadcast inside the state mention the precise nature of the waste. Writers for national publications, however, indulged themselves in scatological puns and jokes at South Dakota's expense. Our position as the home of the Shrine of Democracy didn't stop the quips or protect our dignity in the face of the smut. State officials remained complacent, seasoning any discussion with the words "jobs" and "gold."

Meanwhile, CMC officials ran up bills all over the state: they paid for nothing, putting it all on the tab to be paid when the gold started flowing out of the sewage. Instead of gold fever, we had sewage silliness.

I AM, AS DAVE BARRY SAYS, not making any of this up. I am also deleting and revising furiously to resist obvious puns. If only we who opposed this scheme could have hired George Carlin as our spokesperson. He might have built quite an act to follow his two-liner: "Why do they bother saying 'raw sewage'? Do some people actually cook that stuff?"

BEGINNING IN 1986, the waste was dumped into train cars and hauled west to Igloo, South Dakota. The town's convoluted history has included munitions storage and uranium mining, so city officials welcomed this new industry with no visible dread. Local workers were issued the advanced high-tech equipment they'd been promised, but few needed much training; they moved the crud with shiny new shovels, just the way they'd done most of the jobs they'd held in their lives. In Dakota's ceaseless winds, they first scooped ash from the railroad cars to the ground; then they moved it from the ground to open trucks, and from the open trucks to rickety sheds, one shovelful at a time, laughing as the wind carried most of the load aloft. They wore no protective clothing, no breathing apparatus.

At night, when they gathered at local hangouts to discuss their jobs and chat about their prospects for career advancement, environmentalists waiting to interview them gleaned a few additional facts.

Apparently, sewage incineration is not an exact science. The contents of those railroad cars included a lot of things most people would rather not see more than once, and would prefer not to smell after they have been hauled five hundred miles in a boxcar, including bloody menstrual supplies, uncooked sewage, and used condoms.

At that time, the state's isolation, innocence, and devotion to family was legendary, and mostly true. Not long before, having breakfast in a local café, I had heard a rancher providing his son with some fatherly advice before the boy's upcoming trip to Minneapolis. The lad should, said daddy in a warmly paternal tone, avoid sexual congress—not quite the terms he used—because them Minneapolis girls might have diseases. "You don't know where them pussies have been," he said, "and some of them might be on drugs and using the same needles them queers with AIDS use. You stick to screwing the local girls," daddy admonished sternly but lovingly.

Naturally, then, the fellows shoveling the sewage ash at Igloo assured each other they were safe from drugs and diseases because they lived in South Dakota, but they were a little nervous about the contents of the rail cars. They reasoned grimly that those queers in Minneapolis might use toilets and condoms too. Then they'd swig another beer and fall to figuring out how they might get some of that gold, and how much they needed the jobs. They kept shoveling until they'd unloaded nearly 300,000 tons of the gunk.

Soon after the last railroad car was unloaded, CMC accepted its last check from Minnesota officials, acknowledging that they'd been paid in full for hauling the sewage ash away.

Away. Minnesota officials were pleased to have solved their problem.

Almost before the ink was dry, CMC declared itself $3.5 million in debt. Sorry folks, they said to South Dakota. We can't afford to build a mill to process the waste to obtain the gold. Overnight, CMCwas gone, but the debts remained.

So did the sewage ash. Well, no. South Dakota is a windy state. A lot of it blew away before the leftovers were buried—at taxpayer expense—late in 1989.

Attempting to find a way to create something from nothing in the way our pioneer ancestors made famous, a member of the state's Board of Minerals and Environment collected a little of the ash, mixed it with feldspar and clay, and made pottery—and headlines.

Thousands of tourists headed for Mount Rushmore and Crazy Horse, a couple of beautiful Black Hills mountains hacked into resemblance to famous people, drive past the sewage ash site every year, but Igloo is hard to spot even if you know where to look. On top of the hill where the sewage ash depository is most visible, most drivers are probably looking at the blue sky, the air so pure it provides views of Wyoming's sage and mountains, the rolling blue waves of trees. Some probably say, "It sure looks empty."

And then they inhale. How much, I always wonder as I hold my breath and punch the accelerator, how much of that ash deposited in those roofless concrete bunkers is still floating around?

In retrospect, I apologize to the pottery maker for my laughter. As is often the case, we were closer to agreement than we knew: she didn't want the stuff in South Dakota any more than I do, and her scheme for exporting it at a profit was pretty smart. If she'd hired the marketing geniuses who sold the state on the idea of gold in human manure, she'd probably have cleaned up the ash and been retired to some other state by now. I'm sure there's plenty of material left, if any crafty people would like to give that pottery another try.

Moving garbage of any kind from one spot to another makes no sense unless the aim is to pretend it's gone because we can't see it. Somebody lives wherever we might take it. Americans crow about "wide open spaces," but crowded countries have found ways to use a lot of the stuff we throw away, including sewage, a reliably renewable resource.

SOME DAYS ON MY RANCH, I can believe the TV news is occurring on another planet. Looking up at the blue sky and breathing air scented only by wild grasses, I believe my private world is astonishingly pure. I can take some pride in its cleanliness, because my neighbors and I are thoughtful about what we discard. Residents of cities have learned to Call Somebody to handle particular jobs, especially the unpleasant ones like cleaning up garbage or shooting bad guys. Even recyclers can take their waste Away and turn it over to Someone Else.

Rural folks have always known that waste disposal is just another of our jobs, in the same way we learn to protect ourselves because the sheriff is a long distance away. We're not against organized law enforcement and sewage disposal, but we usually have to do it ourselves anyway. We still dump sewage in the fields to improve cattle forage, and we're careful what we bring home, since most of it will never leave the ranch.

The habits of even old-time country dwellers are changing as "sanitation" companies—denying their real function even in their names—extend their services. I didn't trust the tenants of my parents' old ranch house to burn their garbage safely, so I removed our burn barrels and contracted for a monster waste receptacle. Every month it overflowed with excess packaging, beer bottles, spoiled food, and soft drink containers. Like their city cousins, they paid to have it hauled Away.

Still, waste—excrement, junk, crap, garbage—is eternal; it lasts longer than most marriages and some nations.

Now that my tenants are gone and I'm planning my move back to the ranch, I'm reconsidering my relationship with waste. By the time I'd collected what the tenants left behind in the yard, I'd filled the dumpster about ten more times. Then I cancelled the garbage service. I plan to re-create some of my father's habits, finding ways to minimize the garbage we bring into the ranch, and to reuse whatever we can. I may have to step down into my septic tank to clear the outflow, mumbling to myself that there is no "away."

Pray for Me I Drive Highway 79

After my husband George died, my father became unpredictable, pounding the table with rage every day, sometimes weeping sentimentally. Later, I realized his heart was misbehaving, but at the time his actions were confusing and often seemed mean. Sometimes he called me "child," and ordered me to follow him around all day. At other times he treated me like a partner in the ranch.

I still had a small cow herd, but the only land I owned was my five-acre homesite. The county raised my taxes because the acreage was too small to be considered agricultural land. When I told my father I couldn't afford the increase, he refused to sell me another thirty-five acres so I could meet the ag requirement.

Meanwhile, I kept up a good front; the family and the culture had taught me that: chin up, stiff upper lip, never let 'em see ya sweat, an attitude that can be therapeutic. I was so busy making sure nobody saw me suffering that I hardly had time to suffer. The only time I could be myself was at night with the shades pulled, the doors locked, and the phone off the hook. Then I'd put on one of George's shirts and cry into the dog's thick neck.

Following a rule I read somewhere about making no major changes within a year after the death of a loved one, I stayed on the ranch and kept on working for my dad. I believe I was hoping so hard that he would go back to behaving normally that I saw what I was looking for. He'd never even taken me along when he bought bulls, for example, but when he asked me to find some good black Angus bulls to put with our heifers, I assumed he had decided to make me a real partner. Surely, I thought, he was at last realizing that he needed to give me more responsibility for running the ranch, rather than using me merely as muscle.

So I went looking for the kind of bulls he had taught me we'd need, black Angus sires bred with no horns and with lithe bodies. We'd put these slick operators in with the heifers, two-year-old cows that had never been bred, so their first calves would have lean bodies and small heads with no horn structure, making their passage down the birth canal easier on them and their young mothers.

I made a few phone calls, but buying bulls from a ranch miles away would require they be hauled to our place. I had little experience driving our old trucks hooked to our horse trailer, and I certainly didn't trust my eighty-two-year-old father to haul them, so I looked for bulls closer to home. Thinking I might persuade him to deliver, I drove to the ranch of a neighbor who often had black bulls to sell. He wasn't home, but the man who worked for him was. As I drove into the yard, he came out of a barn and walked up to the window of my pickup. I told him who I was and that I was looking for bulls to buy. He introduced himself, and then stood by the pickup to visit with me as we both worked up to my purpose.

I WANT TO DESCRIBE this man enough to give the reader a mental picture, but protect his identity and keep his privacy intact. He's part Lakota; his name suggests that among his ancestors was a Frenchman who came into the Great Plains as part of the earliest fur trade, in the 1700s. The French trappers were primarily interested in beaver pelts, turned into felt to make hats for stylish gentlemen of the era. Unlike some of the later trappers, the French treated the resident Indians with respect. In our neighborhood, that usually meant marrying Lakota women and settling into a particular tribal band. Once or twice a year the trappers took their furs to St. Louis where some kept big houses and white wives and children. Many returned, year after year, to their Lakota wives. By the time the Lakota were finally put on reservations in the late 1890s, the descendants of the French trappers, thoroughly assimilated, considered themselves Indian.

So I'll call the man Merle Courier. I know nothing of Merle's personal history, but his name indicates his descent, and he was probably raised on the nearby Pine Ridge Reservation. The reservation has churches, schools, and law enforcement in several small towns, and Lakota students rarely attended school in Hermosa. We saw Indians mostly when families stopped for groceries, beer, or gas on their way to Rapid City. Many of the men worked for ranchers in the neighborhood, either occasionally or regularly, so I'd always thought of the reservation as distantly connected to our community. Thus its stories are part of our chronicle. As Minnesotan Paul Gruchow remarks, "All history is ultimately local and personal." When we tell what we remember, we keep the past alive; if we didn't do so, "we could not know, in the deepest sense, how to inhabit a place."

Still, my parents flatly forbade me to date a mixed-blood boy in high school. For a while, when I stayed overnight with certain girlfriends who would lie for me, we'd double-date with other couples. Both my parents believed anyone with "colored" skin was inferior, though my father once bought me a doll baby who was black. He thought it was a fine joke; my mother wanted to throw it away. I named her Dementina, after my playmate and best friend in Texas, and she is the only doll I still have.

Still, Merle Courier and I, though we might have heard each other's names once or twice, had never met. I remember a survey of forty communities and regions in twenty-nine states that said South Dakota ranked highest in the nation for "social trust," the confidence people in the state have in one another. According to the survey, the state's people also showed the highest level of religious involvement, and of giving and volunteering, and ranked first in civic leadership. But South Dakotans were next to last (just above Bismarck, ND) in having friendships with diverse groups. That's because South Dakotans bear a marked resemblance to one another—not just racially, but in every other way, according to the study.

Merle is clearly Lakota, a tall man with that impressive aquiline nose. That day his short black hair, speckled with gray, was mostly hidden under an expensive broad-brimmed hat that showed its quality despite having been walked on by horses a few times. He wore jeans and a western shirt, like any other man of the neighborhood.

AFTER WE'D EXCHANGED the proper amount of small talk required for doing ranch business, I said I was looking for black Angus bulls for my father. The introduction of this serious new topic made a brief conversation about available bulls, cattle prices, and weather necessary. Eventually, we concluded that the ranch owner might be at the Lunch Box Café, situated in a double-wide trailer in Hermosa, run by a white woman with her good friend, a Lakota woman. If the rancher wasn't at the café, someone there would know where to find him. The Lakota woman, Merle said, was his wife.

My bumper was decorated with the sticker two friends had printed with ironic humor: PRAY FOR ME I DRIVE HIGHWAY 79. Everyone who had lived in Hermosa very long knew someone who had died on the two-lane highway. Merle chuckled at the sticker and mentioned a friend who had died on the highway.

Gender and hierarchy are influential in my community, as in all other places. As a woman, I would normally have gotten into a man's pickup if I was accompanying him to town. Women don't usually drive a pickup with a man in it. The social situation was complicated by the fact that I was also the potential buyer, a position of power not traditionally occupied by women in our neighborhood. I doubt either of us considered what some of the old codgers—especially my father—might think about a white woman driving a pickup with an Indian man as passenger. I don't know what Merle was thinking, but he walked straight to the passenger side of my truck and got in.

Just then two teenage boys came out of the house and waved at him. "My boys," he said.

The taller one was dark skinned, with a beaky nose and black eyes. Slim and lithe, he wore his straight black hair tied back, and was dressed in a basketball jersey, shorts, and tennis shoes. He wanted to borrow the pickup, and he managed to explain what he wanted, get permission, and accept his father's advice about being careful without once looking full at me. Then he sauntered away.

The younger boy was pudgy and light skinned, with short blond hair that kept blowing into his eyes, blue and concealed by thick glasses. He wore new blue jeans and a sweater over an open-necked shirt. He stared at me while he asked his father for permission to walk somewhere to borrow a musical tape. He continued to stare at me while he listened to his father's permission and cautions.

As the boys walked away, Merle and I both looked after them. I was wondering if one was adopted, or was a relative taken into the household informally, as the Indian families often do. Merle may have sighed. And then, while I was thinking about his sons, he said something I almost didn't catch about how difficult things could get when parents started to get old. With no more warning than that, he started to tell me about his parents.

I hadn't said a word about my father's behavior to this man. While we'd talked about finding the ranch owner, I'd wondered how much the community had observed about my father's behavior, and thought that if I bought the bulls, my father might forget telling me to do so, exactly what happened a couple of weeks later. I had not yet told anyone except my father's sister and brother how unpredictable his behavior had become; my mother wouldn't admit it.

And I had told no one at all that when I explained to my father why I needed to be part owner of the family land, he'd said I was "just trying to steal" his ranch.

Suddenly Merle was telling me that when his father started to become senile, he began distrusting his wife, accusing her of "trying to steal his ranch." He glanced at me from under his hat brim when he said that key phrase, the same phrase my father had used to me with no one else to hear. I think my mouth dropped open.

Merle's mother's name wasn't on the deeds to the family ranch as a co-owner, he said, so his father was able to sell the ranch before anyone realized what he was doing. Then, distrustful of his whole family, he ordered his wife and sons off the place. Merle nodded at the neat ranch buildings around us, telling me without words, I assumed, that this displacement accounted for his being here, working for a white rancher.

Once his mother recovered from the shock of being booted out of her own home and accused of dishonesty by the husband to whom she had been married for forty years, she hired a lawyer and got the ranch back. Now, he said, his father went everywhere saying how she'd stolen it from him.

I was struck dumb, and my mouth was probably still hanging open. Merle and I had never met before. His father had behaved precisely as mine was doing. He apparently knew that, and moreover, knew where my father's behavior might lead, something none of us in the family were admitting yet.

Somehow, he knew enough about my father's actions, and my puzzlement, to make connections I had not made. Furthermore, he was offering me reassurance, testifying from his own experience that my father's behavior was not so strange when compared to the behavior of other men of his age and station. I know now, as I did not know then, that people who suffer strokes often turn against those who are closest and most beloved. Still, puzzling over how he could know something I hadn't told a soul, I don't recall if I responded to his story, or if I was silent as we drove to the café. I know we walked in together, greeted his wife and her white friend.

We didn't find the ranch owner or anyone who knew where he was, but after we sat awhile in the café, eating pie and drinking coffee, I no longer cared. Merle continued to talk in his quiet voice about how oddly his father had behaved. I stared at him, aware of the contrast we made, astonished how deeply he understood what I was feeling, and how openly he spoke of his own situation. No one interrupted us; the café owner and her friend slapped hamburgers together and laughed with customers and may have deflected nosier neighbors, but neither approached except to refill our coffee cups.

Somehow, through the grapevine that meanders through every true community, Merle knew more about my situation at that time than my own family did. He knew more than I did, and understood how to make me feel as if I could survive the situation. Caught up in events I saw as my personal tragedy, I suddenly realized that Merle was offering me his friendship by disclosing that he'd lived through something similar.

Merle might easily have kept silent; I probably would never have known the story of his father's behavior. He cared enough to violate his own sense of privacy to tell me his story.

One of the oldest of rules in our stoic neighborhood is that we don't talk about the difficult times. We don't even talk to each other if a family member is drinking or beating the kids, and we certainly don't talk to neighbors, or counselors, or any other "outsiders."

Once when I was in graduate school, and my first husband was regularly sleeping with other women, I felt so helpless and worthless that I wanted to kill myself. So I talked to some kind of therapist. While I was still thinking therapy might work—because I believed the problem was with me—I told my father that I was getting counseling for my mental health.

"You must be crazy," he said, "to do something like that."

"That's the general idea," I said.

He shook his head impatiently. "No, there's nothing wrong with your mind. But you're crazy to tell some guy in an office your business."

He probably also suggested that I wasn't getting enough exercise since I didn't work outdoors much in graduate school; that was his standard cure for any ill. Anyway, he was correct. The therapist recorded our sessions and played the tapes to his friends, some of whom were my friends and told me.

I don't know what Merle was thinking, but I believe that a healthy community like ours functions best by blending a decent respect for privacy with a generous dose of concern for the welfare of neighbors. By talking to me, Merle allowed me to see for myself that I was not alone. He offered no advice, no drugs, no therapy. He didn't suggest we get together again. He gave me the simple and profound gift of trust by telling me his story. And he did this despite the fact that we both lived in a little town in a state often accused, with plenty of accuracy, of racism. Lakota man and white woman, we talked in that café as friends, a situation so unusual I can't remember seeing it before or since.

I don't know if I thanked Merle, or if he could tell how astonished and moved I was. I can't recall a single sentence he said, and I've never seen him again. I didn't buy bulls from his boss, because when I told my father that I was going to do so, he denied telling me to buy any bulls, and accused me again of plotting to steal his ranch.

I WISH THIS STORY ENDED DIFFERENTLY; if I had stayed on the ranch, perhaps it would have. A couple of years later, when the buoyant white woman who owned the café died suddenly, Merle's wife, her trusted partner, wanted to buy it. But she was an Indian woman in South Dakota; she couldn't get a loan. The white woman's children hadn't approved of the friendship and sold the trailer before I learned what had happened.

By then, despite the damage my father had done to his own estate, I had stabilized the financial situation enough that I could, and would, have guaranteed a loan to her, or given her the money myself. That didn't happen. I don't know where Merle and his wife are now. Only a few stiff-necked old-timers still refer to the Heartland Expressway as Highway 79, and I know of only one—me—who still has the bumper sticker.

The Stolen Canoe Mystery

My father had neglected ranch repairs, or done them poorly, for a long time. So one of my first tasks after I acquired the ranch was to decide what needed fixing first, and to earn enough money to pay for repairs.

The siding on both my mother's house and my own needed replacement, so I followed local custom by gathering recommendations from neighbors and friends. Trusting my informants, I hired a contractor without meeting him.

Scrambling to pay expenses, I also accepted invitations to give several readings in the eastern part of the state while the siding was being applied. I planned to return while the work was going on, but a blizzard delayed me in eastern South Dakota and forced me to change my route home to Wyoming. By the time I came back to the ranch, the siding was in place, and I'd already paid for the job.

Walking around both houses to look at the finished work, I was annoyed to find cigarette butts, empty soft drink cans, pieces of metal, and tools scattered everywhere, apparently the price I'd paid for being an absentee employer. Scrutinizing my own house, however, I suddenly missed the eighteen-foot Grumman canoe that had belonged to George. For years we'd stored it behind the garage, handy whenever we wanted to slide it on top of the van. To keep it from blowing away, George tied it to a block of concrete. Both had vanished.

I hadn't used the canoe since George died, so with plenty of other problems on my mind, I considered forgetting the theft. Since the whole community knew I was living in Cheyenne, though, the consequences of ignoring this larceny might be more vandalism. The ranch residents might not be able to stop it. The couple renting my mother's house had rural backgrounds, and were settling into the community, putting their children in school, attending church. The couple renting my house were strangers; the woman worked in the nearby town and the man was a writer who stayed home. Rumor said he seldom went outside and wouldn't notice if a helicopter landed on the roof. I'd heard disparaging comments about them leaving the garage door open all day, the shades up and all the lights on at night. I needed to demonstrate to the neighborhood, I thought, that I was paying attention.

The woman living in my mother's house complained that the workers who applied the siding threw their tools and garbage around and cursed in front of her children. She didn't trust them, but she couldn't honestly swear they had stolen the canoe.

So I ate lunch with the senior citizens at the VFW hall. I started conversations in the traditional format, asking about the families, their children's jobs, new grandchildren. They'd always wondered why I spent so much time on my hilltop writing, and seemed pleased I'd moved to Cheyenne. Was I going to stay there?

Looking at these kindly elders who had known me all my life, I hesitated. I didn't want to go into detail about my companionship with Jerry or the mess my father had made of his estate, but I didn't want to lie.

Then someone asked, "Have you got a job?"

I heard myself saying "Yes," without adding the qualification that my job was, as usual, my own writing.

Everyone nodded and smiled, and the questions stopped.

Warmed by their approval, I chattered about the disappearance of my husband's canoe. I told them about my new security system, how I sometimes drove to the ranch late at night and stayed in the basement of my house. I mentioned that I always carry a pistol; maybe I even batted my eyelashes as I observed that a lone woman, and a widow at that, can't trust anybody these days.

Several men immediately suggested that if I caught anybody on my property, I should shoot without regard for warning shots. Several offered to loan me a shotgun, repeating the old maxim about how a nervous woman with a shotgun strikes fear in the hearts of evildoers. Declining politely, I demurely admitted that I kept George's loaded shotgun by the bed.

Later that week, I phoned the siding contractor to ask if he knew anything about the canoe's disappearance. He was surprised and apologized for not calling me when one of the men asked about buying the canoe. If he'd asked, I might have sold the canoe and had no story to tell.

The contractor knew where one of the men lived; he offered to sneak over there and peek into the garage.

No, I said. Leave it to me.

After three or four days of intensely casual chat with my helpful and observant neighbors, on the telephone, in the post office, and in local hangouts, I understood the canoe caper, and even felt a little guilty.

Absentee landowners and people who have more than one home are a relatively new phenomenon in our area, but already we have accepted certain unexamined stereotypes. They are wealthy, therefore they don't take care of their property. They aren't from our community, so they don't know who does good work, or whom to trust; they hire strangers and treat them like servants.

Friends had recommended the contractor I hired, but he'd hired new workers for my job, didn't know them well, and fired them as soon as they finished the work. I knew the names of both men, and knew where they lived on the nearby reservation.

I could also picture them smoking cigarettes, drinking a beer as they walked around my house looking at the view, and building up dislike for the person who hadn't bothered to come see their work. Packing up, probably glad to be finished with the job, they talked about taking a little break, maybe going fishing. As I walked through the windbreak trees picking up their soft drink cans and cigarette butts, I stumbled over George's concrete anchor, a hundred yards from the garage. I was grateful it hadn't been thrown through a window.

On my way back to the ranch after a business trip to town, I stopped at a campground a half mile from my home, operated by a local rancher who supplements his income by making pizza: modern diversification in action. When I was in high school, this man was a skinny, freckled tyke with a runny nose. He grew more than six feet tall, with broad shoulders and a neck like the trunk of a Ponderosa pine. He owns and rides a Harley, has appeared in several low-budget biker movies, and is a legend among our volunteer firefighters. Someone also told me he serves as an unofficial bodyguard to the local sheriff's deputy.

"Oh," he said modestly, "I kinda ride along with him if he thinks things are gonna be tough, like domestics and bar fights."

He's also a state legislator, and though we disagree on almost every single issue about which he speaks publicly, I admire his achievements and consider him one of my most trustworthy neighbors. So while he deftly spread cheese and pepperoni over homemade crust, I told him about the canoe's disappearance.

Then we chatted amiably about the illusion that one is alone in the country. A stranger listening would have thought we'd dropped the subject of the canoe, but, country style, we were letting it rest a bit while we both considered our next move.

I commented that most folks driving through the country don't know that strangers catch someone's attention immediately. Often, I told him, I stop on my way back to the ranch to walk in a cemetery in Hartville, Wyoming. Strolling among the headstones, following my dog, I usually feel the hair on the back of my neck rise and glance up to see someone on a hilltop, obviously fixing fence—while noticing what's happening in the cemetery. Sometimes a pickup on the nearby road slows while the driver looks at my license plate. When I stand up and wave, the driver waves back as the pickup gathers speed; I've proven I'm OK, one of them. "Folks from town think because it looks empty, nobody's paying attention," we agreed.

Next I related a story about two women, guests of a New Mexico retreat where I'd been staying. They took a picnic to a hill above a nearby ranch and enjoyed the sunshine so much they took off their clothes. The ranch woman in the valley below noticed her pre-teenage boys staring at the hillside and looked through her binoculars. Annoyed at the nude display, she fired a few rounds from her shotgun in the air.

I was in the kitchen when the women sprinted through the door, still mostly naked and shrieking about attempted murder. Trying not to laugh, I explained that I hadn't met the ranch woman, but was sure that if she'd been aiming at them, they'd be picking shotgun pellets from tender spots. She was merely providing educational information, which I helpfully translated: You are not invisible in the country, and we don't consider being naked without invitation near our homes and children to be acceptable behavior.

Serving my pizza, my neighbor laughed and said the men who'd applied the siding had stopped at his place for pizza several times. He'd heard them talk about how handy a canoe would be for fishing the Missouri River near their reservation homes. Sure, they'd been arrested once or twice, but only for petty theft, a crime involving property, not injury to people. A typical westerner, he conveyed information without mentioning their names or revealing how much more he knew about them.

I mused aloud, reminding him of the time when someone harassed local women who lived alone. Several of us regularly received obscene phone calls after going to bed. Our dogs were restless each night, and we heard whistles in the darkness. Mornings, we'd find cigarette butts near our windows or around the yard. One night, sick of being nervous, I jerked open the door to the deck, pointed the shotgun at my woodpile twenty feet away, and fired one round. Then I shoved in another shell and slammed the door. After I talked with my neighbors, several other women fired shotguns in the air. None of us were disturbed after that.

Finishing a slice of pizza, I remarked that he'd helped me make a decision. I wanted my canoe back, but I wasn't interested in revenge or causing the men any more trouble. So I wouldn't report the theft to the sheriff or my insurance company for two more weeks. If the canoe re-appeared during that time, I could forget it had been gone and forget the men's names. He might mention to anyone interested that, when returning borrowed tools to the home of a lone woman, one should do so in daylight in case she was nervous and had a gun.

The next day I went back to Cheyenne. Two weeks later, while I was composing a letter to the sheriff, trying to explain why I hadn't reported the theft sooner, the phone rang.

The tenant in my mother's house reported that a pickup had just driven toward my house carrying a canoe and driven away without it.

SOON AFTER I GOT THE CANOE BACK, my cousin and I worked out a kind of barter. He borrowed the canoe so he could take his children fishing, and brought me a johnboat, a stable, flat-bottomed craft easier to handle than a canoe.

Sometimes I wish my neighbors and I knew less about each other's business, but that's how this community functions. Cooperation and trust grow from knowledge. We can rely on each other because we've proven to be reliable. We give and therefore we receive. It's not necessary to contribute for a hundred years as my family has, but you do have to give.

Playing Pool with the Cat Men

On my five-hour drives between Cheyenne and the ranch, I had a lot of time to consider the concept of home. Determined to make a life with Jerry, whose career was in Cheyenne, I also wanted to stay connected to my ranch community. No matter how carefully I read the county newspaper, though, I can't keep track of the community mood as I could when I went to church or visited on the phone with my relatives and neighbors. Yet my attempts to fit into city society were mixed at best.

Driving back and forth, I often wondered if I should work harder at making friends in Cheyenne. One late fall day when I was headed back there from the ranch, I left the main highway at Manville for a slower back road to Guernsey. Looked up, I realized that the winding road ahead disappeared into fog that was flowing over the low, rounded hills. The scene might have come from the album of my trip with Jerry to northern Scotland, and the thought took me back to that night with Duncan and his friends.

CLOUDS HUNG DARK AS PEAT OVER THE OCEAN, shining with the last of the sun's light, and I was shivering as Jerry drove into the village of Lybster. We were traveling in the district of Caithness, Scotland, originally named for the ancient "Cat Men"; I noted testily in my journal that guidebooks didn't mention "Cat Women."

The highway formed one street of the little town, running parallel to the shore. Another street plunged down toward the harbor where convulsive North Sea waves burst against a stone pier. I expected to see Viking boats slide out of the mist, red sunset light flickering on the raised sword blades of warriors crowding the gunwales.

Jerry pulled into the parking lot of the Portland Arms Hotel, muttering, "Probably expensive." Tall windows with Gothic arches glowed yellow against gray stone walls. Steep stone steps led up to massive double doors of oak. In a town so small, so late in the tourist season, we would probably find no other hostelry, so we took our bags and climbed the stairs. Our feet slid naturally into footprints worn in the stone by travelers who must originally have arrived by horseback or by horse-drawn coach.

A room, including breakfast, cost forty-two pounds, nearly eighty-five American dollars, our most expensive stay to that date. We toted our bags three flights up a walnut stairway, resting on both landings, whispering as we looked at the ornate mirrors and dark, carved chests. Our room, too, was crowded with heavy old furniture, two double beds and a dresser. The mirror frame was coagulated with carvings. The bathroom was nearly filled by a tub six feet long. I longed for a hot bath, but we were too hungry. Later, we promised ourselves, knowing that this far north the water would be stained brown by the peat in the soil.

Salivating, we trotted downstairs to the dining room just in time for high tea. A coal fire burned in a massive fireplace, the hearth surrounded by ornate walnut panels carved to resemble shrubs and trees. On the mantel stood old brass teapots and urns polished until they hummed with reflected light. Several red velvet armchairs faced the fire. Steaming teapots and plates of pastries crowded a table, and the air smelled of freshly baked bread. Two or three other couples sat at widely separated tables. We chose a velvet-curtained alcove near the fireplace and served ourselves again and again, tasting finnan haddie for the first time, finishing with fairy cakes and hot tea sweetened with brown sugar. "Happy Thanksgiving," we murmured to one another.

After tea, we looked around the lobby and sampled the stilted conversation of two university professors carrying computers and fax machines. In the private lounge, two more fireplaces faced one another. One was topped by deep green tile, with a surrounding panel of walnut. The other was of oak carved with tumbling winged figures entangled in tendrils, blossoms, curlicues, and ribbons; every figure was female, richly endowed with all the equipment a gentleman might desire. The furniture was heavy and soft;

the bar in the corner indicated the place would fill with hotel guests on expense accounts later. So we kept moving. In a dark corner of the room, we found an almost hidden door to the public bar, and entered the haven of the locals.

I paused, getting my bearings in a murk of cigarette smoke. The room was much larger than the private bar, though the bartender could serve both by stepping through a connecting door. Immediately in front of me was a tiny pool table with one man stooping for a shot while others watched from bar stools. I edged over to a table in the far corner, facing the tall windows we'd seen from the parking lot, while Jerry went to the bar.

Outside, the view was clearly Scotland: the town's stone buildings stood cold and gray along both sides of the street leading to the harbor, silhouetted in mist against the wavering blue of the sea. Inside, our location was less clear. The table tops were cheap Formica, and cigarette smoke is international.

During the next few minutes, each bar patron scanned us. Hotel guests usually remain in the private bar, sheltered from the common folk in the public one. We are working people, and had discovered at our first overnight stop in Scotland that we enjoyed being among ordinary citizens more than among tourists and business travelers, usually American or British, who would fill the other bar. Like the pool players, Jerry was dressed in jeans and a sweater. I wore a long skirt as do Scottish women and for the same reason: central heating is rare. We presented a puzzle.

Just as Jerry returned with our drinks, a man appeared at my elbow. His face was so lined and tan it might have belonged to one of my ranching neighbors; his straight black hair was gray streaked. He bowed slightly at the waist, then noticed Jerry. Smoothly, he introduced himself to both of us, as if that's what he'd intended all along. Duncan, he said, adding with a Highland trill, "I used t'be in the merchant marine." He gestured with a drink we could tell wasn't his first, but his questions were indirect and polite. We responded with our own names and admitted we were Americans. He'd been to America several times with the ships, he said, and mentioned bars in New Orleans and New York, hoping we'd recognize his favorite places.

Sorry, we'd never been either place, we said. In the states we consider home, Wyoming and South Dakota, cities are small and scattered, water and ships virtually fables. He loved the sea, he said, demonstrating how hard it is to walk on a slippery deck in high seas. When he swayed, both of us drew back a little.

He laughed. "That's what the ship does in rough seas," he said. "You thought I was drunk; well, I am, but not about to fall over. I'm used to this. What are you drinking?"

"Famous Grouse," I answered, proud to be able to name a local scotch; "Murphy's," said Jerry, naming a local lager.

"English shit," Duncan snapped, loud enough to turn heads at the bar. "Excuse my language, ma'am," he said tenderly, "but you shouldn't be drinking that stuff." He waved his own glass, filled with a deep brown liquid and turned back toward the bar.

We looked at each other, but before we could speak Duncan set two glasses lightly on the table, saying, "This is Glenmorangie, real Scottish whisky. Wire rope on the top. Taste it; go on." I picked mine up and let a drop roll down my tongue, half expecting it to burn. The Scotch was so smooth I thought he'd brought me an aged brandy. Jerry tried his, then set it firmly in front of me; he prefers beer or ale.

We invited Duncan to sit down, but he remained standing beside my chair, pitching a little as if on a deck, and asked what we thought of then–President Bush the First. I made a face and pointed at Jerry. "*He* voted for him."

Duncan took a deep breath and precisely outlined Bush's economic policies, analyzing their probable devastating effect on poor Scots. "And he's going to get us in a war in the Middle East," he fumed. "That's OK for you Americans, but the bombs'll be dropping here." He looked up at the ceiling, as if a bomb might appear directly. "What do you think of Maggie?"

Jerry had been reading local newspapers as we traveled northern Scotland, and he quoted folks who said England's Prime Minister Thatcher wasn't doing a bad job. (Two days later, when she resigned, a former member of the Black Watch, a regiment of Highlanders, said to us, "She's lucky. We used to behead 'em.")

Jerry and Duncan debated the merits of the men who might succeed her as prime minister. Duncan had nothing good to say about either leader, but he apologized whenever he slipped into profanity, bending a little at the waist each time to look into my face. My neck knotted as I kept looking up to talk.

In the American West, particularly in bars, conversations involving liquor and politics frequently lead to bloodshed. Jerry, like me, is adept at recognizing, and escaping from, such surroundings unscathed. We were anxious to avoid confrontation in an unfamiliar country. We bought a drink for Duncan each time he came from the bar with two for us but worried that the international exchange might last all night, or escalate.

Several times, when Duncan wandered away for a few minutes, Jerry studied the pool players and I eavesdropped on the growing crowd. I suspected Jerry wanted to approach the pool table, but he wasn't sure of the protocol and didn't want to abandon me to Duncan. Several men played darts while others watched televised soccer. The patrons slugged single malt whisky or ale, sneaking covert glances at us every now and then. The room was bright with good cheer, but the noise level remained so low I might have been listening from outside the stone walls.

Taking the table beside ours, a man and woman nodded and smiled. The man brought drinks from the bar, then went to lean against it, visiting with his cronies while the woman sat alone, tapping her foot in time to jukebox music. I recognized the situation from my own dating experiences. Perhaps, I thought, I could move over and talk to her, so Jerry could feel free to scout the pool party, and we'd both slip away from Duncan. Just then, Duncan brought another pair of drinks and began to question Jerry about the Great Plains.

When Duncan disappeared down a corridor toward the bathroom, we consulted quickly. He was growing more intoxicated, and we'd had enough liquor, so we decided to escape his generosity before we hurt ourselves, or his mood changed. We decided to take our drinks, perhaps finish them in the private bar, where Duncan could not follow. We stood, pushed in our chairs, and headed for the door in the corner.

As we passed the pool table, one of the players stepped in front of Jerry and asked, "Are ye Americans then?" Wary after Duncan's denunciation of Bush, we nodded.

The man nodded. "Well, give us some help here." He took Jerry's arm and drew him toward the pool table. "We're wondering how American rules

are different from ours." I perched on a bar stool while Jerry examined the
pool table and the four players introduced themselves. Happily, they all de-
liberated on the intricacies of snooker, pool, and billiards, while I thought
about the things that transcend barriers of language and law—games,
laughter, some jokes. After a moment, one of the Scots handed Jerry a cue
and sat at the bar so Jerry could play.

Another man moved to the end of the pool table nearest me and we
introduced ourselves—he was Robin—between his shots. Adjusting his
wire-rim spectacles, he looked like a man who might play a British accoun-
tant on stage, but said he was a welder on an oil rig in the North Sea.

"You could see the lights from here if it wasn't foggy," he said, gesturing. I told him I'd seen the gaunt steel shapes rising from offshore mist
during our drive north that day. Robin explained how the Scots originally
welcomed oil discoveries; they hoped the oil would improve the economy,
maybe make them independent of England.

"But about all we've got out of it is the filthy oil on the beaches," he
said. "Ruined the fishing, it has. And all the money goes south." Reminds
me of the way a lot of commercial development goes in the states, I said;
if the companies promise "money and jobs," the citizens will let them do
almost anything, but the money departs while the locals live with the consequences. He nodded.

Originally from Edinburgh, he'd moved north for the oil work and married a local girl. Between his turns with the cue, he told me he worked ten
days straight on the platform, followed by four days off. His first stop after
work was always this friendly bar in the hotel, where he called his wife and
played a little pool before going home.

When Jerry glanced our way, Robin nodded and called encouragement
to him and said, "I'm a happily married man, Jerry; don't worry about your
lady."

Then Duncan appeared, lurching a little, to introduce himself to me
again, wanting to buy me a drink, suggesting we might take "a wee walk
together." I waved my Glenmorangie, "You bought me this one, remember?"

"Now Duncan," said Robin, "her friend Jerry doesn't like her walking
out with strangers while he's playing pool." Duncan blinked at him and
leaned against my shoulder. I pushed him away gently and he shambled

off. I knew I could knock him across the room if necessary, but his advance was so polite I hesitated.

The next time Duncan approached, Robin had just finished a shot; deftly, he stepped in front of me, steering Duncan in a circle back toward the other end of the bar. Adjusting his spectacles, he said, "Excuse me for standing in front of you, miss, but I thought maybe he'd listen to me a bit better." I thanked him. He watched Jerry shoot and turned back to say, "I hope I didn't offend you. Are you a liberated lady that doesn't like a gentleman's interference, ma'am?"

With a mental apology to feminists who might disagree, I smiled sweetly and told him I wasn't so liberated I didn't appreciate his gentlemanly help.

Robin rocketed a ball across the table and turned again. "I know protecting you is Jerry's business and I wouldn't stand in his way, but being as he's a wee bit busy now, I was just being a stand-in, so to speak. Not meaning to be forward, I assure you."

Fearing an unseemly giggle, I gulped Glenmorangie. I haven't been treated with such courtliness in years, never in a bar, and never in that rich Gaelic accent. Several times during the next hour or two, Duncan approached me, and Robin stepped between us to divert him, each time apologizing over his shoulder for turning his back on me. And every time, Duncan bought another drink and wandered off.

Finally, the woman bartender refused Duncan's drink order and said quietly that it was closing time. She wiped her hands and went through a gate in the bar to drop the shades over the front windows. Bustling back to the bar, she turned her back on Duncan to wash glasses and wipe the polished walnut. Duncan politely asked for another drink. "Bar's closed," she snapped over her shoulder.

I reached to finish my drink, but Robin whispered, "No rush." He nodded at the bartender, who was selling Duncan a pint bottle. He tucked it into his pocket and glanced my way. Robin shook his head. Duncan shrugged and marched to the door. He turned and waved; the entire crowd called good-byes as he wobbled into the night. Everyone waved or nodded.

Jerry was putting down his pool cue when the bartender placed fresh drinks in front of all of us. Four young men came in the back door, laughing and calling for beer. Another man hung his coat on the rack and helped the woman don her coat while she murmured something about Duncan. As she left by the back door, the new bartender raised the blinds.

Jerry and I stared at each other. I turned to Robin. "They closed the bar, but just to Duncan?"

Robin nodded.

"The whole crowd knew? Everyone?"

He nodded again, ducking his head a little. "We all know him. Since he was made redundant, retired against his will, he can't get other work. He doesn't do any harm. One way or another, he drinks what he can hold and then goes home. He walks, so he's no danger to others. He's got his pint for tomorrow. When he gets home his wife will put him to bed. If he's not home in time, she'll call." He looked anxiously at me. "I suppose an American might say he needs therapy or something." He raised an eyebrow.

"Jerry and I both come from little towns in the West, where everyone knew everyone else," I said. "In those towns, we once handled problems this way."

Robin nodded thoughtfully. "It's changing, then?"

I nodded, still so astonished I stumbled over my words. "Since we all have TV, everyone knows about therapy, even country folks; I've heard some people drive three hundred miles to see their therapists. People drive a hundred miles to shop for groceries, so all the little towns are losing their stores, and that's where we used to visit with each other and keep up with the news." Still not right. I searched for words. "It's more than that. Lots of city folks are moving in," I said. "They don't know about doing things themselves. They call a plumber from the city. They call AA for a flat tire. They call the sheriff if they see a cow on the highway."

I still wasn't saying quite what I meant, though Robin was nodding. "They've gotten used to not knowing their neighbors. They tell themselves not to get involved. They see trouble, all they can think of is calling professional help, a cop. It would never occur to them to fix it themselves. They might say Duncan needed to join an alcoholics group, or go to a shrink. But they'd never tell him, or think of doing this."

Robin nodded and rose from the stool. "Sounds like what's happening in England, even in southern Scotland."

He called his wife as the new customers plunked money into the jukebox for louder music. Jerry and his pool-playing partners put down their cues and the young men picked them up. After a round of mutual thanks and hand-shaking with Robin and his friends, we drew ourselves upright and headed for the hidden door.

"I'm carrying a bit too much Scottish hospitality," Jerry mumbled. "I'm not sure I can make it up those stairs."

"Remember the code of the West," I whispered as the door shut behind us. "Always remain upright in a bar, or something." The private bar was empty. With no light but the glow of a few pieces of peat in the fireplace, we navigated carefully among the big soft chairs. At the foot of the towering stairs, we looked up into darkness. Three flights to our room.

I said, "We could crawl."

Jerry shook his head, "Somebody might see us and I've already done enough damage to the honor of American pool players. Just remember that bathtub. At the top of the stairs."

We filled the tub with water the color of good scotch, and each time we have sipped Glenmorangie since, we have spilled a drop in tribute to Duncan and the people who cared about him.

On my car is the bumper sticker I bought that day:

ENGLAND FOREVER

SCOTLAND A WEE BIT LONGER.

Sounding the Writing Mudhole

In Cheyenne, I met two women who'd read my first book, *Windbreak,* and wanted to see its setting. We agreed that they'd come with me on a visit to my South Dakota house in June of 1995. They knew me only through my diary of a year of my life on the ranch with my second husband. On the drive, I told them more about coming back to the ranch with my first husband, our divorce, and how I built and then left my house after George died.

WRITING ABOUT OUR LIVES, I had described them as circular because our work gave us a financial return as well as food, just as we fed the cows we sold for money. Some days the weather or the needs of the cows dictated the work we did; at other times we could plan days we particularly enjoyed. Always our schedules revolved around light and dark, spring turning toward fall, wind bringing rain, around natural cycles rather than the dictates of the clock.

After surviving our first marriages, George and I thought we'd learned enough to stay happily married the rest of our lives. Naturally, we wanted our own house instead of living crammed into an apartment at the side of my parents' house. The first winter after we were married, we began to discuss every aspect of the way we wanted to live, how to include space for George's camping and shooting gear and for my writing and books; for his woodworking tools and my sewing. We wanted our home to accommodate our avocations, our friends and neighbors, our dogs and cats.

Laughing, we listed the best and worst features of past residences, compared and combined our visions, estimated costs and began again, and again and again. We erased my dormers and window seats, omitted George's lookout tower, postponed the sauna and greenhouse. We enlarged the living room to fit the nine-foot couch I'd bought at a yard sale because it accommodated intoxicated friends like Jerry who occasionally needed to stay overnight. We even considered the future, sketching doors wide enough to admit a wheelchair.

Once we started building, we balanced desire against practicality, tackling some of the work instead of hiring professionals, and getting help from friends skilled at carpentry, plumbing, and electricity. I proudly announced, too often, that we were the sole support of a local concrete company. Anyone who has built a house would find the details painfully familiar.

During a long winter of shoveling snow and pitching hay to cows, we considered minutiae woven into an enormous question: What makes a house a home? With cattle prices down and our savings dwindling, we spent most of our time figuring out how many two-by-fours we could afford, but some of the principles we articulated then have guided my thinking about "home" ever since.

We were pleased at how we were able to make the modest house part of the landscape. We angled the rectangle, putting one corner into the prevailing northwest winds, digging the basement into the south slope of a hill. On all sides we could look at grassland, but the house was backed against the hill, not standing on its top.

Each choice we made for the house was appropriate for the climate and for conservation of energy, the best we could do at the time for the money we had to spend. Twenty-six windows gave us sunlight and passive solar energy; woven blinds reflected summer sun and retained winter heat. I could keep an eye on the weather and the cattle, watch light and shade move across the grass beneath cruising hawks. George, raised in the trees of Michigan, and veteran of some scary armed confrontations, mentioned that the open hilltop offered "a good field of fire."

We painted inside walls in greens and tans, colors natural to the plains; daybreak flared in peach sunrise walls in our bedroom. Everywhere, comfortable chairs sat under wall-mounted reading lights. My sewing room doubled as an extra bedroom. Because I'd grown up watching how ranch women were isolated from conversations as they worked in the kitchen, the wall between the kitchen and dining room was low enough to see over. Guests usually leaned on it, visiting and peering into my pans while I prepared meals, so I couldn't hide my mistakes.

Because George enjoyed cutting and splitting wood, and a nearby cottonwood grove was reaching the end of its natural life, we installed a wood/coal furnace with propane for ignition only. A wide deck offered shelter to the basement door and helped cool my basement study. We left the basement ceiling open so we could access pipes and wiring, and store snowshoes, rifles, and other gear in the rafters. We tucked a half-bath beside the laundry room, and stashed an old iron bathtub in an adjacent pasture as a horse-watering trough until we could install it. Some day, after feeding cows, we'd be able to come in the basement door and leave our filthy clothes by the washer on our way to soaking in the tub.

FITTING THE HOUSE into its landscape and conditions, we planted windbreaks of native trees and shrubs to break the wind, keep snow out of our driveway, and provide shelter and food for wildlife and songbirds. I mulched the windbreaks with mail-order catalogs under discarded carpet, watering frugally with drip hoses. Rather than use chemical sprays, I pulled thistles. Instead of planting a lawn, we transplanted plugs of short native grass to the ground around the house, scarred by our construction. While our neighbors installed lights that automatically come on at dusk, we used spotlights on individual switches, aiming them down to minimize light pollution.

At the dining room table, we could look down over my father's house, barn, and corrals, and see our future. I was content to fit writing into the corners of my life before and after ranch work, and during blizzards. Yes, I was definitely smug about how well I'd recovered from my first marriage.

AFTER GEORGE'S DEATH, I wrapped the house and the ranch around me like a blanket against my father's erratic behavior. When he ordered me to give up my writing or permanently leave the ranch, I took refuge with Jerry three hundred miles away and rented my house so I'd have some income. In my locked ranch house study, I left books and furniture, keepsakes of my life with George. When friends called or wrote to ask when I was moving back home, I gave evasive answers. As my friendship with Jerry turned into a lifetime companionship, I told myself I was prepared to lose the ranch. I didn't list my name in the Cheyenne telephone book.

Whenever I visited the house, the renters had a new request: Could they paint the living room walls black? Did I mean to leave that room locked? They needed the space, so they'd broken in. Rare books disappeared. When I asked them to roll up a hose in front of the house before winter, they ignorantly ripped up hundreds of feet of pipe from my windbreak drip irrigation system.

During one period of harmony, though, they told me about friends who'd stayed overnight with a sick son. The child awakened in the morning feeling better. "This is a healing house," he said.

Eventually, my father died, I moved my mother to a nursing home, the renters left. Back in South Dakota for negotiations with lawyers and accountants, I'd camp a night or two in the house, cleaning and throwing out the renters' unpaid bills. One morning, I was awakened by the furnace exploding; they'd destroyed the firebox by burning propane for heat instead of using it only to ignite wood or coal. George's big woodpile stood intact twenty feet from the back door.

On the drive home to the ranch, I often entertained fantasies of setting the house on fire; surely burning it would be easier than cleaning it, I said, insisting that only lifelong fears of prairie fire and prison stopped me. For two years, each time I visited, I spent most of my time cleaning and weeping. Each time I had left the ranch, I'd come back, but this time I could see no pathway.

BY THE TIME I ARRIVED HOME with the two women from Cheyenne, they knew more than they'd counted on. We worked together cleaning, taking breaks to giggle at photographs in my high school yearbooks and drink coffee on the deck. The dam below my house was nearly half full that year, decorated with cruising ducks. I told them its history: built in the 1930s by my uncle with a team of horses pulling a scoop called a "slip," never full until the year we built the house. We christened it Lake Linda; later I learned the tenants called it "the mudhole."

Then Diane said, "You should make this a writing retreat for women."

Without hesitation, I propped the camera on the deck railing and took a picture of us to record that moment. "A healing house," the boy had said. Perhaps the house could heal me.

WORKING WITH WRITING STUDENTS of various ages, I'd always explained that "revision" means more than correcting errors in spelling and grammar. Each time I revise, I examine my original inspiration again, I try to really see again whatever I am writing about, pretending I have not yet written a word. Each version of the writing adds layers of meaning as the poem or essay matures. As I worked on turning my home into a writing retreat, I tried to apply the same technique.

Each time I returned to the house after moving to Cheyenne, though, I felt uneasy, as though the house itself was malevolent. So I borrowed the idea of a cleansing ritual from Lakota and Wiccan friends. Praying for peace and calm, I carried a smoldering bowl of native sagebrush and sweetgrass through each room and around the hillside. The fresh, wild scent hung in the air, on the furnishings; my despair vanished. Now I regularly reconsecrate the house, and picture its roots reaching, like those of the buffaloberry, deep into the broken limestone of the hillside.

Both cleaning the house and the long drive between Wyoming and South Dakota gave me time to consider how to conduct writing retreats. Naturally, I'd often encountered the belief that rural life and hard work are synonymous with ignorance. I'd also met women who wanted to write but had been discouraged by officious teachers in high school or college. I could empathize; one of my graduate school professors advised me to go back to the ranch and have babies, because I wasn't smart enough for advanced education. Women who read my published work sometimes thanked me for telling *their* stories, for showing, as one said, "that ranch women aren't just big dumb cows." Perhaps I could usefully encourage these women to write about their lives, helping to add more voices, different viewpoints, to the stories that are our culture and history.

FROM THE FIRST, part of my motive was selfish: to dedicate Windbreak House to writing so I'd have an excuse to return to write there. I worried, though, that I am too serious about my writing to be patient with novices. I agree with Margaret Laurence, a Canadian novelist, who says, "When I say 'work' I only mean writing. Everything else is just odd jobs." Trying to work in the city, I was easily distracted by daily life. Dogs barked, salesmen phoned, religious spokespersons knocked on the door, and sirens screamed, distractions excluded from Windbreak House. Writing had been my salvation after George's death, but now I had to figure out if it could produce enough income to live on. I could not run the ranch alone; I have no cattle, my horses all died, and I am no longer willing, and probably not physically able, to do the required work. Yet I was and am convinced I must keep my roots in that arid soil, to learn from it all I can, in order to continue to grow as a writer and as a human being.

I'd had modest success as a writer before leaving the ranch, submitting essays and poems in a rush whenever the ranch work allowed. Now, with nearly forty years' ranching experience, I thought I might be ready to write full-time, to become more aggressive about publishing. Perhaps I could speak more comprehensively for ranchers, especially women. It seemed to me the country has become "citified" so fast its citizens are forgetting where food originates, but I could explain how ranching works, how grazing can enhance the natural environment if done correctly.

Conversely, perhaps my environmental writing could help to clarify some useful ideas for ranchers who feel, and are, threatened by change. A considerable amount of controversy is based on ignorance, a correctable condition.

For years, my so-called writing income came primarily from honoraria as a visiting writer for a day, week, or month. After the isolation of writing, I enjoy the travel, meeting new people, eager discussions of writing. But I hate long absences from home, unfamiliar surroundings where I cannot write, and classrooms filled with indifferent students. Therefore, a retreat would have to replace my income from itinerant teaching. Otherwise, it would be only another job, worse because it would occupy a place I loved.

Even those closest to me—my parents, neighbors, and friends—never accepted the idea that writing is work. Forgetting that my father made me choose between the ranch and writing, my ninety-year-old mother often asked if I'd "gotten a job yet." Many women who live in rural areas of the Great Plains understand that writing can influence political change, but few have learned to take their own writing seriously enough to devote time or money to it. Perhaps working with western women who wanted to write would provide my own keep as well as giving rural families a stronger voice.

THEN ANOTHER PROBLEM AROSE with my homecomings. Each time I returned, my phone started to ring. Everyone knew I'd sold my cows to buy the ranch and had leased the land to a neighbor. Reasoning I had nothing to do, they'd tell me about vacant teaching jobs, or ask me to bake cookies for school functions. "Had any books out lately?" they might ask, but my explanations of how publishing works made their eyes cross and their attention wander. Besides convincing prospective writers to come to my retreat, I had to define its purpose and methods.

The rancher who leased my land sometimes drove to my house, where tradition demanded I invite him in for coffee, or lean on his pickup while he worked up to asking a question about tearing out fences or expanding water systems. One morning when three writers were in residence, I saw him with his wife in the corral sorting cattle, and walked down to see them, determined to find a way to explain why they should not interrupt retreats.

"You know," I began after we'd discussed local news and I'd told them I had three women in residence, "I have to get back pretty soon; I have an appointment in a few minutes. They pay a lot of money to come here to work with me."

They blurted in unison, "They *pay* to come here?"

Of course! People who don't consider writing a profession would hardly imagine its study to be a business. I explained how the retreat worked, perhaps emphasizing my interest in the profit motive rather heavily, and sent them copies of the advertising fliers. My neighbors learned to leave messages on my voice mail, but when they ask how my retreats are going, they grin and chuckle, shaking their heads.

SOMETIMES I MEET WOMEN WHO SAY, "I'm coming to your retreat for a vacation," as if it's a bed and breakfast. Retreats are by invitation only, though; my house isn't a public space available to anyone with the whim and the fee. Women who apply for admission send samples of their work, and I suggest they read mine to decide whether my style and outlook will help them. During our orientation walk, they all learn something about how a ranch operates. While the public often knows something of lobster fishing and ocean pollution, logging and rain forests, oil production and the Arctic, few know much about the vast grassland prairie at the heart of our country. Many "save the environment" efforts concentrate on photogenic critters like grizzly bears, wolves, mountain lions, and whales, but ignore the plains where much of our food is produced. Some folks glimpse its native animals, flattened by speeding cars, only on their way to Yellowstone to visit the tame elk herd that has reduced an elaborate ecosystem to a zoo.

During our walk through the house, I explain how the stove works as well as pointing out the diagram of the perched aquifer above the kitchen sink. House policy, I say, is to conserve water at all times, since I have no idea how limited our water supply may be. One afternoon I was sorting papers for the retreat that had begun that day when I realized that the shower had been running for a long time. I said nothing that evening, but the next noon I was upstairs when the same writer said she was going to take a bath; I looked at the clock. An hour later, she was still in the bathroom; every now and then, I'd hear water running down the drain, and then more water running into the bathtub. When she emerged after two hours, I waited until the other writer in residence rushed into the bathroom and shut the door. "She's been waiting quite awhile," I said mildly.

The woman shrugged. "She could have used yours," she said.

"True, but remember, we have to conserve water here. Using that much water for a single bath might drain the well."

She was inside her room with the door shut before I'd finished the sentence. At breakfast, I asked her again to be careful with her water use. "But I take a bath every day to relax," she said, "to calm my spirit so that I can be receptive to the vibrations of the prairie."

Two hours later, I was startled by a knock at the door. Outside stood a massage therapist, a tall young woman whose last name I recognized; she was the daughter of another of my former Sunday school students. When she'd finished her work, I learned she is a single mother. Several weary writers had jokingly suggested I keep a masseuse on call, but without the Water Waster I might never have found her; now I keep her card on my bulletin board.

Women who come to Windbreak House usually surprise me somehow.

W. came from Montana to work on a book about eight women who drove two Model Ts from Iowa to California and back in 1924. G. worked on a memoir, but also spent hours copying information from my teaching files to use in her own classes. T. wrote for her children, explaining some of the tough choices she's made. Mary said she really came to "hang out" with me, but began writing poems with encouragement from S. who was putting together another book. R. came hoping I'd tell her if her work was good enough to publish. After I convinced her that publishing might not be the most important objective of writing, she returned to write more poems, and later began writing prose, and has published both. English teachers from Missouri, Nebraska, South Dakota, Colorado, and other Great Plains states have come because they agree with me that writing will help them be better teachers. Sometimes themes emerge from the writers' minds or from circumstances. The April Fools retreat began on April 1 and featured a blizzard. The Cow-Tippers of Colorado learned, reluctantly, that cow tipping is a myth. And when my mother died, two women were already on retreat; they mourned with me, attended the funeral, and we all talked and wrote about our mothers for the rest of their retreat.

IN ORDER FOR MY ACTIONS to furnish lessons to visiting writers, I must discipline myself. At home, I can easily sabotage my writing. Pausing to think about a difficult phrase, I may do the breakfast dishes, scour the kitchen sink, put the garbage outside, and sweep snow off the steps. Three hours later, when I return to that perplexing paragraph, I can blame no one but myself for the lost time. "Picking up" a living space is more depressing than doing laundry since it's not *really* cleaning, just beating back chaos. At Windbreak House, I must not only resist the urge, but find a way to point out that I am standing firm against the temptation, and why. Knowing we are inclined to tidy up helps us discuss and understand why more women do housework than appear on the best-seller lists.

The simple abdication of responsibility for neatness has, I think, profound results. We all benefit more from making writing our first priority than we would from having perfect order. This realization alone can create a quiet revolution in a writer's life.

At first, the women carry their books and papers from the bedroom to the dining room to the deck, or to the windbreak, and back. Eventually, most choose a favorite nesting spot. I remind them the house is dedicated to writing and to confidentiality; they can leave a book or a journal behind and find it still there, untouched, hours later. Understanding the importance of such continuity and privacy can help them create the same conditions in their lives once they return home.

When writers arrive at Windbreak House in midafternoon, I greet them in the driveway. Some women have been so nervous I feared a wrong word or gesture might make them bolt for home. One woman said she'd had her hair done the day before. Helplessly, I giggled, explaining she was unlikely to see anyone but me and a few cows. She laughed with me, and we talked about how and why women learn that looks are more important than brains or skill.

After I've helped each woman move in, I explain that I will not enter her room again without invitation. The promise of privacy reminds them of our purpose, and almost none invite me into their rooms; we meet elsewhere in the house.

Most work so hard before arriving that my first job is persuading them to relax enough to allow for creative thought. My teaching varies in response to individual needs and my observations of the women. B., for example, was so physically and emotionally exhausted from her work with adoptive children that she couldn't face her computer. We walked together, talking about writing. That spring the dam below the house was full of water for the first time in its history, and chorus frogs sang all night. I'd never seen them, so we launched the flat boat and had a hilarious time measuring the depth of the water. Then she insisted I sit perfectly still while mosquitoes gnawed our flesh, until I spotted the first frog, then another, and another. She wrote in the house journal, "When the blue waters in my life have contracted to a mere mudhole, I'll remember sounding Lake Linda . . . and I'll have faith that the dry spell will come to an end eventually." Her trip home took longer than usual, though, because she kept stopping to write poems, staying overnight in little towns and sending me postcards about how much she was enjoying herself.

When I realized that Y. had washed dishes twice, I seized the excuse for a brief lecture. "You didn't pay good money to wash dishes," I reminded her. "We have so many dishes we can let them pile up." In fact, after the writers head home, I read their evaluations, then analyze the retreat while

I wash dishes and ease into my five-hour drive back to Cheyenne, remembering R., who wrote, "Every time I sit down to write, I'm back on retreat."

MY WRITING TENDS TOWARD PRACTICAL ACTION rather than purely philosophical ideas. I like to accomplish a goal, to finish a job, just as my father taught me to do. May Sarton said, "A poet *never* feels useful," but both my nonfiction and my poetry often emphasize my belief that we must all take responsibility for our actions. So I teach environmental efficiency by example. Because I wanted visiting writers to feel comfortable, and also because I had little money, I furnished the house from thrift stores. The secondhand nine-foot couch George and I bought to keep friends from driving when they shouldn't holds three writers with their books and writing paraphernalia.

When the container beside the kitchen sink is full of vegetable peelings and coffee grounds, each writer knows where to dump it for compost. Recycling bins line the pantry. A drawer full of secondhand napkin rings and napkins reminds us that wasting paper squanders trees. Most of the women resist using the cloth napkins at first, since they require laundering, but I believe that washing uses fewer resources than paper towels.

I also see the house as a metaphor for the way a writer's life should be organized: orderly but not immaculate. Bare dressers and tables invite writers to keep their books and papers at hand. Decorative objects must also be useful, and include crocheted shawls, rocking chairs, the mahogany bookshelves my father built in high school, several antique trunks, and a handmade box containing my latest collection of letterpress books. Women who suggest I put away the handmade quilts so they will be safe provide me with an excuse to discuss "using" or "saving" all kinds of things, including great poetic lines and talents.

If anything irreplaceable is damaged, I say, I will find something less fragile to fulfill its function, and recall the antique with pleasure. Meanwhile, seeing these objects enables me to picture the people who made them, memories that may lead to writing that will last longer than any hoarded keepsake. Thus the house mirrors the inspiration of writing by ordinary life.

PABLO PICASSO MAY HAVE SAID, "Without great solitude, no serious work is possible," but whoever made the statement, I believe silence and solitude are essential to clear thinking, and may be the most important contributor to good writing. To encourage quiet at Windbreak House, I begin each retreat by yanking the upstairs phone off the wall. I ask writers to turn off their cell phones, and I silence the bell on the basement phone, though I check voice mail each evening in case of emergency. Windbreak House has no television, and no Internet connections; a weather band radio warns me of severe storms.

On the first afternoon of each retreat, I lead an orientation walk inside and outside the house. While I demonstrate practical details of the house's operation, I convey information about the environment. Writers who have never lived in the country may not know, for instance, how they might inadvertently disable the septic system, ending our retreat at once because plumbers are an endangered species in this neighborhood. Such gritty details can lead to a discussion of the types and amounts of waste we each generate, and our options for disposal, all topics that might lead to writing.

Outside, I talk about weather, native plants and animals, as well as the community's culture and economics. Under windbreak trees now ten feet tall, I display the remains of the carpet-and-catalog mulch to show how it caught and held moisture until the trees could support themselves. I point out badger dens, and suggest listening at night for splashes and honking as the badger catches frogs and ducks at the pond below the house. With retreat residents, I've watched hawks and water birds, coyotes hunting moles down the draw, two fawns playing tag among the haystacks.

Sheltered from wind and highway noises, we sit to meditate on the coming retreat. Each of us selects something she's never before examined closely—a rock, an insect, a plant, a thought—to study and sketch, or write about. Even after living on this prairie for forty years, and conducting this exercise a hundred times just on this hill, I always see something new, a lesson rarely lost on the other writers. At a mother-daughter retreat, two thirteen-year-olds carried observation to its ultimate when they photographed and identified the first nest of the common snipe ever found in western South Dakota.

Later, I direct the writers to resource books, leading us into a discussion of research, and how my observations as a child led me to specific information in my essays and tied me to this homeland. Writing, I say as we stand on the deck at night, requires awareness of your surroundings, no matter where you live. When they look up and see stars still visible despite the lights of the subdivision across the highway, we discuss choices that might prevent light pollution.

The importance of becoming intimate with a place has become a fundamental part of my teaching. No matter what the topic, a writer's attachment to a specific place helps her determine her relationship to the rest of the world; specific details strengthen writing. I don't care if Windbreak House writers are concerned with the praying mantis, Hmong embroidery, or dog breeds, as long as each acknowledges her surroundings. The woman writing about the sea coast of Maine drew my attention no less than the women writing about South Dakota, Nebraska, Montana, Oregon, Kansas, and Missouri. When each goes home, I want her to be paying attention to her own home ground, therefore more inclined to be attentive to, and respectful of, its needs.

DIFFERENCES AND SIMILARITIES among the women of Windbreak House lead us into penetrating discussions about our place in the world and our responsibilities as writers. Moving to the city forced me to search all over again for ground to stand on, and made me realize that I didn't have to climb a mountain or return to the ranch to connect with nature. I simply needed to go outside, or breathe, or listen, or plant something. I learned to find natural life around me no matter where I was; learned that something wild is always near, even if it's only a ladybug.

Since each writer brings and prepares her own food, I may not discover a writer is a vegetarian until our first evening meal together, which always makes for interesting dialogue. Sometimes when I discover a woman's specific fears—of ticks, rattlesnakes, Native Americans, the treeless horizon, or admitting she works for an oil company—I can suggest ways to write about them.

After the orientation walk and dinner the first evening, we meet to discuss each writer's goals, and to plan a schedule. I provide long written commentaries on each woman's writing, so she may revise or create new work during her retreat. Freshly inspired by returning to the house, I divide my time between these comments and my own writing projects. At meals, we discuss our progress, altering the schedule if necessary. "Our conversations on issues," wrote a Kansas environmental activist, "were as beneficial to me as our conversations on writing." A conversation is never interrupted by the telephone, by someone at the door, by an appointment.

Not every writer understands the need for quiet, of course. One early retreat guest drank three pots of coffee a day, and her jangled nerves sent her pacing the upstairs hallway in heavy shoes until I pointed out that doing so disturbed both of the other residents. Then she paced back and forth on the carpet in her room, directly above my study. Most writers who want to talk with me come downstairs and knock on my door; this woman bellowed down the stairwell, "Are you busy?" Not until she was gone did I realize I had the power to ask her to leave, but the incident helped me make a mental list of behavior I will not tolerate.

Most of the interruptions that keep us from writing at home are self-created. I use anecdotes from my experiences to help writers understand that a determined writer can make time for herself. Many guests tell me that once they've been to retreat, they find it easier to respect their work enough to make space and time to write at home.

By talk and example, I remind them that an obstruction in their work may indicate the brain needs variety: a nap, a walk, or a prowl through the bookshelves. One bird-watcher alternated writing with hours on the deck, binoculars in hand, improving her tan while she added to the list of birds she'd seen in her lifetime. Another woman wrote, "The most important and empowering thing for me is to be in a house with a working writer. Together we generate energy which pushes each on, saying yes, this is important to do—if not for the world, at least for you, here, now."

I've seldom found it necessary to suggest, after a lively conversation over lunch, that it's time for us all to get back to work; the talks energize us. Most conversations naturally center on ideas, and concurrences have become common. It's not unusual for three or four of us to discover similar reasons for fear, guilt, or divorce, to learn we have the same birthdays, or that several of us have stepchildren. Talking about what we have in common is often good preparation for our writing.

Going to the kitchen for a late-night snack, I may meet another woman doing the same. Wearing nightgowns at two in the morning, we talk with an intimacy that illuminates and expands the work we do as individuals. We are working hard at our writing even after normal hours, but such happy accidents would be unlikely with men or children in residence.

One day at lunch, four of us learned we were all writing about our mothers. During the ensuing honest discussion, we performed a considerable amount of what I'd call homegrown therapy. A couple of us convinced the others not to feel guilty about their anger over particular incidents from the past, and we all discovered reasons we behave as we do. We went back to work refreshed, convinced that what we were doing was worthwhile. I've read two publishable essays enriched by that unplanned, leaderless talk. On departure day, writers often exchange addresses, information on contacts, publishing, and other useful topics.

Waiting for the first writers to arrive, I wondered if inviting strangers to my most private space was evidence I'd completely lost my mind. Now I remember Edith Wharton's observation that we can spread light by being a candle, or by being the mirror that reflects it. I realize how fortunate I was to hear the idea of a retreat at the perfect time for my own development as a writer, when I had the space to devote to it. I am not the retreat hostess; I am a writer, sharing an inspiring place with other writers, a mirror.

VISITING WRITERS who reincarnated Windbreak House became a community outside of space and time. The air crackles with energy during retreats, and we each go home with new respect for the power of writing. Some of us will unplug the telephone when we're writing, or leave the dishes in the sink or see the neighborhood more clearly. We are all connected by the ley lines of writing.

On the final night of each retreat, soaking in the old iron bathtub in the basement bathroom, I realize that my understanding of the writing process has expanded again. Each writer, living in a house dedicated to writing, interprets the experience differently. Eileen, who played her violin each evening, wrote in the house journal about the sounds different grasses made as she walked a mile every day to the old stone house. Wendy keeps a chunk of white quartz on her desk at school to help her visualize the badger den where she collected it. These objects are more than souvenirs;

they reverberate with prairie life, and their music will influence writing for years in the future.

Each woman writes in the house journal before she leaves. "I feel as if the huge rock I've been pushing against has begun not only to budge, but gain a bit of momentum," wrote W. "A door has opened," wrote M.; "I never expected to write poetry." J said, "You are user-friendly. Your retreat is at once a sanctuary . . . and a place of creative invention."

DESPITE THE INSPIRATION OF THE IDEA, healing is not the purpose of Windbreak House, nor do I intend to dispense therapy. The women who have come to write have made it a place where they grow stronger. Like a buffaloberry bush in the windbreak, the retreat continues to wind its roots deep into the native sod, stretch its branches toward the sky.

In the Windbreak House journal, K. once wrote, "The dry brown plants, with their intricate and tangled shapes, spoke to me this morning as we walked through the pastures—and the wide sky reminds me how much room I have to grow." Like her, I see messages in the tawny growth. Buffaloberries ripen among long thorns; they are too tart to eat from the bush, but combined in the right proportion with other ingredients, they are uniquely flavorful. Just like the women of Windbreak House.

Investigating the Heron Murders

Life in the country is almost guaranteed to make one cautious about leaping to conclusions. So I knew better than to make the particular mistake I made about the herons. Even as a child, I'd often overheard my mother tell my father a juicy piece of gossip she'd gleaned at a church gathering or on the party-line telephone. "Remember," he'd say, "there may be more to that story."

My best excuse for the heron fiasco is that I was so busy learning how to be part of a city community that I was less attentive to my ranch neighborhood.

I'D BEEN IMMERSED, that summer, in learning how to live and work with the women who traveled to Windbreak House to work with me on their writing. Slowly I realized we were creating a temporary society within my old community. We watched from the deck, for example, as my neighbors moved cattle through my pastures. If I'd been alone, I'd have gone down to help, but my primary job working with writers meant I couldn't be neighborly in the old way. The rural ranching life I'd always known was going by my windows while I worked at my job of writing and teaching. Once a resident writer who walked the grasslands around the house encountered one of my neighbors in a pickup. After introductions, he said cheerfully, "Oh! You're one of Linda's women! Well, have a nice walk. If you want to ride a horse, my place is just up the road." I liked to think my new community was fitting into the old.

That year, during the final week of August, only Emmy was in residence with me. We lived the writer's fantasy, rising early for breakfast together before turning to writing projects in separate rooms. While we ate lunch, she'd hand me several revised pages from her manuscript. In the afternoon, I'd read and reread the new work, writing comments to help her revise again. Late in the afternoon, we often took a walk together, toward the old stone house or down the willow-choked draw hoping to see deer. She'd ask questions about ranching and grasslands wildlife. Evenings, when she played her violin in practice for an upcoming competition, I'd sit on the deck, wrapping myself in the symphony of her glorious playing, the bass notes of the nighthawks diving in the dark, coyotes howling on the ridge, wind plucking the strings of the grass lute.

One afternoon, she reminded me that I'd promised to show her the great blue herons nesting along the creek that ran through some of our alfalfa fields, and asked to see the rookery. We drove north to Hermosa, then east while I explained how we harvested hay from these fields in summer, hauling some to other areas of the ranch and leaving several stacks in a hay yard under the tall cottonwoods near the creek. In late fall, we'd move our pregnant cows to this acreage, leaving them to graze on the grass left between plots of alfalfa, to drink from the creek, and to find shelter in the gullies and among the trees. Before the first snow, my father would make the hazardous highway drive on the old John Deere A with its hydraulic grapple fork, parking it under the trees. Even if the winter was stormy, we could usually get to the fields every few days in a pickup, and then use the tractor to scatter hay.

During the drive, I also told Emmy about some of my conversations with local folks who hated the herons, declaring they "ate all the fish in the creek." Ranchers or farmers who shoot hawks and owls are unaware that all these earn their place on our land by eating mice, pocket gophers, and other pests. I'd countered these arguments on several occasions by reminding them of the upstream neighbor who piles corral waste on the stream bank. The manure washes into the creek with each rain; I suppose that's what killed the fish, not the herons. When our right to irrigate from the creek was canceled by the state, the same dairy farmer went right on pumping the water without a permit. No one wanted to call the authorities, uncomfortable about interfering with what they saw as the landowner's "right to do what he wanted on his own land." The passing water, however, does not belong to any of us.

The cottonwoods are a huge asset to this winter pasture. As soon as settlement came to this valley in the late 1800s, the homesteaders dug ditches from Battle Creek to carry water to their crops; the cottonwoods seeded themselves along the edges. As we walked toward the heart of the cottonwood grove, I pointed to the lopsided heron nests from previous years, describing how the huge birds flew in convoys from the creek, bringing frogs to their nestlings.

We pulled our hats low to shield us from the twigs, droppings, and bits of spoiled rations that usually rained from the nests. Only then, gazing up, did I realize that the treetops were silent. No soaring shadows flickered as the herons settled on nests. No young birds squawked. As soon as we looked up, the grove seemed so ominously still that I returned to the car, slipped my pistol holster onto my belt, and got my camera, prepared for several unpleasant alternatives. Walking back past Emmy, I stumbled in the tall grass, and my brain finally admitted that we'd been smelling putrefying flesh.

A dead heron with feathers matted and bones askew lay at my feet. Breathing deep to calm myself, I took a picture. With every step, we found more bones. They were everywhere, slender and fragile as the stems of the brome grass around them. The feathers were matted and decomposing; the long beaks lay like broken swords in the grass. By the time I'd photographed two dozen, I was clenching my teeth and Emmy was weeping.

Since I'd been talking about how the neighbors hated the herons without reason, my first thought was that someone had shot the birds.

MY ASSUMPTION WAS LOGICAL, but with that handy item, hindsight, I think I also leapt to my conviction because I felt guilty about living away from the ranch. When my father walked the fence lines several times a year, carrying his repair tools, he talked to hunters, neighbors, and children he found in our fields. He probably considered these visits an important part of ownership; since we can't post a twenty-four-hour guard over every acre, our best hope for avoiding vandalism is to keep up good relations with those who live next door. He never kicked anybody out, or posted the land against hunting. Instead, when he met a hunter, he might casually remark how some folks thoughtlessly killed hawks and owls. Or he'd pretend to be astonished at people who didn't know that the pocket gophers built the foot-high mounds that foul our mowers when we're cutting hay. Shaking his head, he'd remark how some folks are so unobservant they didn't realize those hawks and owls ate pocket gophers and mice, helping cut their numbers much more efficiently than any traps or poisons.

I'd grown up walking these fence lines with him, but since he died my walks in the fields had been less frequent, and less pleasant; I'd had to kill several wounded deer and found the rotting remains of others that hunters had wounded and left to die. Recently, I'd read a half dozen newspaper stories about state law enforcement officials in the area finding the bullet-torn corpses of endangered predators like golden eagles or mountain lions. After moving to Cheyenne, I left the fencing job to the man leasing my land, reasoning that he needed to develop his own relationship with the neighbors.

So part of the blame for the heron murders was clearly mine. I hadn't talked to my neighbors much since my dad died, but I'd heard intriguing rumors: that I was selling the ranch, that I'd gotten a teaching job in Wyoming, that I'd sold my ranch house and moved to the Coast (always capitalized by gossips, especially if they have no idea which coast but are afraid you mean California, Where All Evil Originates). Perhaps the area's larcenous inhabitants, believing I was gone for good, thought my ranch was open for their amusement.

My theory seemed sound, and my imagination furnished a picture of the pickup that brought the killers; my prejudices raised it on tall tires, installed big speakers, and decorated the cab with a row of red and yellow lights. The driver was a teenager—no, one of the good old boys who called me "little lady"—with a rifle rack in his back window. In my imagination, he pulled up in sight of the grove, and several teenage boys perched on the hood, firing rifles, laughing, and tossing beer cans over their shoulders as the birds plummeted. I kicked through the tangled grass listening for the clatter of beer cans. On hands and knees I poked among maggot-infested skeletal remains, searching for bullets. I found nothing.

The lack of evidence should have troubled me.

I considered alternatives. What else might have killed the birds? My eye fell on the town's uncovered sewage lagoon in the field next to ours. I leapt to another environmentally correct possibility based on my own bias: perhaps some toxic substance in the waste pond was the killer.

As Emmy and I drove down the gravel road to the ranch, I met the rancher who rents my land. We idled our pickups side by side while I told him about the herons. I swore to report the killing to officials and reminded him of the heavy fines assessed for shooting wildlife. I ranted about revenge, about penalties for those who had violated my land and beliefs. I wasn't sure he agreed with me, but I knew he'd spread the word. No one could return the herons, but maybe I'd learn the truth while the community gnawed on the news.

That afternoon I telephoned old environmental comrades, collecting telephone numbers and advice. One federal wildlife official consulted his maps and said he didn't even know there was a rookery in that area. I had to confess that my father wanted it kept secret from wildlife officials, fearing "they'd take my ranch to protect some snail."

With a jolt, I realized that since the land is now mine, this incident was a challenge to my theory that information can be protection. By contacting wildlife officials, I had violated the customs of the community and my own family. Some neighbors share the fear that if "the Feds" know endangered species live on private land, "the government will take it away from us." However, I concluded that attracting official notice to the land might help punish the heron killers, and maybe even help me find a way to protect the ranch and its wildlife after my death.

One scientist said that if I'd send him some heron corpses, he might be able to determine the cause of death. Because killing herons is a federal crime under the Migratory Waterfowl Act, if humans were the killers, he'd try to discover their identities. I was grimly heartened to know the culprits might be punished. And if he concluded that the birds had been poisoned by the sewage lagoon instead of shot, I thought, perhaps my town and county would have to confront the consequences of allowing development without imposing rules.

Late that afternoon I drove back to the heron rookery, gathered carcasses into garbage bags, and tied each bag shut.

Then, somewhat calmer, I continued my own investigation. I drove down the gravel road a half mile west of my hay field to a rural trailer subdivision. Whenever I saw people working outside, I stopped to introduce myself and hand out my business card. I talked about the herons and asked if anyone had heard gunshots, or found other dead animals, and explained that I didn't mind responsible hunters in those fields. After a couple of hours, I'd met a lot of people who lived next to my land and gleaned considerable community gossip, none of it related to herons. I laughed at myself for trying to imitate my dad's ability to acquire information through casual conversation. But I hadn't wasted the afternoon. The absentee landowner across the fence now had a face, and maybe some of them would call me if they saw trouble.

I drove on to the last place on the road, a house and mobile home backed against the creek and cottonwoods, owned by two children of an upstream neighbor. I'd talked with the owner several times by telephone and given her permission to cut downed cottonwoods for firewood. In return, she called me if she saw a strange car in our fields. As I pulled up, she was irrigating her lawn from the creek. As we walked around the house to look at her wild flowers, she pointed out how the creek had undercut its bank that summer.

Then she mentioned the hailstorm two weeks before, told me the chunks of ice that fell had been the size of baseballs, and showed me fist-sized holes pounded in her siding, a security light hammered into a lump of metal.

I felt as if I'd been hit on the head by one of those hail stones.

Had she noticed the herons after the storm? I asked.

She waved toward my cottonwoods. "We always call them shitepokes at home," she said, adding that she'd been gone that day, but her father told her he'd seen "lots of dead shitepokes hanging in those trees."

I went straight home, slung the heron corpses into the freezer, and called everyone I'd talked to earlier. Wildlife experts agreed that large hail, a natural plains disaster, could account for the carnage. Half-grown heron chicks, if they survived, would leave, anxious to escape the smell of death, and might not return for several years, if ever.

A mental picture of the dead herons hanging from the high branches immediately replaced my vision of the trigger-happy teenagers, and haunts me still. I'm an old-timer on the prairie; I've seen hail storms that damaged buildings and cars, killed wildlife, flooded dry washes.

As soon as I composed myself, as soon as I started paying attention the way the prairie and my father had trained me to do, I could see signs of the hail everywhere: broken tree branches and stripped leaves, chopped-off alfalfa, and dents in vehicles.

Blinded by theory and prejudice, I'd done just what I'd ranted against for years. Instead of looking with an open mind, so that I could see reality, I'd created my own myth, supplied answers that were incorrect. Worse, I acted on my mistake. I learned the truth only because I was forced to collect more evidence.

Instead of thinking of natural phenomena, I behaved like some ignoramus who'd never seen hail. Now I remembered that one neighbor had mentioned the hail, but because I had not experienced it, because I had not heard those particular icy stones *whock whock* against the roof or felt the chill in the air, I forgot about it. I failed to consider the consequences.

Worse, I mumbled as I paced the floor waiting to complete another phone call, I behaved like an absentee landowner by calling authorities before investigating personally and completely.

Only at that moment did I realize I *am* an absentee landowner. I am no longer part of the daily life of my land, only a periodic visitor. I am literally "out of touch." Scrutinizing a mystery, I leapt to a solution based purely on prejudice, rather than asking questions and listening to the answers. I allowed my knowledge of the right way to learn about a community to be overcome by righteous fury. My father had taught me, though, that mistakes are part of being human, and useful if a person is alert enough to learn from them.

I took the herons out of my freezer, hauled them to an open field, dumped them out of their black plastic shrouds, and apologized for taking them away from their homes. The odor of their deaths lingered in my car for weeks, reminder and punishment.

AS THE SUN SHONE ON THE HERON CORPSES, I was thinking hard. Decisions affecting western lands are made every day by people who have never lived here. The news is filled with stories of people who zealously pursue the wrong course, hampered by ignorance or incorrect information, but believing wholeheartedly in their own view. I've joined my neighbors in complaining about the effects of ignorance on western land policies. As we have so often said, "meaning well" often causes harm that may not be reversed.

Writers, I've often said, must have experienced what they write about, so I'd also gone against what I preach as a writer: that you shouldn't be able to write about a river if you haven't walked its banks, floated and tasted its waters. And you definitely shouldn't be able to dam it.

Because I learned patience from traditional old-timers, I saved myself from the worst effects of my error by standing around all afternoon visiting with strangers, listening more than I talked, "wasting time." If I'd skipped the last neighbor, I would have brought in federal officers, causing suspicion and irritation among my neighbors. The quiet approach demonstrated respect and concern for the people who live on and near my land, as well as interest in their opinions and belief in their honesty. My conversations that afternoon, and the information I was able to spread about the crime of shooting the birds, may help protect the remaining wildlife from casual shootists.

I found the truth only because I kept asking questions, kept listening to the answers. I followed the road to the very end.

Who's Driving the Subdivision?

In July 2007, I celebrated my sixty-fourth birthday at the ranch with Jerry, contemplating our move back to my home when he retired in 2008. We decided to live in Windbreak House, and to move the writing retreats to my parents' ranch home, tidied up and renamed Homestead House. We'd brought along a trailer load of possessions: his blacksmith and woodworking tools, furniture, some of my books and writing files. For a week, we cleaned the ranch outbuildings, picked up trash, hauled hundreds of canning jars to the recycling bins in town, installed new locks, and generally got reacquainted with the place. We speculated about how our lives might change once he becomes a woodworker and blacksmith instead of an engineer. I'll still be a writer, but I can walk to work at the retreat house.

Looking at the old bunkhouse, we visualized a garden shed and rustic writing room. I told Jerry how I first met John and Anna Lindsay when my dad took me to their ranch house east of the tracks. Anna told me they'd started with a one-room cabin. First they built a cattle shed and a cellar for food storage. Then when they had enough money, they added on a little room that became her kitchen. John wasn't a very energetic rancher, so Anna worked at the telephone exchange in Hermosa. Unable to resist the temptation of gossip, she became part of my education in how to use a telephone: never say anything you don't want the whole town to know.

After my father bought their ranch, he tore down the rest of the house and dragged the kitchen to our place behind his team of horses. He built an end wall, and installed a woodstove and a narrow bed for our hired man, and called it the bunkhouse. After the hired man got drunk and drove through some fences, my father decided we could no longer afford to hire help, so the building became a storage area until I moved back to the ranch with my first husband. We built a two-room apartment on my parents' house, and I used the little building for a writing room and office for my Lame Johnny Press. When my husband's three children visited, we put sleeping bags in the bunkhouse. Both my mother and the tenants who lived in the ranch house after she moved to the nursing home had kept cats inside it without providing a litter box, so my first job was scrubbing the floor with ammonia.

Because I'd heard Anna's voice every time I made a call on the party-line phone—"Central!"—I wasn't surprised to hear it behind my left shoulder as I scrubbed the floor. "Land's sakes, I've never seen the beat of this filth!" Or was that my grandmother?

Leaning out the door for fresh air, I could see the wide willow tree to the east where the ranch cats once took refuge during a flood following a bad hail. I rode my mare through the knee-deep water to grab felines out of the branches, stuffing them inside my jacket. Then I had to convince the mare to tippytoe back through the water, ignoring the screeching, squirming, scratching cargo. All week, cleaning the ranch house and yard, I kept seeing reminders of my past life. I found a wastebasket I remembered from the room I had when I was five. Sometimes scenes shifted so quickly I wasn't sure whether I was fourteen, forty, or sixty-four. The yellow stool in the utility room still held the shoe polish I'd last used on my saddle oxfords in high school; still good, too.

We worked coughing on smoke from what turned out to be the worst local fire of the summer. Started by lightning in a tree-filled canyon subdivision near Hot Springs, our closest town to the south, the fire eventually covered more than fifteen square miles. It burned thirty-three homes, the most ever lost in a Black Hills fire; killed a resident, and injured two firefighters. We read newspaper accounts of confusion as volunteer firemen tried to evacuate residents in the dark from homes on twisty, unmarked dirt roads among burning trees. National newscasters used the fire as an occasion to warn of the dangers of building in such high-risk areas without fuel-free zones, fireproof roofs, street signs, and escape routes. Later in the summer, they made the same comments during the standard California fires. I reminded Jerry that, on our way to the ranch, we'd passed close to the subdivision. Homemade signs line both sides of the highway: NO ZONING. Later, we learned subdivision residents had repeatedly ignored the sensible advice of rancher neighbors to cut firebreaks around their homes.

A MONTH AFTER MY BIRTHDAY WORKWEEK, a storm roared down the east side of the Black Hills, pouring rain into communities on the edge of the hills. Rain gauges collected from five to ten inches of water in a few hours. We were back in Cheyenne, sweltering in the August heat, when I read national headlines about devastation in a subdivision along Battle Creek east of Hermosa. Since no one died, the headlines weren't very big, but the disaster produced the usual heart-warming stories as strangers helped each other swim out of their living rooms. Also as usual, a few lowlifes vandalized the damaged houses.

The National Guard brought trucks; the governor toured; various state and federal officials and political hopefuls made statements; and everybody's blood pressure went up. Eventually, authorities concluded that fifty homes were damaged or destroyed and a couple of thousand tons of debris were hauled to landfills in other counties. The nearest dump, in Rapid City, is twenty miles from the housing development in another county, so citizens who didn't live in a floodplain were paying part of the expenses for the poor judgment of those who did, though no one was cynical enough to mention that while the heartwarming volunteer efforts continued.

Town officials blamed Mother Nature with the standard platitude: "There's no way you could ever plan for it."

OFFICIALLY, the average annual rainfall at the ranch is about sixteen inches, though my father's records show that as little as ten or twelve inches a year is not unusual. We've collected considerably less than average in the past decade of drought. During the 1990s, we figured that a cow and her calf consumed the equivalent of the grass grown on twenty-five acres of pasture a year. Now the drought has so stunted the grass we must allow as much as forty acres to feed one cow unit. Some ranchers have reduced their herds and bought feed, trying to hold onto the land until the rains have returned. Others bought more grazing land on credit. Some have sold part of their land, remarking they could make more money on one subdivision than they ever made from cows.

These days, land values don't necessarily reflect the land's true resources, and what it "produces" may be reckoned in short-lived greenbacks rather than ancient grass. Land that sold for $400 an acre in the 1990s, for example, is now considered to be "worth" $550 an acre, but its purpose has likely changed; homesites produce only trash where pasture land produced food, wildlife habitat, open space, and free air purification. I heard that the new owner of the ranch where I'd tried to buy black bulls had financed his ranch dream by selling a parcel next to the creek for another subdivision.

WHEN THIS TOWN WAS SETTLED in the 1880s, settlers saw the Battle Creek valley as both an asset and a danger. Some of them could barely speak American, but they recognized the broad fertile fields alongside the creek as evidence of centuries of flooding. They built their town on a nearby plateau. With shovels and horse-drawn machinery, they carved ditches leading from the creek so the inevitable floodwaters would flow gently, without destruction, into those fields to water their crops.

In 1972, a powerful thunderstorm overwhelmed several Black Hills communities, killing 238 people. Battle Creek rampaged through Hermosa during that flood and roared on through the hayland owned by several ranchers, including my father. We knew the land had been repeatedly flooded for aeons; the rich silt grew better forage than we could grow on the arid uplands where we lived. Rather than try to grow crops on the drier soil, we used the naturally enriched creek bottom to grow most of the hay to feed our cattle herds. Almost every year brought some floodwaters, and the settlers' ditches spread the water out so it could soak into the ground slowly. Every year, floodwaters tore out some of our fences; every year, we rebuilt them, figuring the moisture we gained was compensation for the work and expense.

In 1972, the tangled flood debris deposited in our hayfields included tents and sleeping bags from a campground and pigs from a farm upstream; the mess smelled horrible until volunteers helped bury it. For the rest of his life, my father worried that in their haste to be rid of the waste, the bulldozers had buried some of the five people still missing almost forty years later.

In August of 2007, the deluge jammed debris against a railroad trestle south of town until the water drilled through the embankment. Then the logjam and floodwater blasted into the subdivision on the other side of the tracks. Of the subdivision's thirty-six homesites, thirty-four homes were damaged or destroyed. Three floated off their foundations, and one of those sailed more than a mile, passing the sewage lagoon, until it crashed into a fence and a power pole, dousing the lights for miles as it settled into my hayfield. The old spreader ditches slowed the flood just enough so that most of the debris landed in my meadows: car bumpers, leaking cans of gasoline and antifreeze, freezers, doghouses, children's plastic toys, clothing, suitcases, furniture, siding, beehives, and golf clubs.

As soon as the field dried a bit, my lessee and our ranching neighbors brought tractors, trucks, and loaders and pushed the mess into a pile, along with downed trees and fence, eventually covering a half acre six feet deep. Meanwhile, the National Guard and other volunteers helped residents clean up the subdivision and the county fairgrounds next door. Town officials, however, told me the Guard couldn't come onto my private property, and the dump closed before the field was dry enough for machinery to remove the mess. So the debris, in a pile six feet deep, seventy-five feet wide, and a hundred feet long, remains.

WHEN I DRIVE MY SUV, the law requires me to be responsible for my actions; so if I drive into your yard, I'm liable for the damage I do. No matter how sorry or sober I am, or how sincerely I promise never to do it again, you want cold hard cash. Moreover, you expect me to remove my truck and debris promptly. You require compensation for your losses, including the work of replacing your favorite rose bush, rebuilding the picket fence, filling the gouges my tires made in your lawn. We might say to friends, "the insurance paid," but we both know insurance is really my money, and ultimately, yours. Responsible people are accountable, in both the moral and the financial sense of the term, for their actions.

Who drove the subdivision into my garden? The event was no "act of nature," but an inevitable disaster caused by city planners and developers.

Since subdivision development started along the creek about ten years ago, old-timers have shaken their heads and predicted a flood would destroy the houses. Yet the home buyers who lost homes and possessions say they were told the area had been "taken out of the floodplain." They were right: the town gave the developer a permit requiring him to build the houses one foot above the official floodplain level.

Driving through the subdivision a couple of weeks after the flood, I saw that the houses indeed stood a foot or two off the ground. Where the metal skirting around the houses had been ripped away by the water, I could see how the developer raised them. Two concrete blocks stacked one atop another stood under each of the four corners. Two more blocks supported the center front and center back of each house. So twelve concrete blocks, unsecured, apparently satisfied the town's requirement to raise the homes out of the floodplain.

The day I visited the wrecked subdivision, workers were installing electric and sewage lines for a sixty-lot subdivision next to the swamped houses, on another piece of the ranch where I'd gone to buy bulls. This development is even closer to my hayfields. City officials issued a statement saying that they still considered the floodplain "prime real estate for housing development," though they were "considering" delaying construction until an independent hydrology study was completed. Someone speculated about the possibility of containment dams upstream to hold the water back. Such dams would, of course, have to be built on property owned by people who choose not to live in the floodplain.

ALL OVER THE WEST, developments are appearing in areas nature has made unsuitable for human occupation, places our ancestors left unchanged for good reasons. A creek is bound to inundate its floodplain, even if the house beside it cost two million bucks. Trees will, if conditions are right, burn. No one wants to take responsibility for deciding that some places should be placed off-limits to human habitation, so lives and property are endangered if there's money to be made.

The county newspaper reported that costs to the county of flood-related emergency services had topped $25,000 within a couple weeks after the flood, only the beginning of the eventual costs. A month later, few of the subdivision residents spoke of rebuilding. Many had learned that their insurance was inadequate.

The owners of the house in my hayfield, and their relatives, attacked me for writing about the flood; other writers spread the blame more widely. Observed one citizen, "You folks from Hermosa begged for our help, and here's your help: "DO NOT BUILD OR REBUILD IN A FLOODPLAIN."

"Lunacy lurks," wrote another; "there should be no insurance for homes built in a floodplain." Recalling the most recent New Orleans hurricane, one writer recommended that neither state nor federal agencies should provide rescues "rewarding greed and stupidity."

A South Dakotan mentioned that, "A permit doesn't require Mother Nature's cooperation."

"The waters will come again, but the insurers may not," said another.

"Angry Hermosa Resident" mocked the city's assertion that the floodplain was prime real estate, and said that neither homes nor lots were selling before the flood, adding, "The message to home buyers: Do your research."

A Nebraskan said, "Too bad all this misdirected energy couldn't be focused on revamping zoning regs to avoid similar problems." For weeks, frustrated citizens expressed themselves freely in letters to newspapers and on the Internet, reminding me of Mark Twain's remark in his *Notebook* that "irreverence is the champion of liberty and its only sure defense." I've heard of no legal action against the town or the developer, and many of the residents are stuck with their flood-damaged homes because they had no flood insurance and cannot afford to move.

COULD WE CALCULATE how much the development benefited the county, just as we figure taxes against inflation every year? If we balanced the income from the development against the costs of the flood and the cleanup, perhaps an honest account would show such developments aren't good business for the majority of citizens. A mathematical calculation wouldn't take into consideration the emotional harm done to the floodplain residents, or losses like confidence and keepsakes.

Our ancestors didn't have hydrology studies or zoning, but they used common sense. They gambled in the casinos in Deadwood, but they didn't build houses in floodplains.

LATER THAT FALL, I read about the plan devised by citizens of Burlington, Vermont, to cope with floods on the Winooski River in the heart of town. No one "dared to build homes there, despite its prime location." Instead, a 354-acre parcel became Intervale Center, a place where beginning farmers can create environmentally sustainable farms and gardens. Townspeople and visitors come to the riverbank to dance in a barn, play with their dogs on the lawn, and splash in the fountain behind the stalls selling produce. Between floods, visitors can pay money or food stamps for food grown on the floodplain: shitake mushrooms, heirloom tomatoes, purple potatoes, blueberries, organic beef burgers, and pizzas made of beets and goat cheese. None of these ventures are hurt much by the occasional high water, and the entire town and region benefit.

While I wasn't able to drive from Cheyenne to help subdivision residents collect their underwear from my hayfields, I've been working to make Battle Creek a better citizen of Hermosa. With the Rocky Mountain Bird Observatory, I've established a riparian habitat that should benefit birds as well as reduce flooding, constructing fences that keep the cows from grazing on the steep slopes but allow them to safely cross the creek. The flood destroyed the habitat fence, but my hired crew rebuilt it, at my expense, the next month. Ironically, this wildlife habitat has already made the hayfields and the meandering creek more attractive to those who wish to put houses there, and observers report that residents amble through my acreage as if it were a public park.

A neighbor bought the derelict house that floated onto my property, and someone salvaged the plumbing and light fixtures. However, when the new owner jacked up the cheapjack structure, it broke apart. Then vandals kicked holes in the walls and broke out the windows. The town marshal said he could follow a clear trail where kids on four-wheelers have visited the crumbling structure, and he knows who they are. The house's current owner has given up, says the marshal. "He's not planning to move it now."

"But it's my land," I say. "I'd like to be neighborly, but somebody made a lot of money off that development and I'm storing someone else's garbage."

Meanwhile, the minutes of Hermosa's town council meetings reveal plans to expand the sewage lagoon to accommodate more people in more houses along the creek. Councilpersons suggest I burn the subdivision's flood garbage, including the derelict house, and then bury it in my hayfield where it might be unearthed by future owners or another flood. If the county raises my property taxes to compare with those in the proposed subdivision, I probably won't get a discount for sheltering wildlife. As taxes rise, I'll have to work hard to make enough money to keep the land at all.

Overlooking Antelope Ridge

Finally home on the ranch, I wake before dawn when a Say's phoebe perches on the deck railing to announce its hunting plans. My hair flows across the pillow, ruffled by a breeze sweet with scents from drying grass. Unusually heavy rains all spring have nourished smooth bromegrass nearly as tall as Jerry. The lightest breeze makes the bobbing seed heads ripple, like a dense pack of tawny animals running ahead of the wind. Beautiful, but as the summer grows hotter and drier, these grasses will be transformed into an acute fire danger.

When I was growing up here, the native grass was usually no more than four inches tall, so I could see my feet in case a rattlesnake was using the same route. Walking through this lush growth makes me nervous; my feet tangle in bindweed, goosefoot, and mullein grown larger than I've ever seen it. Invasive grasses like crested wheatgrass and smooth bromegrass tower over the native big bluestem, sideoats grama, and blue grama, and the air is dense with pollen. The Westies' ears and noses collect sharp seeds from the weed we call beggar's-lice; needles of cheatgrass seed burrow into their flesh. Russian thistle is growing in our two-track road. Almost daily I spot some species of grass I usually see only in pictures, grown from seed that has waited in the soil for decades. Besides our usual plains pricklypear, we now have colonies of fragile pricklypear, a cactus I believe may be capable of leaping several feet to embed itself in the paw of an innocent city dog. The spiny fruits stick so tightly to a pant leg or boot that they can be removed only with pliers.

CONTRADICTIONS. Naturally, since I've called this rural town home all my life, I've been as happy and exasperated with my neighbors' opinions as they have been with mine. They rolled their eyes when I married George, with his headband, long hair, earring, and beard. When I was traveling the state speaking against uranium mining and the disposal of nuclear waste in Fall River County, I got telephoned death threats from people whose voices I recognized, while other neighbors surreptitiously handed me cash and thanked me for speaking for them. On the first Memorial Day after George died, I visited the cemetery and noticed his grave didn't have a flag like those of the other military veterans. A couple of phone calls revealed that the local vets had judged by appearances, drawing the wrong conclusion from his long hair; since then, the flag has appeared on schedule.

Friends from more populous areas roll their eyes when I insist I'm a South Dakotan. Why do we hate environmentalists, Indians, women, and Democrats? they ask. Why are we so anxious to pollute our air and water? I'd like to join in the county conversation about our future, because I believe Francis Bacon was right: "Things alter for the worse spontaneously, if they be not altered for the better designedly."

How, though, do I reconnect? I can start with the people I used to neighbor with who are still here, though their situations have changed. A couple of families whose pioneering grandfathers crossed the plains in the same wagon train with mine have found that the fourth generation can't get along, and divided their land, just as my father and uncle did. In other cases, deaths, education, or marriage have changed the way a family does business. While I've steadily increased my contributions to several local fire departments, helped with cemetery upkeep, donated anonymously to the flood cleanup and other local causes, I haven't been visible at meetings. We probably won't begin attending church or join fraternal lodges. If I want to connect with other residents of the community, I have to do more than disapprove of their choices, but this may not be easy.

Contradictions. My district has three state legislators. When I began speaking on the uranium mining and waste issues, one of them poked me hard in the chest and told me to "go home and have babies." His job, he insisted, was not to represent the opinions of the voters in the district, but to use his best judgment on their behalf. He's still in office, and I hope to

get the opportunity to vote against him again. The legislator who started
the pizza restaurant introduced a bill a few years ago that would have made
conservation easements illegal. I've explained to him my Battle Creek
riparian project and my concern about development, and look forward
to discussing some of these issues over pizza. The third legislator is,
hallelujah, a woman; some things have changed.

Perhaps Jerry's patience as well as his tools and generosity will help
open doors; he's also related to some of my longtime neighbors. When a
farming friend came to plow my garden the same day Jerry arrived from
Cheyenne with a load of tools, they were soon visiting over the equipment
in the garage. Now that Jerry has stored away the plaques and certificates
honoring his thirty years of bridge engineering, he's started fixing, tidying up, stacking, mowing, digging, remodeling, and otherwise enjoying his
retirement.

ON THE COUNTY MAP, the land I own is a small part of an unusually
large blank space, about fifty square miles broken mostly by the thin brown
lines of gravel roads. The ranch buildings stand on a different drainage six
miles from the damaged hay meadows, but the August 2007 storm poured
floodwaters down all the gullies leading out of the Black Hills, tearing out
miles of fence. Several of the sparse cottonwoods that probably got their
start from similar floods blew down. Gradually, my lessee is rebuilding all
the fences we lost; that work is part of the normal operating cost of ranching; our problem, not that of other taxpayers.

On the plus side, the flood left a fresh layer of silt on the garden where
I hated hoeing weeds as a child; I'm looking forward to sifting it between
my fingers as I plant seeds. For now, I've planted tomatoes in a six-inch
layer of silt and twigs the flood left, going down daily to rip out more of the
weeds the flood brought with it.

All of this work is my direct responsibility, to do or authorize, because
a deed somewhere says I own this land. I think of the land as a job, not as
an asset; I'd work for its best interests because I live here, even if I didn't
own it. Not far away, a realtor may be looking at it, and tapping the keys of
his calculator. I don't need all the acreage that I own in order to live, but
knowing that it's there keeps me as sane as I'm ever likely to be. Unseen
by me or anyone else, its true inhabitants—the grasses and bushes, the un-

derground water, the antelope, deer, rabbits, skunks, snakes, toads, mead-owlarks, and dung beetles—are going about the business of living as they should. Part of my job is leaving them alone to do theirs.

HOME ON THE RANCH, Jerry takes a call from the realtor selling our Cheyenne house while I open the mail we picked up at the post office box in town. We don't use the highway mailbox because neighbors tell us they've lost mail, especially checks, from those. In one letter, the Chey-enne Police Department informs me that our property has been declared in violation of an ordinance prohibiting "weeds/grass" more than six inches tall. The rain has encouraged my wildflowers, and I haven't been there to pull the grass between them. In previous years I posted a sign explaining that these are native plants and required no extra water. A year ago, I'd have stormed the police station, wildflower books in one hand and the cita-tion in the other, to explain the benefits of native vegetation where water is scarce. Instead, I ask the realtor to chop the growth to a length accept-able to city statute. I hope the neighbors and passersby who always col-lected seed will grow their own gardens, violating city codes if necessary until they are changed to reflect the realities of water use on the plains. I protested the building of a "spray park" in arid Cheyenne, too, but on this hot day the park is no doubt full of children exchanging germs and getting the impression water is so abundant we can afford to spray it into the air.

Moving back to the ranch completes the circle begun when I moved here as a child; I expect to die in the house on the hill overlooking the ranch. But change is everywhere. The old brick school I attended was torn down recently, replaced by flimsy boxes. From the Hermosa cemetery, I can still see Battle Creek winding through the riparian habitat I've created. Perhaps I'll be tucked into that final resting place before the rich bottom-land of the floodplain is completely covered by subdivisions and sewage lagoons. Another development stands only a few feet from the cemetery gates, so I'm probably lucky I bought my plot before someone decides we can't afford to waste expensive real estate on dead neighbors.

Like most western landowners, I'm choking on options for the future of this land. Environmental magazines and organizations extol the virtues of conservation easements, while my neighbors e-mail diatribes insisting easements are a plot to give the land back to the government. (Why would the government want more land? The federal budgets can't pay to care for the land it owns now.) Several organizations are working to remove fences and replace cattle with bison, and a few deranged people want to introduce African lions, cheetahs, and wildebeest. Realtors lurk under every clump of crested wheatgrass proclaiming the wonders of fresh air and open space while filling it. I hear that a county committee is finally discussing zoning, but they've never responded to my requests for information, nor have I seen any news of their activities in the county paper.

Meanwhile, I've agreed with the Great Plains Native Plant Society to establish the only botanic garden in the world so far that will help preserve species native to the prairie, help educate the public about their beauties and benefits. On this ordinary grassland pasture where cattle have grazed since the late 1800s, volunteers found almost 250 species of native plants thriving. They've spent the past few years reconstructing an antique cedar log cabin for a visitor center that will stand in symbolic contrast to the giant horse arena with the shiny green metal roof across the highway. To the south, the houses of the Heartland Country Ranchettes are visible on pointy hills that dissolve a little every day in the rain and wind.

WE HAVE FALLEN quickly into the country habit of going to town with a long list of necessary errands and hurrying through them so we can get home to the evening's work and to walk the dogs. Still, one day I take extra time to explore a used book store in Rapid City where I open a copy of one of my books and am momentarily stunned to see my loving dedication to a close friend. But I knew that when she died a year ago, friends adopted her pets and helped clear her house, so it's logical her books were sold. Change is constant.

Karl Hasselstrom emigrated from Sweden to Iowa, where he worked for a cousin who had paid for his ship passage. By the time he registered his cattle brand in western South Dakota to celebrate the year, 1899, that he proved up his homestead, he called himself Charles. He'd kept his cobbler's tools, including a full set of lasts on which he made shoes for his children. The ranch he established has, in just over a century, dwindled down to me, a childless woman not of his blood. His grandchildren and great-grandchildren, nieces and nephews and their offspring, all follow other professions in other places. My childless uncle Harold sold the ranch where Karl raised his family to the man who helped him during the last few years of his life. The same man leases my adjoining ranch. His daughters are building other lives, but he expects his son to join him in a ranching partnership. My most logical action would be to sell this ranch to him. However, I'm worried about the burden of debt he assumed when he made the successful bid for the piece of Paul's land I called the "wildlife pasture."

Temporarily, I am responsible in the deepest sense for this land, and for all its inhabitants. Thinking over those obligations reminds me of one cold winter afternoon when George walked to our calving pasture with his rifle, hunkered down, and waited for the coyote that had been eating the carcass of a stillborn calf. We don't allow coyote hunting on our land, and coyotes are rarely able to kill healthy calves, but this coyote was too bold; we'd found his tracks near where several cows had calved during the cold nights. So we'd reluctantly decided to kill him, afraid he'd attack a cow who was struggling to give birth. The coyote didn't appear until almost full dark. George said he shot at a silhouette and a glint of eye, and saw the shot strike the coyote's shoulder, but the animal ran off before he could fire again. A month later, we began seeing a coyote every day in the field below the house, catching mice, but his gait was strange: a bippety-boppity hobble. Looking through the glasses, we realized he had only three legs; the fourth was missing at the shoulder.

The descendants of that coyote are my heirs, as are the offspring of the badger who dug the hole on my neighbor's land where I fell while walking in the dark after George died. The grizzled beasts still haunt the miniature limestone canyon north of my house; signs indicate they share it with the occasional passing mountain lion or bobcat. Like the ghost of prairie past, a badger from the neighbor's pasture may waddle down the gully to drink from the spring, meander through the ranch yard, gobble a few frogs by the pond, and then in the tall grass around Windbreak House dig up a thirteen-striped ground squirrel for dessert.

These survivors of the plains ecosystem appreciate the land for what it is, not as real estate. Without them, without its native plants, the prairie is dead, whether it's a ranchette yard or a Wal-Mart parking lot.

I must also consider the human future of the land. What's the best use of this ranch? Smart business practice says sell it to the highest bidder and salve my conscience by giving generously to the charity of my choice as

I head for some exciting retirement spot. If I fear that a ranching family might be forced by these inflated real estate prices to sell it, I could entangle it in conservation easements. Such agreements are administered, however, by humans at least as fallible as ranchers and realtors.

AS I WAS REVISING that last paragraph in early 2008, I received a letter from a neighbor offering me an exclusive opportunity to buy nearly five hundred acres of land just north of my home. This is the pasture where I fell into the badger hole, where antelope entertain me as I wash the breakfast dishes. While negotiating, I tell the landowner how much I've enjoyed walks there, enjoyed watching with retreat guests the band of seventy antelope. I tell him about the hawk we watched hunting and returning to her nest in a tree later knocked over by last August's flood. He says his wife mentioned reading in one of my books how my neighbor Margaret and I watched the pine tree near the highway throughout her life.

Simple prairie, the land has been well cared for: never overgrazed. But it is not, as a friend remarked, nearly sexy enough to attract the attention of an environmental group that might buy it to protect it. Whatever happens there will affect my writing retreat, the ranch, any plans we make for the future. By offering me the chance to buy this property, the owner fulfills all the requirements of neighborly behavior. His asking price is reasonable in comparison with the current prices of land intended for subdivision now, four years after Paul's sale.

However, no one could make enough money raising cattle to repay the investment. I begin calling friends and environmental groups, hoping to find a way to save it from development. I even consider buying all or part of the property with borrowed money and the proceeds from the sale of our house in Cheyenne. I could divide the land, keeping a buffer next to my home and selling off enough homesites to pay off the loan. I'd be a developer. "So we're all bastards," says Stephen Trimble of a similar situation. "Paradox makes a better story than a rant." But I choose not to risk the rest of my land to secure a loan I might not be able to pay off if this mad land rush is broken.

On Good Friday in 2008, while my aunt Anne, the last of the Hasselstrom family, is being buried in the Hermosa cemetery, my neighbor informs me by e-mail that I've run out of time. The FOR SALE signs are up by June, when we come home for good: the property is called Antelope Ridge.

AT SUNSET ON SUMMER EVENINGS, we go to the deck with the dogs, cold drinks, and binoculars to watch the live prairie instead of the TV set still boxed in the basement. Sometimes we see several pronghorn does sky-lined on the south ridge, wandering, grazing, and looking around alertly. Inevitably, we glance away and miss the instant when a fawn rises from the grass to nurse. After dining, the antelope fawns leap and twirl and run together as the does graze. As the land darkens, they wander off with the does to lie down in the grass where they will remain hidden until their next feeding.

Sometimes we look down at the ranch buildings, at the house where my parents lived, the barn, the outhouse, and chicken house, all surrounded by tall cottonwood trees. Most of the trees are probably eighty years old or more, nearly at the end of their normal life span. Some trunks stand dead, and all the trees show branches white as old bone against the sky. Most of these probably grew from seeds washed by floodwaters down the draw east of the house; we should have begun planting replacements years ago, but the job is on our mental list now.

When pioneer women came to live on these naturally treeless plains, I've read, they planted cottonwoods because they grew quickly, providing a little shade for a yard and garden. Sometimes I can spot the ruins of old homesteads crumbling beside a lone cottonwood, and know the old tree was once nourished by a housewife's dishwater. Moreover, hardy women who may have missed the sound of flowing water nearly as much as they missed their families may have loved the cottonwoods because their leaves make the sound of a running stream in the slightest breeze. My wind-break trees, chosen for their ability to survive without added water on this rocky hillside, include juniper, cedar, buffaloberry, and plum, but no cottonwoods. Still, if I close my eyes, I can hear the cottonwoods a half mile away well enough to almost believe rain is falling. Among the whispers in the wind I hear the voices of ancient trees, but also something more. The cottonwood is sacred to these plains for many reasons, including the fact that the Lakota, who preceded us here, chose it to be part of their sacred sun dance. Cut crosswise, a cottonwood limb reveals a perfect five-pointed star at its heart, called the "morning star" by the Lakota, the mark of the Great Spirit. Some scholars have seen the star as a Christian symbol, while others called it a pentagram, and linked it to even more ancient religious observances.

My favorite music, though, is the grass refrain that exists nowhere else on earth. Closing my eyes, I worry about the future of the prairie melody. To most botanists, the term "prairie" refers to the tall-grass prairies of the eastern Great Plains; this drier western grassland is properly called a "steppe" or "savanna." Prone to drought, these areas exist only because unique populations of tough grasses, as well as native animals like the pronghorn and bison, have adapted to their stringent conditions. Some of the current changes made by introduced plants and destructive habits may be fatal to that age-old balance. Apparently no one really knows what riches may exist in native vegetation. We've learned the virtues of a few native plants, including echinacea or pale purple coneflower, for example, but few experts have given serious study to the potential uses of prairie plants, medicinal and otherwise. Greedily selling and paving, watering and plowing the grasslands, we may never know what we are losing. All over the world, shortgrass steppe regions are disappearing or threatened by exploding populations, drought, exploitation, and ignorance. Europeans proudly plow their savannas to turn them into "productive agricultural regions;" the South American pampas and the Serengeti of Africa are dwindling fast.

As the sun drops closer to the Black Hills on the west, a breeze ripples the pond below the house. Four families of ducklings float out of the aquatic plants along the edges; I recognize yellow water crowfoot, American sloughgrass, and some sedges, but I've never had to learn the names of the others, since this pond rarely contains enough water to float even a small duck. As the heat slides away, cool air flows up from the pond. Killdeer pipe messages to each other, darting low, dodging the barn swallows sipping from the water's surface. Ten Canada geese sail into the shallows and begin grazing; no matter how greedily they gobble in the mud, one or two heads are always raised like periscopes on long necks, swiveling to watch for threats. Gently, the chorus of the grass rises. Buffalograss sighs, sideoats grama hums, big and little bluestem shimmer on the high notes, and sand muhly whistles as the wind rises. Redtop wails on the hillside, prairie sandreed and thickspike wheatgrass moan in alto, while curly dock clacks and squirreltail chatters out a staccato beat. Intermediate wheatgrass sounds a steady, somber bass, while witchgrass and foxtail barley run up and down the scales. Timothy, Canada bluegrass, Russian wildrye, Nuttall alkaligrass, the dropseeds, fescues and sedges, porcupine grass, green needlegrass. My uncle Harold could recognize them all and spoke easily of where they were found on his ranch and the land that is now mine. I often sit on the deck picking needleandthread seeds out of my socks with my book of grassland plants open on my lap, remembering their names as I listen to their songs rising full-throated into the clear air.

The grasses sing in all seasons, a perpetual choir I appreciate even more in the chill silence of a winter morning when the temperature is thirty below zero. I can almost hear the coughing call and foot-stomping alert of the pronghorn accompanying the grass tunes, the silken whisper of a deer, the castanet clicks of a million rattlesnakes. Perhaps other voices thrum in the background: bison grumbling, fur trappers reminiscing about their lives before they came west, the skreek of wagon wheels. Voices from the future may spill backward into the symphony: children playing in a trailer park where my barn used to stand.

A big blue heron is suddenly standing in the pond; slowly the sleek head turns, as if listening with me.

The ancient Druids are said to have conceived the idea of perpetual choirs, organizing them according to mathematical principles. Twelve singers at a time gathered at sanctuaries such as Stonehenge and Glastonbury. They chanted in shifts, fresh singers slipping into the circle as others grew tired, so the music never died. They conceived the choir as a religious obligation, of course, but singing in those days was not merely ornamental, not just entertainment. The harmony of the universe, they believed, required human participation; the choirs were an ordinary part of daily living, part of the way humans cared for the earth. Early Christians, understanding that their beliefs were not so different from the earth religions of their predecessors, adopted the structure of the choirs as they absorbed other Druid practices. Nervous about the idea of *enchantment* embodied in "chanting," they spoke instead of the music of the spheres, or the heavenly choir, and the necessity of cooperation between several churches to create perpetual choirs as part of their regular worship. The rite was necessary, they believed, to keep their lives stable.

Sitting in the South Dakota sunset, I hear the voices of the perpetual choirs in the chorus of ancient grasses across the centuries. The community of grasses here was developing, becoming interdependent, when those early human singers were tuning up in Europe. The intricately woven tapestry of vegetation was memorizing this particular soil, these infrequent rains, as each member of the family nourished every other, sharing the work of survival. The development sustained all who lived honestly upon it, from early grazers like *Bison latifrons* to the sleek crossbred heifers peering from beyond my southern windbreak. All of us are part of this chorus because, as Wendell Berry says, "eating is an agricultural act." The prairie has fed us all and needs our prayers.

The governor speaks with enthusiasm of how the Heartland Expressway passing through my ranch is at the heart of the "Great Plains International Trade Corridor" stretching from Canada to Mexico, and how the area will become "a regional center for retail and hospitality." None of the buoyant news stories following his announcement mentions grass.

Then the nighthawks appear, rising from the limestone ledges where they lay their eggs, dipping, soaring, gliding, wheeling, booming as they gobble millers and mosquitoes over the pond. Every night, several of them coast by us at eye level. Their crescent bodies sail the wind, silhouetted against the sunset, until we can no longer separate them from the darkness. As the stars emerge above us, we can still hear the Peep! Peep! Peep! of the nighthawks' hunt, and then the boom of a killing strike.

Epilogue: Waiting for the Storm

Middle of July. Ninety degrees. No breeze.
Perfect haying weather said my father as we
leaned on the pickup passing a jug
of water back and forth. The burlap cover
I'd soaked at sunrise was dry, the water warm.
Fifty feet above us, green and yellow leaves
rustled in the sun, flung cottonwood shadows.
We stared westward, toward the Black Hills
trying to foretell the weather.
He told me how his dad came west in ninety-nine
with all those other Swedes and Germans,
settled down near Battle Creek,
began to learn how this Dakota country
differed from the flat black lands
they'd left in Iowa, where they'd paid
their immigration fare by working for their cousins.

With teams and slips they carved out
shallow trenches snaking toward the creek bank
from their fields; cautiously, they shaped them
so that only when a storm
dumped rain the channel couldn't carry
did the irrigation work. Instead
of roaring through the fences,

ripping off the sod, floods dribbled
into spreader ditches, soaking through their fields,
waiting for tomorrow's seeds. For years,
until the Dirty Thirties,
the rains that flooded Battle Creek
spilled gently into ditch and field.
The settlers prospered, learned American,
saved their money, married local women,
and voted every chance they got.

The prairie wind spread every seed it caught;
saplings sprouted everywhere along the stream.
Each trunk grew straight those first good years,
up twenty feet or so. Then, shouldered by prevailing winds
and stunted by the drought, they all began to bend,
to lean into a gentle curve. Wind conspired
with hail and snow and time against them.
Each tree now genuflects from north to south
a row of arcs as even as the outline of a bridge.
"They look like little old ladies going to town,"
my father said, grinning. "All stooping in a row."
We watched a cloud bank rise beyond the Hills,
growing blacker as it towered toward the sun.
The old trees bent their backs, tattered women
hustling toward shelter, tipping toward the earth.
We laughed together; he was forty-six and I was twelve.

Blackbirds shrieked and billowed from the field,
clattering toward the streamside willows.
The air went still. Before the cloud
had covered half the sky, we felt a puff
out of the south, the land inhaling, summoning
the storm. We climbed inside the truck
and headed home. As I strained to close the gate,
rain splattered on my shoulders. The new hay lay
in windrows that would shed the water. When the field dried out,

we'd be back to finish what we'd started. Maybe we'd find
water in the spreader ditches.
                              Let's see now, that's been
forty-five years last July. Some of these old trees
must be a hundred. Their stooping line still charts
the ditch route, but I seldom see it flow now. Too many
houses lie upstream, too many sewer lines drain to the creek.

One or two dead cottonwoods have fallen;
the rest are shaky, showing whitened trunks.
My neighbor, granddaughter of a frugal pioneer,
cuts the dead for firewood—but irrigates her garden
from the creek, water pumped with no permit.
I pat the nearest tree, feel how the bark is ridged,
wrinkled by her years, corrugated by her age.
Just like my skin.
                   My dad was pretty bent himself
before he died; my mother's curled into a comma.
Wheeling down the halls, she holds herself above the earth
as best she can, but not for long.
                                   I straighten up
and pat the tree's old puckered hide once more.
A cloud is rising grim above the hills, a storm
that some of us won't weather through.

Additional Resources

This list of reading material and other resources includes books and organizations that have contributed to my thoughts on community. I hope to encourage you to explore some of the thousands of ways people are creating community. Find a way that satisfies you.

Community, according to most dictionaries, suggests joint or common ownership of resources. The Great Plains savanna belongs to the nation and conceals unknown resources that might help us feed ourselves, cure diseases, power necessary machines. The unique ecosystem of the shortgrass prairie is too valuable to be wasted by shortsighted greed.

Reading and talking about community can provide us with different viewpoints, but the only way to learn how to live in a community is to get out and live in it. Contribute; give that you shall receive the kind of community you visualize.

Berry, Wendell. *Another Turn of the Crank.* Washington DC: Counterpoint Press, 1996. Wendell Berry writes about the importance of local economies, the value of locally produced foods, and the way real communities function. Reading any of his books will give you new insights about your own life and relationship to community.

Butala, Sharon. *The Perfection of the Morning,* HarperSanFrancisco, 1995; *Coyote's Morning Cry,* Toronto: HarperCollins, 1995; *Wild Stone Heart,* Toronto: HarperFlamingo, 2000. Like me, Sharon has spent several decades exploring a specific patch of prairie, becoming intimately acquainted with its past and the community in which it lies. Her insights are always thoughtful and emerge from deep and intimate knowledge of her place.

Dagget, Dan. *Beyond the Rangeland Conflict.* 1995. 2nd ed. Good Stewards Project, 2000. Dist. by University of Nevada Press. Dagget is one of the first environmentalists to dive into the world of ranching and find practical solutions to pressing land-use problems.

Gruchow, Paul. *Grass Roots: The Universe of Home.* Minneapolis: Milkweed Editions, 1995. I found much in Paul's reflections on growing up on a farm, in the center of a traditional farming community that mirrored my own ranch upbringing. Paul's thoughtful responses show he understood what is necessary to keep such communities alive.

Kemmis, Daniel. *Community and the Politics of Place.* Norman: University of Oklahoma Press, 1990. I heard Daniel Kemmis speak on community in the 1990s and have read and reread this book. It's easy to theorize about community, but Kemmis has done what most theorists have not: worked to build community by participating in politics.

Knight, Richard L., Wendell C. Gilgert, and Ed Marston, eds. *Ranching West of the 100th Meridian: Culture, Ecology, and Economics.* Washington DC: Island Press, 2002. Scientific analysis alternates with poetry and prose in this collection of honest, blunt testimonials from folks involved in modern ranching.

Krueger, Frederick W., ed. *Christian Ecology: Building an Environmental Ethic for the Twenty-First Century.* San Francisco: The Conference, 1988. I may have gotten this collection at a conference on stewardship at Assumption Abbey, home of the monks of the Order of St. Benedict in Richardson, North Dakota. Kathleen Norris persuaded Dan O'Brien and me to discuss with Lutheran ministers how Christians might be better stewards of God's earth. The conference was life-changing in many ways. I've been unable to find elsewhere Wendell Berry's comments in "God and Country" on the concept of "usufruct": the idea that stewardship is the responsible care of property belonging to another. Thus, says Berry, God charges us to take good care of the earth because it is His property, and we jeopardize not only our earthly lives but our souls when we do not.

Meloy, Ellen. *The Anthropology of Turquoise: Reflections on Desert, Sea, Stone, and Sky.* New York: Vintage, 2003. I'd read several of Ellen's books and exchanged letters with her before her sudden death in 2004. By that time, I'd been writing about community for nearly fourteen years. Her death seemed too much; I lost heart for the work of trying to explain why we must not destroy the natural western landscape. Then, in 2006, I discovered this book, and, though I had never heard her living voice, was struck again by how many of her ideas coincided with my own. Her words cheered me on.

Putnam. Robert D. *Bowling Alone: The Collapse and Revival of American Community.* New York: Simon and Schuster, 2000. Putnam discusses the old dichotomy, community versus individual: "Our national myths often exaggerate the role of individual heroes and understate the importance of collective effort," he says. "Social capital is created when people combine short-term altruism with long-term self-interest, doing good unto others knowing that at some future time others may return the favor. He notes that "all prominent moral codes contain some equivalent of the Golden Rule," and provides a graph showing that violent crime is rare where the social capital is high, often in states with many rural areas, like Oregon, Washington, Wyoming, and Utah. The social capital is—or was at the time of this book—very, very high in North and South Dakota. See also www.BowlingAlone.com.

Robinson, Jo. *Pasture Perfect: The Far-Reaching Benefits of Choosing Meat, Eggs, and Dairy Products from Grass-Fed Animals.* Vashon, WA: Vashon Island Press, 2007. I could recommend this book for its recipes alone. Grassfed beef contains more vitamin E (an antioxidant that boosts immunity, and may lower risk of coronary heart disease) and more beta-carotene (good for eyes) than grainfed beef, and is rich in the "good fats" shown to stave off cancer, depression, obesity, diabetes, arthritis, allergies, asthma, dementia, and high blood pressure. Recent studies show grassfed meat also has more conjugated linoleic acid (CLA), which may help prevent breast cancer. Most of the beneficial effects of grassfed meat disappear when animals are fattened with grain. The reason? Cows—and bison, pigs, sheep, and chickens—didn't evolve in cornfields. Also, in feedlots cows are fed such waste products as stale bubblegum in aluminum foil wrappers, leftover pizza, hamburger buns, potato chips, newsprint, cardboard, "sanitized" municipal garbage, chicken feathers, and manure. Think about that while you run on the treadmill to get rid of the extra weight from those "well-marbled" steaks. Robinson's Web site, www.eatwild.com, offers clear information on the importance of prairie grass to the health of animals we eat for meat, and thus to our own health.

Ryden, Kent C. *Mapping the Invisible Landscape: Folklore, Writing, and the Sense of Place.* Iowa City: University of Iowa Press, 1993. Ryden discusses the importance of all the stories of its past to any place, showing us how human experiences in any locale shape its character as well as its future.

Sanders, Scott Russell. *Staying Put: Making a Home in a Restless World.* Boston: Beacon Press, 1993. Discussing the "virtue and discipline of staying put," Sanders says that although he has lived in the same place for twenty years, he is "still discovering what it means to be a citizen."

Van der Ryn, Sim. *The Toilet Papers: Recycling Waste and Conserving Water.* Foreword by Wendell Berry. Sausalito, CA: Ecological Design Press, 2000. A 1970s back-to-the-land classic back in print, with practical information on the history of waste disposal, gardening with waste, composting toilets, urban sewers, and more.

Zwinger, Ann Haymond. *Credo: Shaped by Wind and Water: Reflections of a Naturalist.* Minneapolis: Milkweed Editions, 2000. This gem of a book is filled with practical as well as philosophical wisdom.

ORGANIZATIONS

These are only a few of the hundreds of organizations working on similar problems all over the world. Look in your community; if you don't find one, create it.

The Grass-fed Party, www.grassfedparty.org, supports grass-fed ranching and raising the standards of the American cattle industry. Founded in 2008, the group works to focus attention on humane animal treatment, strengthening the rural economy, better use of corn and grain crops, healthier meat, sustainable ranching, and the preservation of working landscape. A blog focuses on news, views, recipes, event announcements, action initiatives, policy, and investigation of grass-fed topics. "We believe that creating conversation is the first step to making real, working, grass-fed change in our food system."

The Heartland Center for Leadership Development in Lincoln, Nebraska, www.heartlandcenter.info, studies ways to make small towns and communities succeed. Their "20 Clues to Rural Community Survival" includes such ideas as "Knowledge of the physical environment," "Acceptance of women in leadership roles," "Strong multi-generational family orientation," and "Conviction that, in the long run, you have to do it yourself."

The International Dark-Sky Association (IDA), 3225 North First Avenue, Tucson, AZ 85719; (520) 293-3198; www.darksky.org. IDA works to protect the nighttime environment and our heritage of dark skies. It lists as its goals to "stop the adverse effects of light pollution on dark skies, including energy waste and the air and water pollution caused by energy waste; harm to human health; harm to nocturnal wildlife and ecosystems; reduced safety and security; reduced visibility at night; poor nighttime ambience; raise awareness about light pollution, its adverse effects, and its solutions; educate everyone, everywhere, about the values of quality outdoor lighting; help stop other threats to our view of the universe, such as radio frequency interference (RFI) and space debris." IDA works with "communities, astronomers, ecologists, and lighting professionals" and is active locally, nationally, and internationally.

Astronomical associations often work against the light pollution that is damaging prairie views of the night sky, but bans exist only in Arizona, California, and Connecticut. In February 2002, the Czech Republic became the first country in the world to enact a national law against light pollution, as reported by *National Geographic* in October 2002. I didn't find a local group working on this issue, but the New Jersey Astronomical Association (www.njaa.org) often posts news about light pollution in the world, with links to organizations working on the problem.

In the 2008 collection *Let There Be Night: Testimony on Behalf of the Dark*, edited by Paul Bogard (University of Nevada Press), some of the country's best writers celebrate the beauty and importance of dark skies.

Loading Dock, www.loadingdock.org. "You could build a house with what people throw away," says the Web site for this facility dedicated to making building materials available for reuse at low cost. Slogan: "Don't Dump, Donate!"

The Minnesota Institute for Sustainable Agriculture at the University of Minnesota (www.misa.umn.edu) sponsors a variety of programs. I particularly like *Time, Soil, and Children: Conversations with the Second Generation of Sustainable Farm Families in Minnesota*, by Beth E. Waterhouse, 2004.

The National Cowboy Poetry Gathering, Elko, Nevada, www.westernfolklife. org. The Gathering provides one of the most energetic and varied forums available for the discussion of land issues in the West. Panel discussions always include participants from every possible viewpoint. Check the Web site for upcoming programs.

Pacifica News Service, www.pacifica.org, established in 1949, offers a wide variety of alternative news reporting, as does www.indymedia.org, a guide to the independent media movement. As with all news, consider the information and ideas presented and compare them with that available from other sources, but alternatives to the large news organizations offer useful perspectives, data, and opinions.

Quivira Coalition, 1413 Second Street, Suite 1, Santa Fe, NM 87505;(505) 820–2544; admin@quiviracoalition.org. "The mission of The Quivira Coalition is to build resilience by fostering ecological, economic, and social health on western landscapes through education, innovation, collaboration, and progressive public and private land stewardship." The organization works very successfully to build cooperation among ranchers, environmentalists, federal and state agency personnel, academics and members of the public, with workshops, tours, projects that demonstrate their principles on the real landscape, and conferences.

St. Vincent de Paul of Lane County, Oregon, recycles while creating jobs. For more information, St. Vincent de Paul of Lane County, PO Box 24608, Eugene, OR 97402; www.svdp.us. In "Waste Not: An Oregon Solution to Joblessness and Overflowing Landfills," *Orion Afield,* Autumn 1999: 34–37, Elizabeth Grossman described how the program *daily* takes ten tons of metal and 300,000 pounds of clothing out of the waste stream, along with mattresses, box springs, cardboard, and glass, while creating jobs and skills for low-income residents in a woodshop, appliance center, and mattress factory.